The Design of Children's Technology

Allison Druin, Editor

The Morgan Kaufmann Series in Interactive Technologies

Series Editors

- Stuart Card, Xerox PARC

- Jonathon Grudin, University of California, Irvine

- Mark Linton, Vitria Technology

- Jakob Nielsen, Nielsen Norman Group

- Tim Skelly, Design Happy

The Design of Children's Technology

Allison Druin, Editor

Morgan Kaufmann Publishers, Inc.
San Francisco, CA

Senior Editor: Diane D. Cerra
Director of Production and Manufacturing: Yonie Overton
Production Editor: Elisabeth Beller
Cover Design: Ross Carron
Text Design: Rebecca Evans
Copyeditor: Ken DellaPenta
Proofreader: Jennifer McClain
Composition: UpperCase Publication Services
Illustration: Cherie Plumlee
Indexer: Steve Rath
Printer: Courier Corporation

Designations used by companies to distinguish their products are often claimed as trademarks or registered trademarks. In all instances where Morgan Kaufmann Publishers, Inc. is aware of a claim, the product names appear in initial capital or all capital letters. Readers, however, should contact the appropriate companies for more complete information regarding trademarks and registration.

Morgan Kaufmann Publishers, Inc.
Editorial and Sales Office
340 Pine Street, Sixth Floor
San Francisco, CA 94104-3205
USA

Telephone   415/392-2665
Facsimile   415/982-2665
Email   *mkp@mkp.com*
WWW   *http://www.mkp.com*

Order toll free 800/745-7323

03   02   01   00   99   5   4   3   2   1

Library of Congress Cataloging-in-Publication Data

The design of children's technology / Allison Druin, editor
        p.   cm.
    Includes bibliographical references and index.
    ISBN 1-55860-507-X
    1. Children's software—Development.   I. Druin, Allison, date.
QA76.76.C54D47 1999
005.36—dc21   98-38500
                                                           CIP

Contents

Preface

Beginning a Discussion about Kids, Technology, and Design

Allison Druin

Human-Computer Interaction Lab, Institute for Advanced Computer
Studies and Department of Human Development, College of Education,
University of Maryland, College Park

A Question

One day I had the good fortune to meet an 8-year-old girl named JoAnna. She was a student in a classroom of 8- and 9-year-old children in Albuquerque, New Mexico (Druin and Platt 1997). During the 1995/1996 school year, the students and I were working on how to design Web pages for a class project (see Figure P.1). At the conclusion of one of our 90-minute sessions together, JoAnna asked me a question: "Why don't adults talk more to kids about how to make software for school?"

Figure P.1

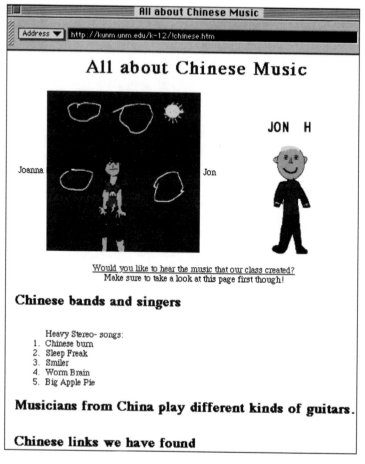

A portion of JoAnna's Web page (kunm.unm.edu/k-12/!chinese.htm)

My young friend posed an interesting question. I believe her curiosity grew out of the limited but satisfying Web design experience she had begun. Thanks to her time spent designing Web pages, JoAnna felt she had something to tell the developers of the design software she used. One particular point she wanted to share was that it would be much easier for her if she could just "talk the words in" as opposed to type on a keyboard.

JoAnna's need to be heard is not unusual among children. It raises a larger question: Why don't we as technology designers spend more time talking with children about what we make for them? When we develop technologies for doctors, astronomers, or graphic artists, we work with them. We observe what they do; we ask them why they do what they do; and we will many times collaborate with them on the design of these new technologies. In the case of children, it is far less common to talk with them about the design process (Druin 1996). Typically, teachers or parents will be consulted, but children are more commonly observed and tested to see how much they have learned using the technology. It is much rarer for researchers or product developers to just ask kids to share their thoughts as design partners.

In fact, when reviewing the literature on technology and children, it is much easier to find books, journal articles, and conference papers on the *impact* that technology has had on children, educational practices, teachers, and learning environments (e.g., Collis 1994; Dwyer, Ringstaff, and Sandholtz 1991; Kay 1996; Lewis 1995; Norton 1992; Papert 1980; Postman 1995; Sheingold 1991; Shneiderman 1992; Spoehr 1994; Stoll 1995; Thompson, Simonson, and Hargrave 1992; Tinker 1993; Turkle 1995). Far fewer discussions are available on the process of designing new technologies for children. Although the impact of technology is an extremely valuable area of research and discussion, so too is the exploration of the technology design process. What do people make for children? Why do they do it? And how do they go about creating it? These are all questions that people are asking.

Routinely, I receive email in response to a column I write for the *SIGCHI Bulletin*, entitled "Kids and Computers" (Druin 1997a). My correspondents typically share with me observations like the following:

> I am doing my graduate research on making a reading program for children. I have had a difficult time finding references in books or papers that discuss the design process. Can you tell me what other people have done? Are there things I should worry about that are specific to technology for children? Are there ways I should work with children? How can I tell when the software is what they want?

Depending on how these questions are answered, the end result affects children. Each time we make decisions about the design process, the final product can change. In turn, if children use these products, this can change how they play, learn, and live for some time in the future. In this book, authors from industry and academia look at this crucial design process. Each author is a professional who focuses on this emerging field of children, computers, and human-computer interaction (HCI).

The Whys

Returning to my young friend JoAnna (see Figure P.2), she also asked me a question on another day that has had me thinking for some time: "Why do you make stuff for kids?" Upon reflection, I realized that for years I had been so concerned with what I could make for kids that, embarrassingly enough, I actually hadn't spent much time asking myself why I did what I did. Upon further reflection, it made me realize that the *why* probably had a lot to do with *what* I ultimately made for children. This question forced me to stand back for a moment and think and to spend some time asking the same question of some of my colleagues. Their answers helped me begin to understand why I choose to do what I do. The thoughts that follow are from a selection of the authors in this book, describing why they make new technologies for children (Druin 1997b; Druin 1998a,b):

> It's the best way to have a big impact on the world. If you can influence the lives of today's kids, you can help shape the world of tomorrow. So designing for kids makes me feel like I'm doing something worthwhile. To help kids understand or learn a new concept, you really have to understand it well yourself. So in addition, designing for kids pushes me to understand things in new and deeper ways.
>
> *Mitchel Resnick, MIT Media Laboratory*

> We've been trying to make a programming language for ordinary people of all ages, people who have never taken a programming class. If we can make it work for kids, I believe we can extend it to adults later. So kids are the cutting-edge users for our approach to programming. It's working out great. They've given us lots of valuable feedback.
>
> *David Smith, Stagecast Software*

> Children are our future, so that's where society, and we, should be concentrating our efforts. As designers, we also find children to be delightful clients: they carry little baggage and few preconceptions and are therefore receptive

Figure **P.2**

JoAnna's letter to email pen pals in Australia, sent from Albuquerque, New Mexico

to new ideas, and their incredible imagination feeds back into the design of new technology. They therefore make us better designers. And working with children is just plain fun!

Ron Baecker, University of Toronto

Children are becoming exposed to computers and technology at an increasingly early age, and most of this technology has not been leveraged to make the child-computer interaction optimal. For instance, early on in the design of children's software products, many companies believed that a successful strategy was to add a new user interface with animation and primary colors on top of an existing adult product. After a few fun animations were discovered, kids would easily become bored or frustrated. I chose to participate in user-centered design focused on children because the opportunities to raise the bar in the user interface are so great, as are the benefits that children receive in terms of learning and staying engaged. It's a gratifying experience.

Mary Czerwinski, Microsoft Corporation

Before I started designing for kids, I was first won over to a design philosophy: *constructionism.* Broadly, it's about empowering users—about assuming your users are intelligent and creative and can achieve great things with quality tools and support. Applying this to adults is unfortunately often viewed as heretical. (As evidence, consider the popularity of the phrase *idiot proofing.*) On the other hand, a constructionist design philosophy makes complete sense to most people if you're designing for kids. Designing for kids is great because you're safe to assume your users are intelligent, creative, witty, and fond of purple. (Adults are too—but many people may not believe you when you say so.)

Amy Bruckman, Georgia Institute of Technology

Too often we tend to equate *education* with skill *acquisition;* but it benefits a student little if he or she has acquired a huge repertoire of mathematical skills, and yet at the same time has learned to loathe mathematics for life. The reason we work on things like HyperGami is to provide children (and adults) with a dignified, rich, mathematical activity—an activity through which they might develop an actual passion for mathematics. Our work, then, is not simply about getting kids to learn faster or more efficiently; that would be too grim an enterprise. Rather, we hope to offer kids the sense that mathematics can be an avenue for self-expression, a source of pleasure, and a vocation.

Mike Eisenberg, University of Colorado

Not surprisingly, my list of "whys" is similar to what my colleagues have just discussed. I too want to make a positive impact and support our future generation with exciting, creative, and compelling learning experiences. I too believe that we can learn a lot from kids about what kids want and need in their lives. And I too believe that kids can teach us what adults might want in their lives (but are too afraid to ask). But most importantly, I believe that making things for kids is less constrained than making things for adults. When you design technologies for adults, typically it is to help the adult be more productive or efficient at their work. There are many specific, often complex, goals that must be met. However, when you design technologies for children, the goals may be complex, but you can also make things that ask for laughter, excitement, or creativity. One 6-year-old boy named Sim once told me that technology for kids has to have *high smile value.* If the smile value is low it is just no good. Imagine if everyone worked on finding a high smile value—what a different world this might be!

Finally, I have come to realize that there is one more reason why I make technology for children. I like working with kids! The phrases "it's not possible" or "that's the wrong way to do that" don't seem to be a part of what kids say. They are design partners who tend to be more open to new possibilities. That is not to say that children have less to discuss. If you give them a chance to tell you what they're thinking, they most certainly will. And from my experience, they will tell you honestly—in fact, they can be brutal in their honesty (Druin 1996). But, through the years, I have found that a polite design partner is far less useful than one who can quickly get to the point.

For all of these reasons, I have come to have a passion for working with and for kids. I have also come to wonder why more people aren't making things for children too. With all of these great reasons, I somehow assumed everyone would be flocking to the field. But in the past, this has not been the case. One reason for this could be that only recently has technology for children become a successful commercial industry. For many years, only small numbers of industry and academic professionals were concerned with children and technology (Druin and Solomon 1996). For the most part, people didn't see this area as a financially lucrative field. They felt that since schools generally didn't have enormous amounts of money, this field would never take off. But today it has, partially because schools and communities now place an importance on acquiring and teaching with new technologies. In addition, computers have found their way into our homes by the millions— and parents have found them to be an important entertainment and educational tool (President's Committee of Advisors 1997).

As these new technologies become an integral part of more schools and homes, the need becomes ever greater to continue to develop new, creative, exciting technologies for children. The questions then become, How will these technologies be created? What design practices are successful in developing these new technologies? And what examples can be found today that suggest new directions for the future? A discussion needs to be started on these questions now. There are exciting opportunities and pressing challenges in finding new design solutions that can support our children with technologies throughout their lives. How we choose to take advantage of these opportunities and meet those challenges will change not only the technologies we make but also the lives of the children that use them.

This Book

The authors in this book are well acquainted with these challenges and opportunities. From their vast experience in academia and industry, they can offer you examples of new processes and products. If you are a professional working in the field, or hope to be one soon, this book can support and challenge you in your current and future work. This book looks at the how, the what, and the why.

Authors from diverse backgrounds with extraordinary experiences tell their stories, relate their practices, and explain their new technologies. Each chapter offers a case study of real-life work in developing new technologies for children. The authors discuss the design methodologies they use, their approach to bringing kids into the development process, and the knowledge base they have developed about children as technology users. They also discuss commercial products and university research projects. These chapters describe everything from new Internet tools, to innovative programming languages for kids, to new computational construction kits made with LEGO bricks. These diverse technologies support children as software designers, scientists, mathematicians, artists, and more. In each chapter, you can see how the technology design process affects the product design, which in turn truly affects the world for our children.

You will find that this book is structured in two parts: Part I, "The Design Process," and Part II, "The Technology of Children." In Part I, the design process is discussed, offering six diverse perspectives from academic and industry professionals. In Chapter 1, industry experts from Microsoft Corporation discuss the role of usability engineers in the development of their products for children. They offer design techniques, guidelines, and real-world product examples of their work at Microsoft. It is a wonderful glimpse into the corporate world of software development for children. In Chapter 2, researchers from the University of Sussex in England discuss their experiences in bringing children into the design process. They examine a framework for working with children in the context of designing software that supports the understanding of ecology and the notion of food webs. In doing so, these researchers ask important questions about the nature of children as informants in the design process. In Chapter 3, researchers from the University of Maryland, University of New Mexico, and Louisiana State University discuss their experiences in partnering with children to develop new technologies. They offer useful guidelines for three research approaches that support an understanding of children's technology wants and needs. An example of their design process is presented in the development of a new drawing tool for children. In Chapter 4, the researcher's role in the design of children's media is discussed by a media research consultant. From product specification to the marketing process, the challenges of the design process are presented. An interesting real-world example of this process is discussed as it relates to an asthma education video game for the Super Nintendo platform. In Chapter 5, researchers from Virginia Polytechnic Institute discuss their work with children and teachers in designing

Internet experiences in the classroom. Researchers discuss their participatory design strategies and scenario-based methods in bringing children and teachers into the design process. The chapter offers an important perspective on what can be done to change the technology tools of our classroom learning environments. Finally, in Chapter 6, experiences at UCLA with children as software developers are discussed. An example is presented of what is possible when children are software designers and testers of their own technologies.

In Part II of this book, the authors focus on examples of technology that they have developed that point in future technology directions. These authors continue to discuss their design process but in the context of explaining their new constructivist tools for children. Each example that is discussed offers children the chance to be authors of their own technology experiences. With these tools, they can build new robotic worlds, design new video presentations, program new simulations, and more.

In Chapter 7, researchers from the MIT Media Laboratory discuss their experiences in creating new construction tool kits for children. The authors present their innovative work in developing programmable LEGO bricks, a new generation of the Logo programming language, and a new virtual world for children built by children. In Chapter 8, researchers from the University of Toronto discuss their work in developing a new video authoring tool for children. Exciting examples are described that show what children created using this tool during multimedia summer camps. In addition, children's feedback about this new technology is examined. In Chapter 9, industry experts from Stagecast Software discuss their experiences in developing a new programming language for children. With the Cocoa technology, children can create simulations with a visual approach to programming. In Chapter 10, ToonTalk, a tool for building animated worlds, is discussed by its creator at Animated Programs. This chapter offers examples of how children with different learning styles can be supported with this special technology. And finally, in Chapter 11, researchers from the University of Colorado discuss their experiences in combining the ancient art of origami with new computer technologies to develop HyperGami. They offer a unique perspective in combining the low-tech materials of paper folding with the high-tech tools of the computer to create what they call a "middle-tech" learning experience for children.

In all, these 11 chapters offer diverse views from academic and industry professionals of what is possible in the technology design process. It is our hope that this book will offer you guidance and inspiration in how you develop your new technologies for children. In addition, we hope that this is only the start of new discussions, new ideas, and new possibilities for the future of kids, technology, and design.

References

Collis, B. 1994. A triple innovation in the Netherlands: Supporting a new curriculum with new technologies through a new kind of strategy for teacher support and stimulation. *Journal of Computing in Teacher Education* 11(1): 12–18.

Druin, A. 1996. A place called childhood. *Interactions* 3(1): 17–22.

Druin, A. 1997a. An introduction. *SIGCHI Bulletin* 29(1): 18–19.

Druin, A. 1997b. Why do we make technologies for kids? *SIGCHI Bulletin* 29(2): 18–19.

Druin, A. 1998a. Private communication.

Druin, A. 1998b. Private communication.

Druin, A., and Platt, M. 1997. Children's online environments. In C. Forsythe, E. Grose, and J. Ratner, eds. *Human factors and Web development.* Mahwah, NJ: Lawrence Erlbaum, 47–55.

Druin, A., and Solomon, C. 1996. *Designing multimedia environments for children: Computers, creativity and kids.* New York: John Wiley & Sons.

Dwyer, D. C., Ringstaff, C., and Sandholtz, J. H. 1991. Change in beliefs and practices in technology-rich classrooms. *Educational Leadership* 48(1): 45–54.

Kay, A. 1996. Revealing the elephant: The use and misuse of computers in education. *Educom Review* 31(4): 22–28.

Lewis, P. 1995. Ill children to get 3-D playground out in cyberspace. *The New York Times,* June 8, p. C3.

Norton, P. 1992. When technology meets subject-matter disciplines in education: Part three: Incorporating the computer as method. *Educational Technology* 32(8): 35–44.

Papert, S. 1980. *Mindstorms: Children, computers and powerful ideas.* New York: Basic Books.

Postman, N. 1995. *The end of education: Redefining the value of school.* New York: Alfred A. Knopf.

President's Committee of Advisors on Science and Technology. 1997. *Report to the President on the use of technology to strengthen K–12 education in the United States.* Washington, DC: President's Committee of Advisors on Science and Technology, Executive Office of the President of the United States.

Sheingold, K. 1991. Restructuring for learning with technology. *Phi Delta Kappan* 73(1): 17–27.

Shneiderman, B. 1992. Engagement and construction: Education strategies for the post-TV era. In *Proceedings of the International Conference on Computer Learning.* New York: Springer-Verlag, 39–45.

Spoehr, K. T. 1994. Enhancing the acquisition of conceptual structures through hypermedia. In K. McGilly, ed. *Classroom lessons: Integrating cognitive theory and classroom practice.* Cambridge, MA: MIT Press, 75–101.

Stoll, C. 1995. *Silicon snake oil: Second thoughts on the information highway.* New York: Doubleday.

Thompson, A. D., Simonson, M. R., and Hargrave, C. P. 1992. *Educational technology: A review of the research,* revised edition. Washington, DC: Association for Educational Communications and Technology.

Tinker, R. F. 1993. Telecommuting as a progressive force in education. In *Technical Education Research Center [TERC] Technical Report.* Cambridge, MA: TERC Publications.

Turkle, S. 1995. *Life on the screen.* New York: Simon & Schuster.

Part I

The Design Process

Chapter One

The Role of Usability Research in Designing Children's Computer Products

Libby Hanna

IMG Usability, Microsoft Corporation

Kirsten Risden

IMG Usability, Microsoft Corporation

Mary Czerwinski

Microsoft Research, Microsoft Corporation

Kristin J. Alexander

Hardware Ergonomics and Usability,
Microsoft Corporation

1.1 Introduction

Usability research with children has often been considered either too difficult to carry out with unruly subjects or not necessary for an audience that is satisfied with gratuitous animations and funny noises. In addition, traditional measures of usability such as productivity indices and speed and efficiency of task completion are not generally appropriate to use for children's products. However, our research at Microsoft indicates that the usability of a product is closely related to children's enjoyment of it. Therefore we have worked hard to develop sound methodologies for usability testing with children. In this chapter, we describe the methods we use during various stages of product development, design guidelines that have resulted from our research, and useful practices that we have learned along the way for working with product teams and upper management.

Microsoft usability engineers have been working on children's products for many years, but it was only recently that usability was formally incorporated as a standard practice during product design. It might be useful to begin this chapter by examining the evolution of children's usability research at Microsoft. At the outset, the Microsoft Kids product teams felt strongly that children's engagement was more important than, or at least as important as, usability. In fact, some product teams were abandoning usability work during the development cycle because it appeared too difficult to evaluate product ideas for "fun." When usability engineers attempted to operationally define engagement for research purposes, it was clear that a stable and consistent definition was not available.

One of the most productive research efforts of the Kids usability staff was to take on this problem. Through literature review, surveys, and response tracking over product generations, the usability engineers were able to define at least some of the components of a fun product (Risden, Hanna, and Kanerva 1997). Factor analyses of children's responses to questions assessing liking and usability of computer software revealed dimensions of engagement such as "familiarity," "control," and "challenge" that fit with research and theoretical discussions of others (e.g., Lepper 1988; Malone 1980; Whalen and Csiksentmihalyi 1991). Most importantly, this research demonstrated that ease of use is a critical determinant of engagement and as such is key to every children's product if it is to be a success. The research also helped product teams value the background and skills that usability engineers could bring to new and difficult issues in the design of children's computer products. Our research was a fabulous mechanism for broadening our argument for why usability work is important during Kids product design.

However, it was not always obvious that the Kids usability group was making progress in establishing a precedent for user-centered design. As with other teams, battles were often lost because of schedule or budget, and these losses were very disappointing given how much effort the team was exerting to get successful products out the door. We knew progress had occurred, however, when one of the usability staff was elevated to a "team lead" role and allowed to attend upper-level staffing meetings. Here the usability lead was able to fight strongly for product redesign, and even schedule changes, when feedback from children demonstrated a need for it. Eventually, all usability issues observed in the laboratory were integrated into a database and given the same kind of high-priority treatment in the company as other software bugs.

At about the same time that the Kids usability engineers were researching the dimensions of engagement, departments within Microsoft were reorganizing into smaller, functionally organized teams. Usability decentralized and the Kids usability engineers moved next door to their teammates on the product teams. Usability engineers now reported to a divisional usability manager as well as having a dotted-line reporting relationship to program managers. This arrangement ensured that usability engineers were rewarded not only for their usability expertise but also for how well they worked with their teams and toward their teams' goals. Over time, it became clear that this dual reporting structure elevated the status of the usability engineers within the Kids product teams. The close proximity to teams is now something that no usability engineer would give up willingly.

The usability engineering staff that works on children's products is uniquely qualified to advocate usability engineering. As developmental and educational psychologists, the staff has adopted an energetic, rigorous approach to product design and research and has been able to attain respect for their contribution to the product design cycle.

In the rest of this chapter, we describe the range of methods we use during the course of product development. Then we discuss some of the child-technology interaction guidelines that we have developed through our work on specific Microsoft children's products. Finally, we suggest ways to work with product teams as a usability engineer. All the expertise in the world will not guarantee success if usability engineers don't know how to communicate effectively with their teams. It is our sincere hope that other children's usability engineers will benefit from the lessons learned by the Microsoft Kids usability team.

1.2   Methods of Usability Research with Children

Usability Research Processes

When we conduct usability research, we follow three basic processes common to the field of human-computer interaction (Dumas and Redish 1993; Nielson 1993; Rubin 1994). The first is to analyze the user—to understand the user's skills, knowledge, and expectations. For children's products, we begin with a targeted age range and supply information about children within that range. One common age range for children's products is 3- to 6-year-olds. We help the team understand both 3-year-olds and 6-year-olds and how they interact with computer programs. A 3-year-old may not understand certain words like "select"; a 6-year-old may resent a "babyish" character on screen. Individual differences in temperament and attention span also have to be taken into account. The product needs to accommodate children who click madly around a screen as well as those who sit back and wait to be told what to do.

The second process is to analyze tasks—to understand the user activities that a product is intended to support. When analyzing usage by children, we look at the goals of the product and the goals of children. The goal of the product may be to teach the alphabet, but children will probably not play with the product because they want to learn the alphabet. A child's goal may be to explore and find out what happens or to win a game.

The third process is to design a product in iterative phases based on the analysis of users and their tasks. This puts the previous two steps into the actual design process. Iterative design is put into practice by testing an idea, revising it according to feedback from the data, and testing the revised idea.

Usability Research Techniques

Table 1.1 lists the techniques we have used in our usability research and when each method is most useful in the product development cycle. The paragraphs that follow provide details and examples of how each technique has been implemented in our work.

Expert Reviews

At the very beginning of the design process, expert reviews routinely provide "quick checks" on design to catch obvious problems. We look at design specifications or storyboards and use child development milestones as well

Table 1.1

Techniques for usability research with children

Research technique	Applicable stage of product development
Expert reviews	Throughout
Site visits	Concept; preliminary design
Survey construction	Concept; preliminary design; beta testing
Card-sorting tasks	Concept; preliminary design
Paper prototype tests	Preliminary design
Iterative laboratory tests	Prototyping; developing
Longitudinal tests	Beta testing; final products

as common usability guidelines to check for violations. For example, a game for 4-year-old children that requires reading is not age-appropriate. A design that provides a simple yellow circle on the screen for help functionality violates a usability guideline of "recognition over recall" (Nielson 1993). The button needs to have an image that gives more information about its function so that a child can immediately recognize its purpose instead of having to memorize it with repeated use. Issues and recommendations can be communicated to the team in a written format or in informal meetings such as "spec bashes." The issues and recommendations generated in this way can also be summarized into general guidelines that other teams can use as a resource as well. When usability engineers sit on a team and participate in design meetings, expert reviews can be incorporated continuously in the design process.

Site Visits

Site visits provide information about children's use of products in context. Site visits for word processing or spreadsheet programs often focus on looking at the work environment and how to increase productivity or efficiency within that environment. For children's products, we tend to focus on how children use products over time, examining what makes a product retain appeal and replayability or how quickly children master certain types of interactivity. Our goal is to increase the chance that children will choose our products over many other options in their free time.

In homes, we have observed children using competitive products in order to gather information about the relative importance of features. For example, when we began designing an educational title that incorporated a unique help system, we observed children at home turning off the help systems in competitive products because the help systems were disrupting

Figure 1.1

*A scale for asking children
to rate software on attributes
of usability and engagement*

game play. This observation helped us to increase the relevance and decrease the intrusiveness of our help system.

We conduct site visits at schools and day care centers to gather group data. This is especially useful for exploring children's preferences and other qualitative reactions to design ideas. We have interviewed children at schools about Internet use and their current interests in commercial products. We have taken character drawings to day care centers and gathered preference data (using a paired-comparison technique, where children are shown all possible pairs of characters and asked to choose which they like better in each pair).

Survey Construction

In some cases, we have had to adapt typical survey methods to be age-appropriate. For example, when asking children between about 5 to 10 years of age to rate attributes of computer products, we have developed the use of a vertical scale with a smiling face on the top and a frowning face on the bottom, shown in Figure 1.1 (Risden, Hanna, and Kanerva 1997).

Researchers can read questionnaire items out loud and then ask children to draw a line across the scale to mark "how much" of something is true of what they are rating. We find that children are able to respond more reliably to a pictorial representation such as this with its meaningful anchors (smiling and sad faces) and concepts of more and less (vertical rather than horizontal presentation of the scale) than to Likert-type scales.

When children under 5 years of age are participating in laboratory tests, we often ask parents to rate features for both their own liking and their children's liking. These ratings can be compared to observations of children's behavior to validate our reports on what the children find appealing. We also create questionnaires for parents to answer specific research questions. For example, before revising a parent-report feature in an educational product, the team wanted to know how much parents actually used the feature and benefited from it. We developed a questionnaire that asked about the feature in the midst of questions about many other features. This helped avoid focusing too much attention on the feature of interest.

Card-Sorting Tasks

Another research technique that can contribute to early product concept design is card sorting. Children as young as 8 can be asked to sort cards, containing pictures or words, into spontaneous or predetermined categories. When software groups features, tools, or activities into preassigned categories and children need to follow the hierarchy to access the tools, this procedure can be used to check how well the preassigned categories fit children's expectations.

This technique was used during the design phase for the revision of Creative Writer (© 1994 Microsoft Corporation), a word processing program for children. Figure 1.2 is a screen shot from the original program, where numerous icons for different categories of tools are displayed across the top of the screen (in the toolbar for a new document). These include such categories as font format tools, clip art, page format tools, editing tools, and so on.

In one of the usability studies done for the redesign, children were asked to sort cards containing the names of word processing tools. The results from a cluster analysis helped the team regroup the tools into four main categories—writing tools, page tools, picture tools, and idea tools—which are represented in four large icons across the top of the screen in Creative Writer2 (© 1996 Microsoft Corporation), shown in Figure 1.3.

Paper Prototype Tests

Even very preliminary functional designs can be tested with children by using paper materials. Screen shots, sketches, or storyboards can be put together in a notebook. Children can "click" on things by pointing to them with their finger. As they click on navigational elements, the researcher can turn the pages to take them to the appropriate place in the program. Active elements can be simulated by cutting out the pieces and allowing children

Figure 1.2

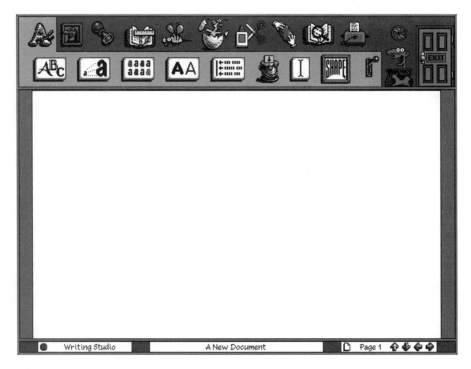

The "new document" screen in the first version of Creative Writer (© 1994 Microsoft Corporation), showing icons for different categories of tools across the top

to manipulate them. Once children are interacting with the design, errors and observed confusion can directly predict errors children will make when using the future computer product.

For example, preliminary designs for the science exploration title *Scholastic's The Magic School Bus Explores in the Age of Dinosaurs* (© 1996 Microsoft Corporation; © 1996 Scholastic Inc.; based on *The Magic School Bus* book series © Joanna Cole and Bruce Degen) were tested using drawings of the front of the bus at various locations (shown in Figures 1.4 through 1.6).

As children navigated to the various locations, it was easy to assess how well they could remember the required sequence to "drive" the bus. When they first entered the bus, they saw an image of the school through the bus window to show them they were in the present (Figure 1.4). Then they had to click on the steering wheel to bring up a destination map in the window (Figure 1.5). After clicking on one of the dots on the map, an image of the resulting location would appear in the window (Figure 1.6). In the test, children had trouble remembering the particular step to bring up a destination map, so the final design included alternate ways to access the map.

Figure 1.3

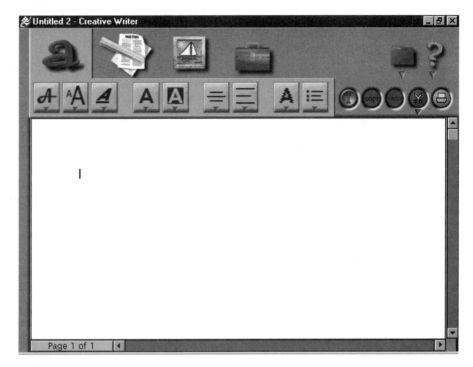

The "new document" screen in Creative Writer2 (© 1996 Microsoft Corporation), showing the reorganization of tool categories after card-sorting studies with children

Team members may discount results from paper tests, feeling that the additional audio and animation of the computer product will eliminate children's confusion. However, these very preliminary stages are the only time at which there is still the possibility of radical redesign. A precise and rigorous simulation of interactivity will usually convince teams that the paper test is an adequate measure and can be achieved with a little forethought and creativity. It also offers the opportunity to observe children interacting with the design almost right from the start.

Iterative Laboratory Tests

Children can participate in traditional laboratory usability tests with only minor adjustments in procedure (see [Hanna, Risden, and Alexander 1997] for guidelines on adapting these tests for children). We use a typical laboratory setup, with a one-way mirror into an observation area for team members and videotaping equipment to record behavior and computer screen captures. Children participate one-on-one with the researcher. During

Figure **1.4**

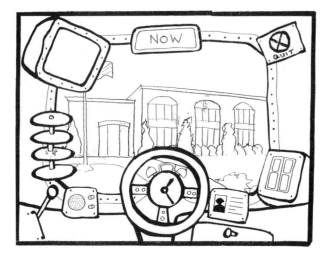

A drawing of the initial "front of the bus" screen used in a paper prototype test for Scholastic's The Magic School Bus Explores in the Age of Dinosaurs *(© 1996 Microsoft Corporation; © 1996 Scholastic Inc.; based on* The Magic School Bus *book series © Joanna Cole and Bruce Degen)*

Figure **1.5**

*A drawing of the destination map that appears in the front of the bus after clicking the steering wheel (*Scholastic's The Magic School Bus Explores in the Age of Dinosaurs, *© 1996 Microsoft Corporation; © 1996 Scholastic Inc.; based on* The Magic School Bus *book series © Joanna Cole and Bruce Degen)*

Figure 1.6

*A drawing of the front of the bus as it appears after clicking "Cretaceous Mongolia" in the destination map (*Scholastic's The Magic School Bus Explores in the Age of Dinosaurs *© 1996 Microsoft Corporation; © 1996 Scholastic Inc.; based on* The Magic School Bus *book series © Joanna Cole and Bruce Degen)*

these tests we can quickly uncover problems by observing children maneuvering through products on their own. Children are very accustomed to asking for and getting help from others when they use new products. However, because our goal is to find out what children can do with the product without intervention, we try to turn the situation around. Instead of helping them progress with the product as it is intended to be used, we try to find out what they want to do with the product.

As products begin to be built, usability is assessed in an iterative research process. A feature is tested, revised, then tested again to make sure that children understand its components. The peekaboo game for the animatronic doll Actimates Interactive Barney (© 1997 Microsoft Corporation; © 1997 Lyons Partnership, L. P.) was tested repeatedly to ensure that the sensors inside the doll were sensitive enough to respond consistently to small children's attempts to cover the doll's eyes. The early learning title *My Personal Tutor Preschool Workshop* (© 1997 Microsoft Corporation) was tested on a monthly basis to make sure that young children could understand audio instructions, recognize and use navigational icons, find hotspots, and complete problems in activities. For example, the icons for returning to the main screen and for changing levels went through several versions, until testing showed consistent success with using the host character pointing backwards for "return" and using a scale with dots representing the 1–3 levels of the game for "levels." The final versions are shown in the screen shot of a sample activity in Figure 1.7 (see also Color Plate).

Laboratory testing can offer a quick check on product appeal, especially for gathering information on how to avoid negative reactions. Although children may not display much positive emotion in the laboratory, any sign of negative emotion deserves attention. Observing signs of disengagement like rocking, sighing, or turning away from the product gives a picture of how much something may or may not appeal to children. For example, when testing Actimates Barney, several children were observed ending their play when the doll wouldn't respond to initiations of the peekaboo game. The doll was presented as a play partner for children, so naturally children expected him to respond to their actions, just like a real partner would. This

Figure 1.7

A screen shot of the "patterns" activity in My Personal Tutor Preschool Workshop *(© 1997 Microsoft Corporation), showing final "return" and "levels" icons (on the bottom of the screen) after iterative testing*

issue was resolved by making all of the doll's routines interruptible whenever children initiated the peekaboo game. With this change, peekaboo became their favorite activity. Figure 1.8 (Color Plate only) shows a child playing with Actimates Barney.

Longitudinal Tests

Longitudinal research on children's products often evaluates the effectiveness of educational content or techniques (e.g., Kulik and Kulik 1991; Lieberman 1997). When a product is completed or nearly completed, we can conduct similar tests under industry time constraints by bringing children into the laboratory for repeat visits over 2 to 3 weeks. We plan for a total amount of time in the lab that approximates the average amount of time children may use the product over 2 to 3 months at home. Pretests and posttests offer quick checks on learning, and comparisons of how quickly children can navigate through products during repeat visits give additional insight into usability.

We have put beta versions of products in homes and surveyed parents over several days or weeks to assess younger children's progress through games and the discoverability of key features. For example, a team designed a product that constrained children to following a set progression of activities. Putting the product in the home and gathering responses from parents about children's frustration with the lack of freedom was crucial feedback to help the team develop a less restrictive design. (Although the team had observed this frustration in earlier lab testing, they felt strongly that children would accept the constraint over time. Home testing persuaded them otherwise.) Survey construction work for gathering this information included both qualitative questionnaires and scale construction involving the use of statistical techniques like factor analysis and reliability assessments.

Designers may approach a product for children with the attitude "I know kids" or "I have kids so I can design for kids," and they may come up with appealing and age-appropriate graphics and humor. But how to design a game that children can easily figure out how to play may still be elusive. Putting the product in the proper context for children and looking at the product through their eyes is the crucial task. Observing even a few children using the product during early product design will catch a substantial number of issues that are difficult to predict ahead of time. Evaluating products with children at the end of the product development cycle provides invaluable information for future directions.

1.3   User Interface Design Guidelines for Children

From our experiences observing children interacting with both successful and unsuccessful UI designs, and the work of others both in academia and the computer industry (Druin and Solomon 1996; Haugland and Shade 1990; Henninger 1994; Robertson 1994; Wright et al. 1989), we have come up with some guidelines to use when designing multimedia environments for children. This is not by any means a complete list. Rather, the guidelines included here reflect helpful principles that have emerged from our work. Table 1.2 contains the general areas and specific guidelines for each.

Activity Design

The best software, like the best play materials, should provide a tool that allows children to explore the world creatively, using their imaginations to manipulate and assimilate knowledge about the world around them. A successful design gives children control of the computer environment and allows them to set the pace of the interaction.

Design activities to be inherently interesting and challenging so children will want to do them for their own sake. The best interactivity models real-world play scenarios that children are most interested in (e.g., for preschoolers, dress-up and fantasy role-playing, construction play, drawing and coloring, action figure and doll play, etc.) and uses intuitive, logical, and familiar procedures for accomplishing activities. Each step should make sense to children so that they can easily remember what to do. Any activity that requires children to signal when they are done should use a logical sequence, such as pulling the chain to the train whistle or opening a gate to let something through.

Design activities to allow for expanding complexity and support children as they move from one level to the next in use of the product. Activities should begin with single-step interactivity, so children do not have to remember several steps in order to complete a problem. As children gain mastery of the activity, steps can slowly be added to increase the challenge and complexity. Support children in mastering the activity by supplying feedback that helps them learn new information. In structured activities where children are asked to supply the correct answer, give feedback for wrong choices to redirect children and teach them the concept (e.g., "That's blue, I need red"). Activities should never jump levels of difficulty without warning or sufficient practice in the preceding level.

Design supportive reward structures that take children's developmental level and context of use into account. The best method for motivating

Table 1.2

UI guidelines for children's computer products

Areas of product design	Guidelines for design
Activities	• Design activities to be inherently interesting and challenging so children will want to do them for their own sake. • Design activities to allow for expanding complexity and support children as they move from one level to the next in use of the product. • Design supportive reward structures that take children's developmental level and context of use into account.
Instructions	• Present instructions in an age-appropriate format. • Design instructions to be easy to comprehend and remember. • On-screen character interventions should be supportive rather than distracting. • Allow children to control access to instructional information.
Screen layout	• Design icons to be visually meaningful to children. • Use cursor design to help communicate functionality. • Use rollover audio, animation, and highlighting to indicate where to find functionality.

children to stick with a computer program may be designing intrinsically rewarding activities in which mastering a challenging problem is rewarding in itself (Lepper 1988; Malone 1980). However, many educational programs make use of extrinsic rewards as well, for example, to encourage children to try an activity that they find less enjoyable. The following guidelines pertain to the design of extrinsic rewards. These can be as simple as congratulatory audio and animations that play when a child has successfully completed a problem or as complicated as intricate point systems that accumulate to offer access to new games or prizes.

Rewards should be given consistently even when children repeat problems or activity levels they have done before. Children may fail at harder levels and will need to be able to reexperience the same success at the easier level to gain confidence in moving forward. Children should never be punished (by the absence of a reward) for repeating activities. Reward structures designed to motivate children to continue will need to address young children's problems with delayed gratification and self-monitoring. Older children (6 years and up) can be highly motivated by point systems and obtaining "high scores." However, younger children are often unable to track their own progress toward end goals unless they are given frequent reminders and intermittent rewards. Finally, humor in rewards should take into account the intellectual level of children in the target age range. The sophistication of the humor should offer both silliness and incongruity humor that they can understand (McGee 1971). Some humor directed at adults is appropriate, as many parents accompany their young children on the computer, and anything that makes the experience enjoyable for both children and adults is commendable. But adult-directed humor should never detract from children's engagement by interrupting progress or confusing children.

Instruction Design

Present instructions in an age-appropriate format. For example, avoid on-screen text when designing products for young children. Add a feature that enables children of all ages to have any on-screen text read aloud for them. Children may be beginning readers through second grade, and even older children are not accustomed to reading on computer screens. They usually will not read text unless they absolutely have to.

Design instructions to be easy to comprehend and remember. The language should be clear and simple without the use of concepts children have not yet learned. For example, don't reference left and right with young children. Use on-screen characters that speak instructions. Children pay more attention to characters than to audio alone, and they can click the characters to hear instructions repeated. Add highlighting or animation of objects that are being referred to in instructions to help direct attention.

On-screen character interventions should be supportive rather than distracting. Make sure the on-screen character's comments are appropriately timed in relation to on-screen content. Prime children for events that are about to happen, comment on events that are in the process of occurring, or reflect on just-completed events. If there is more than one on-screen character, they should not talk over each other. Multiple characters should complement rather than compete with or copy one another. Finally, characters should not animate or talk constantly: such behavior will distract children's attention away from important content or their own accomplishments. (See [Reeves and Nass 1996] for further discussion of the importance of characters and social conventions such as politeness in computer products.)

Allow children to control access to instructional information. Always allow children to terminate animations and interrupt audio with mouse clicks. Children may assume something is broken if their mouse clicks do not do anything. They do not have the patience to sit through lengthy instructions and will not be able to absorb much of the information at any one time. Instructions can be repeated in the form of feedback for incorrect or irrelevant choices or can be accessed by clicking help characters. This feature works well for speeding up game play.

Screen Layout Design

Design icons to be visually meaningful to children. The best icons for children are easily recognizable and familiar, representing items in their everyday world. For example, use doors for going "outside," and stop signs for stopping activities. Design icons and accompanying hotspots to be large to accommodate young children's developing cursor control. A common rule is to make icons at least the size of a quarter. Make icons look "clickable" by using three-dimensional imagery. When you place a "return" button on the screen, do not also have a "quit" button. When both are on the screen simultaneously, children tend to choose the "quit" button to exit activities and then accidentally exit the program.

Use cursor design to help communicate functionality. The cursor optimally has three states: a resting state, a "hot" state when rolling over an active element, and a "wait" state during screen transitions. The wait cursor should use a symbol that children associate with time passing, such as the traditional hourglass, clock, or fingers counting down (make sure these are big enough to be identifiable for children). The cursor also may change into the active element when using sticky-drag-and-drop (when the element sticks to the cursor with the first click and then is placed with the second click) instead of click-and-drag interactivity. Make sure that the cursor is designed with a clearly defined point so children can tell how to activate hotspots. If a wait cursor is not used, find another way to communicate what the computer is doing during transitions. Audio can tell children that things are being set up. When children have not interacted with the computer for a lengthy period of time, signify that the program is waiting with some mild animation or audio (e.g., toe-tapping, humming).

Use rollover audio, animation, and highlighting to indicate where to find functionality. Hotspots on the screen can highlight or animate to indicate to children what is clickable and what is not. Navigational elements can animate on rollover to show children they have their cursor in the right place. Navigational elements can also have rollover audio that tells children what the function is (e.g., "quit"). Add a 0.1–0.5 second delay for rollover audio so children can use it deliberately. Otherwise they tend to randomly hear audio after their cursor is already somewhere else and they fail to make the connection.

1.4 Working with Development Teams

Sound research methods and guidelines based on empirical observation are critical tools for making good usability recommendations to teams. However, even the very best of recommendations will not ensure usable software if a development team is unwilling or unable to incorporate them into the product at the right time. This section discusses what we have learned about integrating with teams at Microsoft and suggests guidelines that can help to ensure that a usability engineer's expertise really benefits the product.

There are several roles that a usability engineer may take on in working with a team. These roles typically grow and evolve over time. Initially, a developmental psychologist in this position may contribute primarily through the collection of data and through the application of the developmental literature to design issues. Team members may even view a usability engineer as having a sort of administrative role in setting up studies to allow the team to have access to target users. As the engineer's position within the team matures, however, he or she can take the lead in mapping out long-term research strategies. The usability engineer may also be a record keeper and disseminator of knowledge gained about users in current and previous design cycles. As roles and responsibilities become more varied, the engineer's influence becomes stronger and more pervasive throughout the design cycle. The engineer may be asked to settle debates objectively, to find the most cost-effective ways of getting usability engineering into a design, to take a hand in design, and so on.

Table 1.3 lists the general guidelines for working with product teams. We have found these practices and approaches to be effective in incorporating usability engineering into products and promoting the growth of a usability engineer's role within a team. These guidelines can be used by usability engineers themselves or by team members who want to facilitate the integration of usability into their teams.

Be Responsive to Team Needs

Most products have well-articulated goals. These goals usually fit into a certain time frame, overall business strategy, and set of technological constraints. Understanding and constantly monitoring the team's goals and the context that these goals arise in is imperative for delivering the right recommendations at the right time to the right people. The key to successfully doing this is working directly with the team (as opposed to through some intermediary) and seeing yourself and being seen as a partner rather than a regulator. The guidelines below suggest ways of developing a partnering role.

Know what the product goals, technology limitations, and development schedules are and align your usability engineering work with them. Figure out, from reading specs, product visions, schedules, and attending meetings, what the critical usability work is and when it needs to be done. Listen hard and ask the right questions so you have a deep rather than a surface-level understanding of where teams are trying to go with features they are proposing. These practices, more than any other, can put you in a position to help the team realize their vision, which is quite different from merely being in a position to make the team aware of usability issues associated with a particular feature.

Table 1.3

Guidelines for working with teams

General guidelines	*Implications*
Be responsive to team needs.	• Know what the product goals, technology limitations, and development schedules are and align your usability engineering work with them. • Develop effective working relationships with key decision makers. • Be aware of how usability work impacts the team's schedule and find ways to make usability fit into that time frame rather than the other way around. • Be flexible and creative in aligning your work with team goals. • Use a variety of methods for getting the team to think deeply about usability issues.
Carve a unique niche for usability engineering on the team.	• Always speak from data, including your own data, that of other usability engineers, and research findings in the developmental and educational literature. • Avoid taking sides in political issues.
Handle conflict constructively.	• Try not to take things personally. • Seek a positive solution for everyone. • Whenever possible, try to resolve conflicts without escalating them to higher levels.

Develop effective working relationships with key decision makers. Figure out who the critical decision makers are and work with them. Note that job titles will not always tell you who the key decision makers are. You will generally have to rely on observations of team dynamics to determine this. When you do identify the key decision makers, make sure they review study proposals, come to usability tests, and attend all results meetings.

Be aware of how usability work impacts the team's schedule and find ways to make usability fit into that time frame rather than the other way around. For example, take on the job of creating study materials (e.g., screen shots, prototypes, etc.) when designers and developers on the team are working on their own deadlines. Get study results to teams as quickly as possible (within 2 days is best), and conduct results meetings as efficiently as possible.

Be flexible and creative in aligning your work with team goals. Create practices around the unique circumstances of the team rather than adopting a one-size-fits-all routine. Be ready to revise plans if the situation calls for it. Check another part of the design if a prototype will not be ready and a study is scheduled. Don't panic if a certain prescribed approach does not, or cannot, work given the way a particular team functions. Always keep in mind that being flexible does not mean you are wishy-washy, but rather means you differentiate between what is and is not important and you are ready to take any route necessary that leads you to what is important.

Use a variety of methods for getting the team to think deeply about usability issues. Phrase your findings and recommendations in ways that the team can quickly understand. Suggest ways to resolve usability problems, but watch for and encourage team members to think of even better ways to address the issue. Creating drawings that reflect the way suggestions could be implemented in design often helps spur constructive discussion and debate. Provide varied and ample opportunities for team members to have contact with users.

Carve a Unique Niche for Usability Engineering on the Team

As the roles of a usability engineer multiply, it is important to have a basic framework that ties these roles together. This is important for the team because it gives them a context within which to interpret the engineer's input to the design. It is important for the engineer as well because it gives a consistent set of assumptions to fall back on for providing that input. The guidelines below suggest practices that have been important in helping us to carve our niches within teams.

Always speak from data, including your own data, that of other usability engineers, and research findings in the developmental and educational literature. Know what to say to provide backups to your claims. You might show additional data, explain how it maps with or replicates previous findings, or use logic. Whatever method you use, do take the time to check backups to support your findings and recommendations. Do not be afraid to acknowledge when you do not have data on an issue and, if appropriate, suggest ways of getting some.

Avoid taking sides in political issues. Taking sides can hurt your standing on the team in at least two ways. First, you never know how the makeup of a team will change. The person you were against one day may be the same person you need to develop an alliance with the next. Second, showing a strong partisan bias will bring your overall objectivity into question. A better approach is to focus on finding an objective way of dealing with issues that pertain directly to your work and the usability of the product. Acknowledge that your role is to present the issues and not to determine the business case for addressing them. You are an unbiased party that provides the data to help the team make decisions.

Handle Conflict Constructively

Conflict is bound to arise in any situation where groups with different backgrounds and values work together dynamically. This conflict may have to do with misunderstandings or disagreements about roles, procedures, or product goals. Even in the most professionally run settings, conflict can arise because of mismatches in personal style. Although conflict is usually considered something to be avoided, dealing directly with the issues that give rise to conflict can be a very constructive process and one that could provide the usability engineer with opportunities for even greater integration with the team. The guidelines below suggest ways of handling conflicts, and potential conflicts, constructively.

Try not to take things personally. Make sure you react out of a concern for the product rather than a concern for ownership. In some cases, it may be wise to ask if the reason for conflict lies in your own working style or ability. The answer may give you valuable information, but make sure you are ready to hear it and use it in a constructive way. Take time to think through how to present a concern you have objectively, and ask questions that help you understand others' perspectives as to why the issue came up.

Seek a positive solution for everyone. Work out a mutually agreed upon way of proceeding. Avoid digging in your heels about a particular situation. Try to negotiate rather than maintain a position, and prepare some constructive solutions to suggest.

Whenever possible, try to resolve conflicts without escalating them to higher levels. Escalation usually adds flame to the fire by threatening everyone and makes the situation even more difficult. At the same time, you need to know when to walk away from a no-win situation or seek help from a supervisor.

In summary, usability engineers can help ensure that a product will benefit from their training, expertise, and research findings by nurturing the development of their position and reputation within a team. Although there is no set formula for doing this, we have found that working proactively to be responsive to team needs, to carve a unique and respected niche within the team, and to deal constructively with conflict when it arises has been effective for us. It is important to note that the whole notion of usability engineers nurturing the development of their position on a team implies that they work on a particular product or set of products for an extended amount of time. This can influence work practices at several levels. At an organizational level, institutions that use queuing methods to distribute usability resources (e.g., engineers are assigned to isolated studies for whatever work requests come in) may want to consider changing to models that dedicate engineers to a specific product line. At an individual level, engineers facing a reorganization should try, if possible, to move to products where they have had good working relationships with key team members in the past. The foundation that engineers have established with these people will carry over to each new product, making them much more effective than they would have been if they had to start from scratch with a completely new team.

1.5 Summary

This chapter has presented the history and work practices of the Microsoft Kids usability group and some lessons learned from our experiences. Establishing a strong and effective program of usability research has meant gaining a foothold in the corporate structure by providing professional expertise in a variety of ways and working well within product teams. We have found it invaluable to have a solid foundation in child development, research techniques, and business production cycles. To know how to gather the essential information is not enough: it is also crucial to know how and when to present it so it can be used. As we continue our research program, we will continue to accumulate guidelines to strengthen our contributions to product design at the start. We will refine usability research techniques to enable us to gather user data from children for all aspects of product design, including conceptual approaches to content development as well as specifics of navigation and game play. And we will strive to maintain children's usability research as a viable and valuable business practice. We hope that others can use the information we have provided here to aid in their own development and evaluation of computer products for children.

References

Druin, A., and Solomon, C. 1996. *Designing multimedia environments for children: Computers, creativity, and kids.* New York: John Wiley & Sons.

Dumas, J. S., and Redish, J. C. 1993. *A practical guide to usability testing.* Norwood, NJ: Ablex.

Hanna, L., Risden, K., and Alexander, K. J. 1997. Guidelines for usability testing with children. *Interactions* (September/October): 9–14.

Haugland, S. W., and Shade, D. D. 1990. *Developmental evaluations of software for young children.* Albany, NY: Delmar.

Henninger, M. L. 1994. Software for the early childhood classroom: What should it look like? *Journal of Computing in Childhood Education* 5: 167–175.

Kulik, C. C., and Kulik, J. A. 1991. Effectiveness of computer-based instruction: An updated analysis. *Computers in Human Behavior* 7: 75–94.

Lepper, M. R. 1988. Motivational considerations in the study of instruction. *Cognition and Instruction* 5: 289–309.

Lieberman, D. A. 1997. Interactive video games for health promotion: Effects on knowledge, self-efficacy, social support, and health. In R. L. Street, Jr., W. R. Gold, and T. Manning, eds., *Health Promotion and Interactive Technology: Theoretical Applications and Future Directions.* Mahwah, NJ: Lawrence Erlbaum.

Malone, T. 1980. What makes things fun to learn? A study of intrinsically motivating computer games. *Cognitive and Instructional Sciences Series.* Research report no. CIS-7 SSL-80-11. Palo Alto, CA: Palo Alto Research Center.

McGee, P. E. 1971. Cognitive development and children's comprehension of humor. *Child Development* 42: 123–138.

Nielson, J. 1993. *Usability engineering.* Chestnut Hill, MA: Academic Press.

Reeves, B., and Nass, C. 1996. *The media equation: How people treat computers, television, and new media like real people and places.* New York: Cambridge University Press.

Risden, K., Hanna, E., and Kanerva, A. 1997. Dimensions of intrinsic motivation in children's favorite computer activities. Poster session presented at the meeting of the Society for Research in Child Development, Washington, DC.

Robertson, J. W. 1994. Usability and children's software: A user-centered design methodology. *Journal of Computing in Childhood Education* 5: 257–271.

Rubin, J. 1994. *Handbook of usability testing: How to plan, design, and conduct effective tests.* New York: John Wiley.

Whalen, S., and Csiksentmihalyi, M. 1991. *Putting flow into educational practice.* Chicago: University of Chicago. ERIC Document Reproduction Service No. PS 019 952.

Wright, J., Shade, D. D., Thouvenelle, S., and Davidson, J. 1989. New directions in software development for young children. *Journal of Computing in Childhood Education* 1: 45–57.

Chapter TWO

Kids as Informants:

Telling Us What We Didn't Know or Confirming What We Knew Already?

Mike Scaife

School of Cognitive and Computing Sciences
University of Sussex, Brighton, UK

Yvonne Rogers

School of Cognitive and Computing Sciences
University of Sussex, Brighton, UK

2.1 Introduction

Joe: "So the pike comes down here and it says, 'Where's my dinner?' . . . It grabs this one . . . 'Yum yum! This is better than going to the fish and chip shop!'"

Alan: "And when everything is finished, it says, 'Only the pike is left'. . . and the pike dies . . . and the pike says, 'Where did all the food go?'. . . then the pike dissolves . . . or you just see it as bones."

This is a small extract from a prototyping design session where we asked pairs of 9-year-olds to create a software game, using laminated cutouts, to teach some basic concepts in ecology to children younger than themselves (see Figure 2.1). As evidenced by hours of videotape material collected, there is no stopping the likes of Joe and Alan once their imagination is fired up. But what are we to make of it all? Is this interaction anything more than kids being loveable? Should we really be using this kind of material to get insight into how to design better educational software? Moreover, how can a design team use such inputs? What criteria can they use to determine whether what children come up with is both pedagogically sound and fun? And why should such observations be of any value anyway? Aren't kids simply emulating what's already out there (Kafai 1996)? Don't we already know—as designers and experts in educational technology—what we need to know?

These questions may seem like just another version of a central concern when designing any kind of system or software—when, whether, and how to involve users in the design process and what the actual benefits are of doing so. But, in addition, the involvement of kids, rather than adults, in designing interactive software raises a number of quite specific considerations, and it is these that we shall focus on in our chapter. We shall do this in the context of our own research, the ECOi project.* We have been developing novel interactive software for teaching 9- to 14-year-olds some of the basic concepts of ecology. Our overall research project has several interrelated, complex aims, but we wish to focus here on the insights we gained into the many pros and cons of involving kids within a multidisciplinary design team and how these led to changes in both the design process and the software developed.

User-Centered Design and Adults: Reactive or Participative?

The conventional user-centered design (UCD) approach has been typically to position users as a testing or evaluation service for designers to ensure those users' needs are met (Norman and Draper 1986; Rubinstein and

*ECOi (External Cognition for Designing and Engineering Interactivity), is a two-year project funded by the U.K. ESRC Cognitive Engineering Initiative (www.cogs.susx. ac.uk/ECOi).

Figure **2.1**

Joe and Alan, 9-year-olds, doing low-tech prototyping

Hersh 1984). By placing users in this reacting role, designers can obtain a range of feedback as to what is good, bad, and ugly about their designs. However, such a setup means that the kind of feedback obtained from users is primarily based on reaction rather than initiation (Müller, Wildman, and White 1993). A further problem with this kind of asymmetrical relationship is that the onus is entirely on the designers to take on board and translate the users' reactions. Many obstacles can prevent this from happening in a beneficial way, ranging from the designers' own reluctance to reconsider and possibly throw away their own design ideas to organizational constraints that demand the product be shipped before any redesign can be put into practice (Landauer 1996). All too often the actual contribution made by users to the redesign of a system/interface is "too little, too late."

In contrast, the more recently popularized participatory design (PD) approach is to respect users more as partners in the design process and, in so doing, explicitly give them a more equal and responsible role. In this way it is hoped that users can jointly work together with the designers to develop a system that will fit their needs (Schuler and Mamioka 1993). Here "the goal is to provide an equal opportunity design environment in which all participants can contribute as peer co-designers"(Müller, Wildman, and White 1993, p. 64).

User-Centered Design and Kids: Same or Different?

A basic assumption behind the PD approach is that users and designers can view each other as equals. Can this hold when the users are children? In particular, can we have design teams where children are given the same kinds of responsibilities as adults are given in other design team setups? Will designers feel comfortable in taking on board the demands and suggestions of kids? Or is it more reasonable to position children in a more traditional reactive role, getting them to say what they like or dislike about prototypes that designers create? These questions are relevant for a number of reasons, including the fact that children can't discuss learning goals that they have not yet reached themselves and the strong possibility that interpreting children's dialogue is not as straightforward as may be assumed. In addition, there is the issue of overturning traditional power relations between adult and child, for example, in having children make contributions about the content and the way they should be taught—something that adults have always been responsible for.

It may seem strange to even pose these questions, given the recent spate of reports describing the impressive achievements of involving children in the process of design and evaluation of software packages and programming languages. For example, Druin and Solomon (1996) have pioneered the whole concept of having children as part of a design team, particularly in terms of suggesting metaphors for the designer (see Chapter 3). Kafai (1995) has also employed fourth-graders as software game developers and other, younger children as evaluators of their products in the Game Design Project (see Chapter 6). Likewise, Cypher and Smith (1995) used fifth-graders to test both their own and other children's examples of the rule set in the programming language called KidSim (now called Cocoa; see Chapter 9). More extensively, Oosterholt, Kusano, and de Vries (1996) describe how they successfully involved children throughout the development cycle of a communication device, pointing out how in order to achieve this co-design it is necessary to "enter their world." What is not in doubt, then, is that children *can* be brought into the design process and make a contribution. What is less clear is whether we can generalize about the relationship that they can be expected to have with designers. Put simply, in terms of the two approaches we discussed above, should we view them more as partners or in a more limited role as testers?

The answer to this question, of course, depends on the context and specifics of a given project because there are likely to be different interplays between children and the various adults involved in the design process. Teachers, psychologists, HCI experts, graphic designers, and software engineers will each have their own relationship with each other, needing to interact in different ways. In turn, they will also have different relationships with the children: some will have more direct involvement than others. What we have to do is to ask what might be the optimum kinds of interactions: How can we most effectively involve each person, including the child, in the design process of creating a software product? For example, teachers can often tell us what children find difficult to learn using traditional materials but not what might be effective using the alternative of interactive multimedia. On the other hand, children are very good at expressing what motivates them in a learning context but perhaps overegg the custard a little and exaggerate when it comes to saying what they find boring. Weighing up and integrating the different contributions is also an important part of the process, and it is unrealistic to take on board everyone's contributions. The design team has to decide how they fit together and whether they fulfill the project's objectives.

Specifying an effective method for involving different people in the design process at different stages is what we have done with our "informant design" framework. Essentially, this involves determining the different phases of design, identifying who will be the informants in these, what their inputs will be, and what methods will be used. Our emphasis is to view different people as informants through our interaction with them. In so doing, it has enabled us as a design team (consisting of an interaction/software designer, an HCI specialist, a developmental psychologist, and an educational technologist) to discover what we did not know rather than try to confirm what we thought we already knew. Such a philosophy is often overlooked by designers following a user-centered design approach in the excitement of demonstrating their own creative designs to users.

To achieve this understanding, however, it is important to consider the nature of the relationship of the informants with different members of the design team. For example, at the beginning of a project, it is necessary to define the domain and learning problems. In our ECOi project, the educational technologist and psychologist in the design team began by working with teachers from local schools to explicate specific learning goals, to identify the problems with current methods of teaching, and to make a comparison between conventional and interactive media for presenting material. They also interacted with children in their school environment, getting them to evaluate existing materials (e.g., CD-ROMs, textbooks) in that domain to identify what they found to be the main learning difficulties and obstacles to understanding. In parallel, the interaction/software designer created some preliminary sketches and storyboards for the domain space, and the HCI expert operationalized theoretical ideas on interactivity.

In subsequent stages of the project, the various members of the design team worked together in different combinations with the children. Full details of our informant design framework are given elsewhere (Scaife et al. 1997). Here we shall outline how our informant framework arose and describe some of its successes and shortcomings in the ECOi project. We shall draw on our experiences to give a view on problems and successes of our form of child involvement that we hope will be valuable for other projects. Our account here concentrates on the place of the child in the process.

2.2 The ECOi Project—First Steps

ECOi arose from our analysis of the problems that kids roughly 9 years and up seemed to have learning basic concepts in ecology, especially the notion of food webs. On the one hand, they have no problem understanding what a food web is (i.e., that within an ecosystem there is a network of different organisms that eat each other). For example, in a pond, where fish, snails, weeds, tadpoles, and slime cohabit, children readily understand that fish eat tadpoles and that tadpoles eat weeds, but that the tadpoles don't eat the fish and the weeds don't eat the tadpoles. But on the other hand, they are not able to use formalisms, like a food web diagram, to reason about the ecosystem as a whole (see Figure 2.2). Often they get it wrong, redrawing the diagram, showing incorrect relationships between organisms. Typically, they are unable to read information from the diagram about which organisms die as a consequence of one of the other organisms being removed from the

Figure 2.2

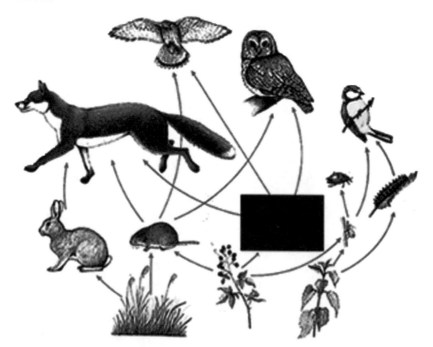

A typical food web diagram used in school textbooks to show who eats whom and, thus, the energy flow between organisms. Here one of the organisms has been shaded out in the diagram in order to pose the question, What would happen to the other creatures if the mouse was gone?

ecosystem. The ability to do this kind of inferential reasoning—using the spatial layout to read off the solution by working through the chains of arrows between the organisms—is a fundamental part of understanding ecological concepts (as opposed to simply memorizing a food web diagram, which is typically what most kids are required to do).

This is an example of a far wider problem since there are many other kinds of formalisms, such as cycle diagrams and flowcharts, that are an inherent part of science domains and that have evolved to enable us to make predictions and inferences about the interrelationships between elements and processes. Yet we discovered that, typically, school children are simply not taught diagram-reading skills, with the result that notations such as arrows linking the parts of a food web are not properly understood. Instead, the children rely on their intuitions as to what different symbols mean and how to use them to make inferences, often wrongly since the conventions used in scientific diagrams are counterintuitive to their everyday assumptions. The result is that there is a large conceptual distance between the diagram and the real world, meaning that they are unable to make correct predictions as to what happens when ecosystems are perturbed in various ways.

2.3 The Pedagogical Challenge: Multimedia as a Solution?

We believed that this conceptual gap between the child's everyday experiences and the abstract formalisms that have evolved in science could be closed by using the potential of multimedia software. We argued that explicitly showing the changes that occur in an animated view of an ecosystem in conjunction with showing how those changes are represented in the abstract formalism should enable children to understand better how they could map the two and thus use the formalism to make inferences. In particular, we believed that multimedia software could be designed to allow them to manipulate and construct the food web diagrams themselves and to provide different kinds of feedback—an innovation that simply cannot be achieved using conventional media (e.g., video, books).

To test our ideas, we began by building a simulation of a simple familiar ecosystem, a pond, creating a suite of software modules that showed a variety of diagrammatic interfaces that were dynamically linked to the simulation such that altering one altered the other. For example, removing the token for the tadpoles in the diagram caused removal of the tadpoles in the pond. By this process of "dynalinking," we aimed to allow the child to see the mapping between "real" events and abstract representations of them.

Our First Designs

The initial approach to the design of the simulation was based on an extensive analysis of the problem space and existing attempts to develop learning material. We looked at curricular material identifying relevant ecology concepts and what levels of comprehension were required. We asked 60 children, from 9 to 14 years of age, about their experience of being taught these concepts, identifying issues and teaching methods they found difficult. We also asked 12 teachers of this age range how they would approach the teaching task, such as food webs, and what conceptual difficulties they typically encountered in class. In addition, we got teachers and children alike to evaluate state-of-the-art commercial CD-ROMs that had been developed to teach ecology (Aldrich, Rogers, and Scaife 1998) in order to get a better understanding of what did and didn't work with existing interactive multimedia.

Together, these data served as inputs for the second phase of the design, building a series of prototypes. In this respect, the input of the children and teachers was very important in terms of clarifying for us what was the problem space and why existing learning methods were not working. We also performed a more general developmental analysis of the cognitive difficulties likely to be posed by different kinds of representation in learning. For example: What kind of diagram could we reasonably expect a 9-year-old to understand? This discussion was linked to our analysis of how any external representation was effective, what the pros and cons of different forms might be (e.g., text versus graphic, diagrams versus animation), and how best to combine them (Scaife and Rogers 1996; Rogers and Scaife 1998).

Thus, even at a preliminary stage, the software designer had a basis to begin sketching out a range of ideas for alternative representations. We then decided on the elements of the ecosystem—what we would put into the pond. These had to be simple and familiar enough to be readily understood. Working from our analysis of how interactivity might support learning, we aimed to provide a simple form of diagrammatic linkage to the pond simulation. Using Macromedia Director, our software designer built a simple pond animation, where a number of organisms were visualized (e.g., tadpoles and fish swimming, pond weed moving). In addition, a series of "radio buttons" were displayed below the animation, each labeled as a type of organism. Clicking on a radio button caused the "death" of that type of organism, the exemplars vanishing from the animated pond (see Figure 2.3). However, the action also had a domino effect, resulting in ecologically appropriate removal of other organisms, so that, for example, if the small fish were removed, the big fish—their predators—would also die. A voice-over provided a simultaneous commentary to the actions (e.g., "The small fish

Figure 2.3

☐ Weeds ☐ Tadpoles ☐ Beetles ☐ Small   ☐ Large
                                      Fish   Fish

The first pondworld prototype

have died . . . now the big fish have died."). In this way the children would be able to see an ecosystem in action.

   To determine if our ideas about dynalinking the abstract representation (radio buttons as tokens for species) with the concrete animation were supported, we took the prototype to schools and tried it on some willing 9- to 10-year-olds. The results were not as we had hoped. Although the children had no difficulties in interacting with the animation, their overall verdict of the prototype was harsh: "this is boring" was a representative view. In addition, they often failed to notice the radio buttons and needed to be instructed to click on them. When asked what the relation was between these and the animation, they had a hard time explaining it. This was a setback, but it did not deter us from exploring other ways of visualizing our idea of dynamic linking between abstract and concrete representations. So we went back to the drawing board and sketched out a number of other ways in which we could achieve this form of dynamic interactivity more effectively. In parallel, we discussed why they considered our first prototype to be boring. We realized that there were two immediate considerations. First, did it matter that the children found the prototype dull? Of course it did. As we all know, motivation is a prerequisite for successful learning. The more difficult second question was, How do we go about fixing this while still sticking to our pedagogical goals?

What we realized was that we were just not on the right wavelength in terms of what the kids found stimulating. So how could we find out? We decided at this stage that it might be fruitful to involve children to inform us in general of what behaviors, features, special effects, and challenges (e.g., games) they enjoyed interacting with at the computer interface. Our idea was that we could usefully employ some of their ideas by integrating them with our own evolving ones about dynamic linking of abstract and concrete representations. Hence, we considered it very important to keep sight of our own goals and not simply hand the design over to the children.

2.4 Low-Tech Prototyping with the Kids

So how did we involve the kids? Clearly, it was totally unfeasible to expect kids to develop software prototypes themselves. Instead, we used a range of low-tech techniques to get the children to imagine what they thought software could be like to teach kids about food webs. One method involved having them make drawings of what the interface might look like and how it might behave. However, this was of limited value, not least because children of this age are in the "literal phase" of drawing (Gardner 1982), spending inordinate amounts of time doing fine details of the creatures and paying little attention to how they would interact and behave. Similar informal observations have been found with many of the Simworld games, where kids enjoy spending much more time creating creatures rather than manipulating their behaviors. Hence, a more productive route turned out to be providing them with already laminated cutouts of the organisms, which the kids could readily manipulate against a background like that of an empty pond (see Figure 2.4; see also Color Plate). In this way, they focused more on the behavior of the ecosystem rather than simply on what the organisms should look like.

A Typical Session

In one session, we asked eight pairs of 9- to 11-year-old children what they thought would make a good CD-ROM for teaching about food webs, encouraging them to use the low-tech materials. We asked them to imagine designing something for children younger than they were, by a year or two;

Figure 2.4

Pond background and creature cutouts used in low-tech prototyping sessions (cutouts not to scale)

they were able to remember their own experiences at this point. Typically they would talk for anywhere between 10 and 20 minutes, coming up with different scenarios for a game or a quiz, which we recorded on audio- or videotape. If they seemed to be stuck, we would ask about the consequences of the imaginary user behaving in a certain way (e.g., making incorrect links in the food chain). At the end, we asked for suggestions about special effects, such as noises made during eating. Throughout the session, the emphasis was on eliciting as many suggestions for animations and games as possible while minimizing input from us.

Results

Working in pairs turned out to be a highly effective way to engender inter-action: the kids sparked off each other, sometimes collaborating to extend each other's ideas, sometimes competing to come up with the "most fun" scenario. For example, one pair kept interrupting each other and saying things like "No, I've got a better idea . . . how about if we had a race-the-clock game where . . ." The majority of children had no problem in using the paper materials to simulate an interactive game, providing animations, special effects, sounds, and feedback. From our point of view, the results of these low-tech sessions were very insightful. Not only were the kids generally very enthusiastic—in contrast to their muted responses to our own first prototypes—but they also revealed a great degree of sophistication in terms of their understanding of the use and potential of interactive software. We can classify the findings into various categories:

Decentered Designs

First, the kids showed a capacity to talk about scenarios in very decentered terms. (The term "decenter" is used in developmental psychology to refer, among other things, to the ability to take another's point of view.) They were able to make comments about the suitability of possible "designs" for a range of audiences. For example:

- If information was delivered as text: "Younger ones wouldn't be able to understand . . . to read it . . . You could have age levels [to adjust the form information is delivered in]."

- On the possibility of gruesome noises for animals dying: "Depends on what age they are . . . If you had them at home they'd have nightmares . . . If they were quite old you could have some really revolting ones . . . Boys prefer more gruesome noises."

- On individual differences: "You could have this go really quick, but then some people like to think about it . . . You could have 'beat the clock' . . . You could choose if you wanted to beat the clock . . . You could pull the hands round so you could have 10 minutes or half an hour."

Structured Learning Designs

Second, they could think in terms not just of special effects, the forte of this age, but also in terms of the metaorganization and aims of a game. For example:

- "You have all the animals lined up like this [shows a food chain], then they go away [i.e., screen clears] . . . then [voice-over] 'Put them in order . . . Who eats who?'"

- "You have questions at the bottom like for [indicates fish], and it says, 'Who do I like to eat?' . . . to see if you've remembered . . . to see if they've been listening or not."

- "You should tell them [users] at the beginning . . . some pond animals eat more than one animal."

Interesting and Controversial Designs

Finally, there were a host of suggestions about how to make the game more interesting by providing lively feedback. For example:

- "So the stickleback looks for food and sees the beetle [zooms the stickleback down onto the prey] . . . grabs it . . . says, 'yum yum' [makes munching noise]."

- "You press return when you are finished . . . [if they've missed a link in the food chain] it says, 'Hey! I eat more than one thing!'"

- "You could have a mouse with three buttons . . . each would have a sticker . . . The left button would start the game up, the right button would finish it, the middle one would save."

One pair also discussed a game where incorrect feeding relationships were permissible, for example, a weed eating a perch. To provide feedback, the children suggested a voice-over narration that would say something like "That's not right, try again." This idea of showing incorrect behaviors that contravened those of an ecosystem became a controversial talking point of the design team. One of the members felt that it might encourage younger kids to believe such behaviors were possible, based on the general assumption that kids are rather gullible and believe what they see on television and other media. The others on the design team disagreed, arguing that, even at such a young age, children have a good knowledge of what is real and what is not, that inanimate objects don't eat live organisms (e.g., weeds do not really eat fish). In the end, we decided to test the latter hypothesis—that providing the wrong feedback in a fun and bizarre way might enable the children to rectify the mistake they had made in trying to sort out the food web and understand why. Thus, in this context, the kids' ideas resonated with some of the conceptual and learning concerns we had ourselves.

Effects on Our Methodology

There were many more suggestions than these. They had two immediate effects on our methodology. First, we were made aware of a valuable resource for design ideas and decided to adopt the procedure in a systematic way.

Second, we realized that we had been misreading the role of the child in the process of developing educational software. Our position had been that we knew what was appropriate for the animation, both in terms of content and interface design. We had seen the children's interactions with the prototypes as doing useful work—validating cognitive assumptions about the comprehensibility of the animation, for example. But we had failed to take on board the extent of their expectations and understanding of both the failings of much of the software they had already encountered (in commercial educational CD-ROMs) and of the potential the medium had (e.g., extrapolating from their experience of electronic games). The most imaginative of the kids could also map this potential onto their insights about learning problems in the domain.

These revelations led us to reconsider how we viewed the child in our design process. The richness of their knowledge about the genre of interactive software and the coupled ability to project this into scenario design led us to view them as analogous to the "native informant" of anthropology. For us this implied that kids are aware of aspects of the use of technology that we are not sensitive to and that we need to be told of. This perspective also holds for others involved in the design process—for example, teachers with their knowledge of the nuts and bolts of what works with a class of 30 or educational psychologists with their understanding of the fit between modules of the curriculum. The end result of this process was to rework our model of collaboration between members of the design team and the user population. So by "informant design," we intend a method for going between privileged observations from potential users and ourselves with another set of skills.

2.5 The ECOi Project—Further Steps

Our interdisciplinary design methodology evolved to incorporate informant design in a number of ways. The most important was to work much more closely with the kids in ways other than having them "just" react to our software prototypes. This was done in two ways.

The first was to systematically use the low-tech prototyping method to develop our suite of software modules, by involving the kids from simple interactions with a pond simulation through to more complex scenarios requiring various manipulations of food web diagrams. The end result of this process was a suite of five modules that the kids worked through in sequence. The first was a simple demonstration of a few creatures in a pond; the last module required them to indicate the effects of deletion of a species from the ecosystem by crossing out any other species that would die out as a result (see Figure 2.5).

The second was to try to involve the software/graphic designer more directly with the kids, rather than just trying to supply him our own filtered versions of their low-tech designs or responses to his prototypes. Initially we had the designer go out to schools and observe the kids doing low-tech prototyping work. This approach had the merit of giving him a feel for their ideas, which can be lost when viewing these encounters on videotape, as well as a chance to float ideas in conversation with the children. A second liaison was to have the kids come to the design studio and sit down with the designer. The idea here was to have the kids look at prototypes in development and, where possible, have the designer make on-the-fly changes. Of course, there are severe constraints on how many changes can be done there and then—for example, 3D rendering is a time-greedy process. However, the process did work very well for some aspects, especially for special effects.

Figure 2.5

"Eraser-web" module in which children have to delete species in the pond by placing a cross on the food web diagram (part of screen only)

One example of on-the-fly, high-tech prototyping was to get the kids to help us co-design some animations to convey various incorrect behaviors in the ecosystem that would have "kid appeal." We wanted the kids to come up with their own ideas for how this kind of "incorrect" feedback should be presented—as discussed earlier, a controversial learning method, but which had, interestingly, been voiced by the kids themselves in the low-tech proto-typing session as something that should be included in a software game. In particular, we wanted them to come up with suggestions of specific details for animations in Pondworld for feeding relationships that did not happen in real life. To do this kind of co-designing with high-tech prototyping, we got pairs of children to work in the studio with the designer. To put them in the picture, he first demonstrated the existing prototype modules to them, explaining the kind of educational software we were developing. In particu-lar, their attention was drawn to the existing animations of correct feeding relationships. They also played with the software prototypes, getting a feel for what could be currently done with them. The designer described to them the incorrect scenario of a weed eating a fish and asked what kinds of things should be included in an animation of this. The kids took immedi-ately to the idea and began discussing how the animation should be quite gruesome, with lots of blood coming out of the fish. They then described what the behavior of the weed should be like and the accompanying sounds. Below is an extract of the conversation that went on between the designer and a pair of 10-year-old girls. It begins at the point where the de-signer asks the girls what the weed should do:

Child 1:   "The weed should get bigger and wrap itself around the fish and pull it down and start eating it." [Child makes lots of gesturing to show how the weed should do this.]

Designer: "OK, and it would make a noise at the same time?"

Child 2:   "Yes!"

Designer: "We could do that. What else? Could we do some different sounds at the end to say it's finished eating or something?"

Child 1:   "Yes, a burp!"

As can be seen, the designer tries to elicit suggestions from the children and then lets them know if he thinks they are doable. Following this ses-sion, the designer set about implementing some of their ideas, including the suggested visual and sound effects (see Figure 2.6; see also Color Plate). This was done using SoundEdit and Director tools. When the kids returned a short while later to the design studio, they watched the new animation in the making, helping out with some of the sounds. They were impressed by how their ideas had been transformed into actual software. We also got other kids to interact with the redesigned software, and when they happened upon the "bloodbath" animation, they burst out laughing, exclaiming, "That's so funny!"

These on-the-fly, high-tech prototyping sessions showed us that it was possible to get the software designer to work more closely with the kids and to take on board some of their more imaginative and kid-appealing ideas. It also made us aware of the value of using kids to react to existing high-tech prototypes by making suggestions as to how specific components could be developed. A possible problem with this approach, however, is that the designer could be led astray by the multitude of ideas elicited from the kids that end up conflicting with the learning goals specified by the psychologists. For example, it was possible that too much emphasis on the special effects in the incorrect animations might distract the child's attention away from the underlying pedagogical goal of the animations—to get them to confront their own incorrect or incomplete understanding of the food web diagram and, in so doing, modify it. However, this did not happen: instead

Figure 2.6

Snapshot taken from "bloodbath" animation, in which the weed eats the fish. The child has deliberately placed the fish and weed in the wrong places in the food web diagram, resulting in a reversal of normal eating behavior. Chomping sounds recorded from children accompany the animation. The fish also shrinks until it eventually disappears with a loud burp.

the kids tested on such modules appeared to benefit from having both dynalinks and "incorrect" animations. They were kept motivated by the fun elements in the animations while also seeming to understand better the relationships between the organisms in the food web diagram—a desirable balance between the fun factor and the learning factor.

These kinds of involvement with the kids in the design process were just one aspect of a complex set of interactions we coordinated between teachers, psychologists, an HCI expert, and the designer (for more details, see Scaife et al. 1997). There were, of course, other kinds of co-design sessions, where contributions were made by different members of the team in collaboration with the designer. The emphasis in this chapter has been to illustrate how kids can make a valuable contribution when they are treated as informants rather than as partners or simply as testers. So where does this leave us in terms of evaluating the role kids can play? If we stand back from the specifics of our own project goals, we believe that there is some value in giving a brief summary of some of the concerns and practical problems that arise with our way of working.

2.6 Being Selective: Which Method and Which Ideas?

At a recent CHI conference where we presented this work, we were asked whether we weren't guilty of romanticizing the potential role of kids in low-tech prototyping. What have children got that adults haven't? This is an issue with a practical face. On the one hand, the kids come up with many wonderful suggestions that the design team would not have come up with and that, in our case, greatly enhanced the interactive software. On the other hand, many of their ideas are completely unworkable in computational terms and, furthermore, could have conflicted with the pedagogical goals of the software. They may also clash with the established feel of the package developed so far, either in terms of the content or the interface. So how do we know when to say yes and when to say no to kids' ideas?

The problem of selection, from a range of suggestions, is indeed a hard one. It is easy to settle on the ideas that are easy to implement, such as sound effects for dying animals, or to focus on just those ideas that gel with what we previously came up with. The latter approach is another version of the "confirming what we thought" motivation for just having them rate the prototypes for usability. However, there is also a Hobson's choice here. Simply relaying the multitude of ideas elicited from the low-tech prototyping sessions, in an unvarnished way, to the designer can be confusing and overwhelming—particularly out of context of the original scenario. But translating the set of ideas into an implementable specification means that we need to make principled decisions about the extent to which the suggestions are compatible with the evolving design blueprint.

Having the kids come into the studio also has its problems. We have already mentioned the constraint of what design work can be implemented on the fly. Like many adult users, kids do not have a good sense of what is possible or not. Also, kids will focus more on the fun aspects of the software, tending to suggest how the sounds can be souped up, more blood can be introduced, and so on. In contrast to the freer format of low-tech prototyping, they don't talk much about learning issues. This trade-off resonates with a point discussed by Wong (1992): interfaces that are presented as rough sketches are often much more appropriate prototypes for eliciting responses from users than more finished interfaces because they prevent users getting too fixated on low-level issues, such as what size a button should be, rather than asking more general questions, such as whether buttons are appropriate for the application in hand. In many ways, the inherent flexibility of the low-tech "design your own software" format lends itself to more general suggestions than eliciting responses with the high-tech software prototypes. When confronted with a piece of software that is already designed by any user—be it child or adult—the evaluating users are constrained to make suggestions at a lower level of detail.

In our view, both low-tech and high-tech methods have their place in the design process. The issue is to know which method to use to best effect when involving children during the design process. In our project we used both in tandem, reviewing the outcome in relation to our own pedagogically and HCI-based evolving designs. We should also stress that our design project was very much driven by our original pedagogical concern—to try to get kids to understand better and be able to make inferences from formalisms. Hence, for us, our selection of kids' ideas was largely influenced by pedagogical criteria. Specifically, we wanted to ensure that the resultant software supported our cognitive assumptions about the learning benefits of using dynamic linking of multiple representations at the interface. Many of the specific design ideas coming from the kids were not used, although those that were proved to be highly motivating. (A side effect of this low-tech exercise was that it provided a chance for the kids to reflect on their learning and hence may in itself be an effective learning method.) At a general level, therefore, we can say that kids' ideas are most useful in helping us design the motivating and fun aspects of the educational software—a genre that we as adults are not necessarily tuned into.

2.7 Revisiting Our Informant Design Framework: Kids as Partners or Testers?

Managing an informant design framework involves making just as many compromises as with any other approach. We had to pay careful attention to the inputs not just from kids but also from teachers and educational advisers to maintain the original educational aims of the whole package. In practice, this meant balancing a number of different aspects: learning goals, interface design, fun factors, and technical feasibility. In effect we came, if not full circle, then at least through 270 degrees, as we became more realistic about the contribution children can make to the design process of our interactive software. In terms of the original dichotomy between user-centered design and participatory design, our position is somewhere between the two. We believe in involving the kids as more than reactive critics because they have much to tell us about motivational and genre expectations that we simply don't have good intuitions about. However, we do not treat kids as full partners either, as we are aware of the extent that they can be involved, because of limitations on their knowledge, time, and experience.

2.8 Some General Concerns for a Kid-Centered Informant Design Framework

Our approach, as this book demonstrates, is just one of many. We don't claim its supremacy over others, not least because different contexts will allow different roles for the kids. However, insofar as there are generalizable lessons for us, we have formulated a set of concerns that we believe will apply to projects where children are involved in the design process. Considering at least some of them may help others to plan projects accordingly, to be realistic about how children can contribute within a design team, and not to overromanticize their potential input.

The Selection Problem

Given the imagination of the kids and the endless stream of suggestions, how does the design team make a principled choice?

Comment

It is important to have criteria to determine what to accept and what not to with respect to the goals of the system. This is especially important for educational software, where interface and fun factors can conflict with learning goals. You need to ask what the trade-offs will be if an idea or set of ideas are implemented in terms of critical "kid" learning factors: that is, how do fun and motivation interact with better understanding? For entertainment software or other technological developments, a different set of criteria and trade-offs will be relevant (e.g., compelling, enjoyable, not boring).

The Focus Problem

Adult assumptions about what is effective may go unnoticed because kids don't necessarily focus on the details of the software that have been designed specifically to support learning goals. How do you deal with this mismatch of expectations?

Comment

Kids may not be sensitive to the learning goals of the software and overlook or use components differently from anticipated. For example, the implementation of dynalinking in one of our prototypes appeared to act more as a mechanical device rather than, as we had hoped, a conceptual learning device. The kids did not pick this up because they were not aware of what it was supposed to be doing. Therefore, involving kids both in the design and evaluation process is important to be able to detect aspects of the software where there are mismatches between expectations.

The Dialogue Problem

Kid talk is not adult talk, and so there can be a translation problem between what they actually say, what they want to say, what we want to hear, and what we actually hear.

Comment

We tend to assume that we can just understand what the kids are getting at, but is this so? We must remember that kids have a different conceptual framework and terminology than adults, and so we need to be aware of the need to speak a common language.

The Individual Problem

How do we design software that caters to the learning needs of the huge variety of kids?

Comment

Clearly, there are big individual differences in what makes learning hard: some kids need more motivation, some get bored very quickly, others need specific educational targets. Furthermore, what works for 7-year-olds may not work for 9-year-olds. So is it possible to design a fully inclusive package for all abilities? Are some formats universally appealing (e.g., quizzes, games)?

The Authoring Problem

Should we just get out of the way and give kids the software tools to do the design?

Comment

There are now software tools geared specifically for kids (e.g., KidPix, HyperStudio). But where should their input end? Again, the extent of their involvement will depend a lot on the kind of product being developed. There may be more scope for involving them as partners for entertainment systems. For educational packages, viewing them as informants is more useful and realistic, particularly when we recall the difficulty of having them define learning goals.

The Single-Method Problem

Is informant design useful for other areas?

Comment

What can kids most usefully help us with (e.g., identifying learning problems, genre expectations)? Is it possible that kid-centered methods can generalize to other areas? For informant design, we realize that it is both cost-effective, targeting expertise in specific areas, but also cost-intensive since not every project will be able to take the time to involve all our informants in the way we did.

2.9 Conclusions

Our experience has been that the involvement of kids at different stages of software development can clearly bring significant benefits. First, the products are developed in a more efficient way, with the use of low-tech prototyping a highly effective means for meshing kids' design ideas with inputs from other informants. Second, the children's inputs ground our initial approaches to the educational issues, reducing the distance between what we might consider a "good" solution to a learning problem and what they actually find effective and motivating from their own perspective. Finally, we have found the informant design framework to be an insightful and effective approach to design, getting us as a design team to stand back and discover what we did not know, rather than simply trying to confirm what we thought we knew already.

Acknowledgments

This work was supported by the U.K. ESRC Cognitive Engineering Initiative award number L12725103. Many thanks are due to the other members of the ECOi team: Matt Davies, for his outstanding design skills, and Frances Aldrich, for her dedicated field work. We also thank schools in East Sussex, U.K., and Los Angeles, California.

References

Aldrich, F., Rogers, Y., and Scaife, M. 1998. Getting to grips with "interactivity": Helping teachers assess the educational value of CD-ROMs. To appear in *British Journal of Educational Technology*.

Cypher, A., and Smith, D. C. 1995. KidSim: End user programming of simulations. In *Proceedings of CHI '95*. New York: ACM Press, 27–34.

Druin, A., and Solomon, C. 1996. *Designing multimedia environments for children: Computers, creativity, and kids*. New York: John Wiley & Sons.

Gardner, H. 1982. *Art, mind and brain*. New York: Basic Books.

Kafai, Y. B. 1995. *Minds in play: Computer game design as a context for learning*. Hillsdale, NJ: Lawrence Erlbaum.

Kafai, Y. B. 1996. Software by kids for kids. *Communications of the ACM* 39: 38–39.

Landauer, T. 1996. *The trouble with computers*. Boston: MIT Press.

Müller, M. J., Wildman, D. M., and White, E. A. 1993. "Equal opportunity" PD using PICTIVE. *Communications of the ACM* 36(4): 64–65.

Norman, D., and Draper, S. 1986. *User centered system design.* Hillsdale, NJ: Lawrence Erlbaum.

Oosterholt, R., Kusano, M., and de Vries, G. 1996. Interaction design and human factors support, in the development of a personal communicator for children. In *Proceedings of CHI '96.* New York: ACM Press, 450–457.

Rogers, Y., and Scaife, M. 1998. How can interactive multimedia facilitate learning? To appear in *CD-ROM Proceedings of the First International Workshop on Multimodality in Multimedia Interfaces.* Menlo Park, CA: AAAI Publications.

Rubinstein, R., and Hersh, H. 1984. *The human factor: Designing computer systems for people.* Burlington, MA: Digital Press.

Scaife, M., and Rogers, Y. 1996. External cognition: How do graphical representations work? *International Journal of Human-Computer Studies* 45: 185–213.

Scaife, M., Rogers, Y., Aldrich, F., and Davies, M. 1997. Designing for or designing with? Informant design for interactive learning environments. In *Proceedings of CHI '97.* New York: ACM Press, 343–350.

Schuler, D., and Mamioka, A., eds. 1993. Participatory design: Principles and practices. Hillsdale, NJ: Lawrence Erlbaum.

Wong, Y. Y. 1992. Rough and ready prototypes: Lessons from graphic design. In *CHI '92 Conference Companion.* New York: ACM Press, 83–84.

Chapter Three

Children as Our Technology Design Partners

Allison Druin
University of Maryland, College Park

Ben Bederson
University of Maryland, College Park

Angela Boltman
University of Maryland, College Park

Adrian Miura
University of New Mexico

Debby Knotts-Callahan
University of New Mexico

Mark Platt
Louisiana State University

3.1 Introduction

"That's silly!" "I'm bored!" "I like that!" "Why do I have to do this?" "What is this for?" These are all important responses or questions that come from children. As our design partners in developing new technologies, children can offer bluntly honest views of their world. They have their own likes, dislikes, and needs that are not the same as adults' (Druin, Stewart, et al. 1997). As the development of new technologies for children becomes commonplace in industry and university research labs, children's input into the design and development process is critical. We need to establish new development methodologies that enable us to stop, listen, and learn to collaborate with children of all ages.

Today, an array of methodologies has been developed to observe and understand adults as users of technology. In general, these are used in a workplace environment where tasks are clearly defined for a required end-user product (Bjerknes, Ehn, and Kyng 1987; Beyer and Holtzblatt 1997; Holtzblatt and Jones 1992; Holtzblatt and Jones 1995; Holtzblatt and Beyer 1997; Müller 1991; Müller, Wildman, and White 1994). The observation and participation methodologies of these experiences do not take into account the difficulty in studying the constantly changing interaction between children and technology. When children are given the chance to use technology in ways they would like, many times they do not have a defined task and their activities are open-ended and exploratory (Druin 1996a).

Interestingly enough, the one environment for children that has typically been well researched is the school environment (e.g., Collis and Carleer 1992; Kay 1996; Norton 1992; Ringstaff et al. 1993; Tinker 1993). We believe that this has been the case because school activities lend themselves to the existing observation and participation methodologies. Schools are generally places where children are asked to carry out directed, adult-specified tasks. Children are typically not in control of when they can have art or what they can write about, or even when they can go home. Ultimately, we believe that researchers can only tell so much about what children want or need in technologies from environments such as these. Therefore, our research has primarily been focused on what happens with children and technology outside of the school environment.

This chapter describes the research methods that were developed and adapted for work with children.* In addition, an example of how these methodologies have been used to develop a prototype drawing tool for

*This work was accomplished by the authors when they were affiliated with the University of New Mexico.

children will also be discussed. This work is based upon a year and a half of frequent and intensive direct contact with children (Druin, Boltman, et al. 1997). Hundreds of children were observed in a wide range of activities in diverse southwestern sites: from urban middle-class homes, to isolated non-English-speaking rural farmhouses, to an intensive 5-day technology camp experience at an international conference. These children varied in age (3–13 years old) as well as ethnic background (e.g., Native American, Hispanic, African American, Caucasian, and children of recent immigrants from Vietnam, China, and Korea).

3.2 Adapting Three Design Methodologies

Based upon a review of the literature and some initial exploratory studies (Druin 1996b), we found it necessary to collect data with children in three different ways. The first methodology was adapted from *contextual inquiry* techniques (Beyer and Holtzblatt 1997; Holtzblatt and Jones 1992; Holtzblatt and Jones 1995; Holtzblatt and Beyer 1997). We found that 3- to 5-year-old children can be, at times, nonverbal or less self-reflective in discussing the world around them. Therefore, in order to understand what these children's needs may be, our observation techniques had to capture children's exploratory activity patterns (Druin, Boltman, et al. 1997). We found that a modified form of contextual inquiry could serve this purpose.

The second methodology that we developed came to be called *technology immersion* (Boltman et al. 1998; Druin, Boltman, et al. 1997). This methodology grew out of our need to see how children use large amounts of technology. We found that if we only observed what children did with what they currently had, we missed what children might do given better circumstances (Druin, Boltman, et al. 1997). Many times, children had minimal contact with technology in their homes or public places. Therefore, by using the observation techniques of contextual inquiry in a technology-rich environment, we found that many patterns emerged in children's use of technology.

Finally, the third methodology was adapted from *participatory design* techniques (Bjerknes, Ehn, and Kyng 1987; Müller 1991; Müller, Wildman, and White 1994). We found that in addition to collecting data through observation, we needed to hear from children directly. We wanted the opportunity to develop a partnership with children much in the same way that we do with our adult users of technology (Druin and Solomon 1996). It is not uncommon to work with artists when developing a drawing program or to work with biologists when developing a tool for biology. Therefore, we wanted to work with

Figure 3.1

Megan's drawing (age 8): what she would like to see in future technologies

Figure 3.2

Cheryl's drawing (age 7): what she would like to see in future technologies

children so that they too could tell us in their own words what they would like to see in the future (see Figures 3.1 and 3.2 for examples). This is not to say that children can tell us everything about what is needed for a new technology. On the other hand, design team members that are, for example, computer scientists or educators are also limited in their range of experience and expertise. However, when all the team members have a say in the design process, including children, a complete range of experiences can be taken into account during the research process. In the sections that follow, a full description of the techniques for each research methodology will be described.

Contextual Inquiry with Children

The methodology of contextual inquiry (CI) calls for researchers to collect data in the users' own environment. Generally, users are observed performing typical activities and researchers ask questions of users when clarification is needed (Beyer and Holtzblatt 1997; Holtzblatt and Jones 1992; Holtzblatt and Jones 1995; Holtzblatt and Beyer 1997). In the case of users who are children, we observed them in their homes and favorite public places (e.g., children's museums, activity centers, game arcades).

With our modified form of CI, the techniques we used were essentially the same whether in a home environment or public place. There were always at least one *interactor* and two *note-takers*. The interactor was always the researcher who initiated discussion and asked questions concerning the activity. The interactor asked questions that were directed to what the user was doing at the moment (e.g., How come you're doing that? Why do you like that? What's this?). The interactor would avoid asking questions that might steer the activities of the child (e.g., Could you show me this? How about doing that?). For research purposes, we found it important that the interaction be led by the child user, not the adult researcher (Druin, Boltman, et al. 1997).

With this form of CI, notes were never taken by the interactor. Children clearly felt uncomfortable and distracted if the interactor was taking notes while talking to them. Note-taking seemed to make children feel that they were in school, being tested by a teacher for wrong or right answers. Instead, we found that the interactor should become a participant observer, talking naturally to children and becoming a part of their active experience (Druin, Boltman, et al. 1997).

Consequently, different researchers acted as the note-takers, recording what the children did and said. One note-taker recorded the activities (what the user does) and the other note-taker recorded quotes (what the user says). Both note-takers recorded the time so that the quotes and activities could be synchronized in later data analysis. It should be understood that at the time of this research, video cameras were not found to be successful in capturing data (Druin, Boltman, et al. 1997). We found that children tended to perform when they saw a video camera in the room. In addition, even with small unobtrusive devices, video was still difficult to use in small private spaces (e.g., bedrooms) because the video image was incomplete: it was difficult to know where to place cameras when it was unknown where the child would sit, stand, or move in their own environment. In large public spaces, the sound was of poor quality and frequently inaudible.

For both interactor and note-takers, we found that informal clothing should be worn (e.g., sweatshirt, jeans). In this way, researchers seemed to represent less of an authority figure and more of a friend or confidant who the children could feel comfortable with sharing their thoughts. In general, children are used to seeing teachers and their parents work in more formal clothes. By wearing informal clothes, researchers had an easier time of developing a more relaxed relationship with their users (Druin, Boltman, et al. 1997).

To summarize, we found 10 contextual inquiry techniques for observing children:

1. *Go to "their territory."* When children are in their own rooms, a playground, or a place that they are familiar with, they feel more in control. They will be more willing to open up and share their thoughts.

2. *Give children time.* Children need to become accustomed to their environment. Do not immediately ask questions about their likes and dislikes. Let them do what they would normally do: play, explore, make up stories, and so on.

3. *Wear informal clothing.* By wearing T-shirts, jeans, and so on, you will avoid being labeled as an authority figure. It will let you be "one of the gang." Children should feel that you are someone they can talk to as a friend.

4. *Do not stand with young children.* Be one of them. Sit on the ground with them. Climb the jungle gym. Lie on the ground while using the computer. This keeps the activity in the child's world. Again, you do not want to represent yourself as an authority figure or outsider.

5. *Use an object as a bridge.* Objects can help researchers to develop a relationship with the children they're observing. The object (e.g., computer, video game, Walkman radio) can become an icebreaker, the frame or reason for developing a relationship. If no technology is present in the environment, bring something that would allow interaction between interviewer and user.

6. *Ask about their opinions and feelings.* The interactor needs to ask questions that can get to the child's thoughts and feelings. By using the phrase "I need your help . . ." the child can feel empowered, important, and more willing and excited to share their thoughts.

7. *Use informal language.* The interactor should use informal language when spending time with children. Such phrases as "Why's that?" should be used, as

opposed to "Why are you doing that?" In this way, children will be more likely to open up and tell you what they are thinking.

8. *The interactor must not take notes.* Children will be too distracted to give honest feedback if the interactor must stop to jot down notes. Children will also associate the researcher with an authority figure or typical teacher. The note-takers must be different people than the interactor.

9. *Use small notepads.* If paper is used for note-taking, use small notepads. Large pads/notebooks remind children of teachers or authority figures. When large pads are used, children may feel as if there are "right answers" that you are looking for, as opposed to sharing thoughts.

10. *Note-takers should not move.* Researchers who take notes need to be close by, but should not move or make eye contact with the children once they are in their initial location. The note-takers must become a background, nonmoving part of their environment—almost invisible. In this way, children will feel more comfortable and may freely do what they would like.

Following a CI session with children, we found it extremely useful to discuss our quick impressions of the research experience (Druin, Boltman, et al. 1997). Many times we would discuss the activity patterns we saw emerging or the process of the research itself. With this technique of quick self-reflection, our research methodology was refined. These discussions were captured in quick notes and used during diagramming sessions. After a digestion period of 1 day to a maximum of 1 week, our research team re-grouped to chart or diagram the experience. Other CI researchers generally develop "task" or "bubble" diagrams to interpret the data (Beyer and Holtz-blatt 1997; Holtzblatt and Jones 1992; Holtzblatt and Jones 1995; Holtzblatt and Beyer 1997). In our case of examining children, we found these visualizations limiting and often too complex to make sense of what occurred. We found children may start a task without finishing it, then start another, and yet another. Then without pause they might go back to the task they started at the beginning and then start something else anew (Druin, Boltman, et al. 1997).

Thanks to these exploratory activities, we found it more understandable to diagram these experiences based on the patterns of activity and the roles that the child played rather than by task. In this way, a more complete picture emerged of the child. We developed a spreadsheet or cell-based diagram (see Figure 3.3) in which the information is broken up into six columns: time, quotes, activities, activity patterns, roles, and design ideas (Druin, Boltman, et al. 1997).

The "time" column is used to synchronize quotes with activities. The "quotes" column contains phrases and sentences said by the child or children

Figure 3.3

Time	Quotes	Activities	Activity patterns	Roles	Design ideas
36:45	Oh, look it, there's a kitty. The kitty meowed. (laughs)	The game begins on the computer. Child sees the kitty on the screen for the first time and is excited by the sound.	Child is sensitive to feedback from computer.	Explorer	Design technology with sound.
37:73	The kitten meowed again!			Explorer	
39:20	I want the playing one.	Child clicks on the scared cat and tries to take out another one. It doesn't work.	Difficulty with mouse dragging.		Look for alternative input devices or don't use dragging with a mouse.
39:50	Awww. The kitten was afraid.	Child clicks on another basket with a cat.	Tells stories about actions on the screen.	Storyteller	Offer children storytelling opportunities with technology.
40:20	Which one's the playful one?	Child looks for a playful cat.	Child knows what she wants to do.	Searcher	
41:00	I don't want to name my kitty.	Child doesn't name her cat when prompted to by the computer.	Child knows what she wants to do.	Searcher	
41:30	That's to give milk.	Child clicks on different icons to see what they do.	Tests out what can be done with the software.	Explorer	Make technology easy to explore.
	I think the kitty wants milk.	Child drags the milk to the cat and is excited to see the cat react to her.	Child is sensitive to feedback from computer.	Explorer	Design technology that is extremely reactive to child users.
42:00	Mmmm. I wonder what he wants. Maybe he wants nothing now?	Child tries to drag another object to the cat on the screen.		Explorer	
42:45	It didn't work. I can't.	Child is not successful in dragging the object.	Difficulty with mouse dragging.	Explorer	Look for alternative input devices or don't use dragging with a mouse.
43:25	Look it. He's playing.		Tells stories about actions on the screen.	Storyteller	
44:20	What happened?	The program window goes the background.	Child is sensitive to feedback from computer.	Explorer	Make it more difficult to accidentally click on the desktop.
45:50	He got very quiet so he doesn't know the mouse is sleeping.	Child watches as the cat follows the mouse, tells a story about why the cat is quiet.	Tells stories about actions on the screen.	Storyteller	Offer children storytelling opportunities with technology.
47:25	Here kitty...here kitty...	Child moves screen toys to the cat.		Storyteller	

An example of a CI diagram (child: female, age 4; Albuquerque, New Mexico; February 1997)

during a session. The "activities" column contains the observed actions of the child or children during a session. The "activity patterns" column is developed by the researchers during data analysis and is based on repetitive patterns that emerge in the "quotes" and "activities" columns. The "roles" column is also developed by the researchers from the data in the "quotes" and "activities" columns. The "roles" column describes "who the children are" when they are interacting with technology (e.g., storyteller, researcher, creator, writer, player). Finally, the last column contains the "design ideas." It is a culmination of all of the information gathered or generated. This column is also the start of the brainstorming process. It offers new ideas for the development of new technology that can be related directly to the observed data.

Each of these columns, from left to right, is a finer interpretation of the data gathered. In general, we would start by diagramming all of our raw data (time, quotes, and activities) and then extrapolate to developing the columns that contained the reflective observations (activity patterns, roles, and design ideas). A sample activity pattern that we witnessed was *user tells a story about what is on the screen*. A sample role was *child as storyteller*. A sample design idea was *more user-initiated storytelling activities need to be developed in our technology* (Druin, Boltman, et al. 1997).

Technology Immersion with Children

The second research methodology that we refined to be used with children is technology immersion. With this methodology, children were provided with a technology-rich environment where they were decision makers. The children were asked to make their own choices concerning what they did with technology. The methodology of technology immersion also offered a time-intensive experience, where children had a great deal of time (10 hours a day, for 5 consecutive days) to explore different kinds of technology and to make decisions about what they liked and did not like. In addition, this methodology supported children with a large amount of technology (e.g., PCs, Macs, scanners, printers, digital cameras, and Internet access). No child ever had to share a computer if he or she did not choose to. No child ever had to wait to accomplish what he or she wanted to—the technology was waiting to be used.

Generally, children do not have this kind of unlimited access to technology in schools. Many children are lucky if they can use a computer for a 45-minute session a day (Fulton 1997). Although it is becoming more common for children to have technology at home, again their time with the technology is limited: generally, children will have access to a home computer only after school, and it is shared with other family members. With technology immersion, however, a combination of technology, time, and freedom of choice offers researchers more opportunity to understand what children do and want with technology (Boltman, Druin, and Miura 1998; Druin et al. 1996).

One such technology immersion experience that we developed is CHIkids (Boltman, Druin, and Miura 1998; Druin et al. 1996; Druin 1996b; Druin, Boltman, et al. 1997). This is an ongoing technology immersion experience offered at ACM's yearly CHI conference on computer-human interaction (see Figures 3.4 [Color Plate only] and 3.5). It is an annual experience that supports up to 100 children (ages 3–13) in four main areas of technology exploration: Multimedia Storytelling, Technology Workouts, CD-ROM Field Trips, and the CHIkids Newsroom. Children explore technology by being multimedia storytellers, software testers, and newsroom reporters. This technology immersion experience was first accomplished at CHI '96 and has since been replicated each year at the CHI conferences.

The actual technology immersion methodology calls for two CHIkids adult leaders, as well as a number of college student volunteers, to support each of the four main CHIkids technology areas. All adult leaders and college volunteers take a "facilitator" approach to working with the children in their area. In our past experience, using this approach encourages children to make their own choices, giving them control over their technology exploration. Some educators would call this a *problem-centered* approach to using technology (Norton 1992). The focus of the children's exploration was not the technology or an adult telling them to follow 10 specific steps to "learn" something new. Instead, the focus was a "problem" of interest to the children, such as to be a newsroom reporter for the CHI conference, or to form a company and create new multimedia software, or even to test the experimental software of the CHI conference attendees. In tackling these so-called problems, children used whatever technology tools they needed, in ways they felt comfortable, and used their adult mentors as resources.

Figure 3.5

The CHIkids program at CHI '97

The adults were there to offer suggestions and provide feedback when the children asked for it.

By offering up to 100 children a flexible, time-intensive, technology-rich environment, each year we have been able to observe children of varying ages in ways not usually available to researchers in schools or at homes. These children shared many important insights with us about their technology experiences. These were not one-shot observations or single occurrences, but rather patterns of activity that each year we consistently witnessed over the 50 hours we spent with these children. Interestingly enough, many of the same activity patterns that emerged in our CI research were seen in the technology immersion experience. In fact, some patterns of activity that we had overlooked in the CI data were more obvious after the technology immersion research. In a later section, we will further describe what we learned from these experiences.

Participatory Design with Children

The third research methodology we refined for children is participatory design (Müller 1991; Müller, Wildman, and White 1994; Druin and Solomon 1996). As opposed to being observed, with this methodology children are directly asked to work with researchers to collaboratively create "low-tech prototypes" out of paper, glue, crayons, and so on (see Figures 3.6 [Color Plate only] and 3.7). In this way, we as adult researchers can identify new technology possibilities that might not have been considered otherwise. At the same time, children who are not well skilled in the development process can be inspired and empowered by their collaboration with adults to generate new ideas. The low-tech tools give equal footing to adults and children as design partners. Both adults and children know how to use these prototyping tools, and these tools act as a bridge or an icebreaker for a more comfortable brainstorming session (Druin and Solomon 1996; Druin, Boltman, et al. 1997).

We have used and refined this methodology for over 8 years in pilot studies in the United States and Europe. We have found that children ages 7–10 make the most effective design partners (Druin and Solomon 1996; Druin, Stewart, et al. 1997). These children are self-reflective and verbal enough to discuss what they are thinking. They can understand the abstract idea of designing something on paper or in clay that will be turned into technology in the future. Children of this age, however, seem not to be too heavily burdened with preconceived notions of the way things "are supposed to be," something we see commonly in children older than 10. Interestingly enough, we have found that children ages 7–10 can be productive

Figure 3.7

A sample participatory design session during a tutorial at ACM's CHI '94 conference

technology designers even when developing software for older or younger children (Druin, Stewart, et al. 1997).

We have also found that two to four children paired with two to three adults create a productive brainstorming experience (Druin and Solomon 1996; Druin, Boltman, et al. 1997). One lone adult should never be placed with two or more children in one design team because the team dynamics take on the feel of a classroom with one teacher and many children. We have also found that a group with a single child is not productive in a collaborative design experience either. The child feels outnumbered or overwhelmed by the adults in the group. In summary, we have found the following participatory design techniques to work with children:

1. *Child design partners: 7–10 years old.* Children ages 7–10 are the ideal design partners because of their ability to develop ideas from abstract concepts, yet remaining open to exploring new ideas. Children younger than this have a more difficult time partnering with adults to develop new design ideas.

2. *More than one child on a team.* One child should never work with numerous adults in a design team. The child can quickly become overwhelmed or overshadowed by the adult design partners.

3. *More than one adult on a team.* One adult should never work in a design team with multiple children because the dynamics of the team become school-like. Two or three adults with three to four children is ideal.

4. *Adult interaction is important.* Adult-to-adult interaction is just as important as adult-to-child and child-to-child interaction. Many times the adults in the group become so concerned with interacting with the children on the team that they forget to consider the other adults in the group.

5. *Low-tech prototyping tools should be diverse.* Low-tech prototyping tools should offer diverse forms of expression (2D, 3D). Familiar art supplies such as crayons, paper, tape, clay, yarn, balloons, and LEGO blocks can be used.

6. *Freely combine low-tech tools.* Children freely combine all media in nontraditional ways to produce the prototypes. Adults should feel just as free to do the same. Don't be afraid to draw on LEGO blocks and wrap clay with yarn.

7. *Introduce low-tech tools quickly.* Ideas grow more quickly when the low-tech prototyping tools are introduced as quickly as possible. When adults or children on a team start building or constructing with the low-tech tools, the prototyping process is accelerated.

8. *More complex ideas can be developed.* The sooner the physical prototyping starts, the more complex the final outcome/product is likely to be. The longer the team waits to start using the prototyping tools, the simpler the final idea seems to be.

9. *Adults can be playful.* When adult team members become more informal and playful, children on the team are more likely to open up faster and feel more comfortable in the design process.

10. *The goal should be flexible.* The outcome for the design session should be flexible. If a very constrained design problem is offered, then children and adults grow restless. More open-ended design problems are better addressed with this methodology.

To gain a better understanding of this research methodology, below is an example participatory design session. It occurred in April 1997 at the University of New Mexico. During this session, four design teams were asked to prototype a computer of the future that could help children understand some aspect of the human body. Each group contained two adults and two or three children, ages 7 or 8. The notes below were recorded by one of the authors of this chapter, D. Knotts-Callahan (Druin, Boltman, et al. 1997, pp. 17–23):

All team members are sitting at a round table. Materials are spread out all over the table in no particular order. All the team members start fiddling with materials and a lively discussion occurs about the body and computers. This team functions like a kids' club, with a secret. Initially, when another adult or this note-taker approaches, a team member makes a comment, "Shhh, don't show or tell them. It's a secret." This game/bonding experience adds to the kid-chemistry of the team dynamics. Despite the secrets, this note-taker catches them off-guard and captures some of their interactions.

Kids (one girl and two boys) are working together building a clay form. Adults are at opposite sides of the table making other parts. They are all working together, with the kids taking more of the lead.

Adult #1 says, "Maybe we could draw all the things we've done and name them." Boy and girl are busily attaching strings of yarn to a clay object: their "brain." The other boy is making a mouse out of clay. Boy steps back, inspects the project, pointing to a piece of yarn asks, "Shouldn't we make this go under the head?"

Adult #1 adds, "Hey, what if we can take this all apart and put it back together?" Adult #2 says, "Like Mister Potato Head?" All of the kids respond, "That's cool!" Adult #1 points to part of their prototype and asks, "What can you do with this?" Adult #2 asks, "What if you have different eye colors? Should we consider genetics?" Adult #1 says, "I guess, but I don't know much about that kind of stuff."

During this whole interaction between the two adults, all three kids continue to focus on what they're working on (e.g., attaching parts, making labels, etc.). One kid says to the other, "What about the mouse?" Another kid produces a clay mouse that has been sitting at the sidelines. The final touches are at hand. Adult #1 adds the last dab of clay . . .

All four teams bring their computers to the central table . . . Team 3 presents their idea. The three kids gather round their prototype. The girl starts, "The title of our project is Touch and Pull." One of the boys moves into place next to the project, and points to a clay form, he says, "This is Roger, our mouse Roger looks like an animal, not your typical computer mouse." An adult from the crowd asks, "What does it do?" The boy responds, "You talk to Roger. You ask him what the body does and he tells you." Girl kid joins in, "And you touch body parts, like the eyes, and Roger tells you what the eyes do."

For photographs showing examples of these participatory design sessions and the final prototypes, see *www.umiacs.umd.edu/~allisond/*.

3.3 Results of Our Field Research

All too often we hear, "That's a nice story about a kid, but how does that tell me what technology to design?" With the research methodologies of contextual inquiry, technology immersion, and participatory design, we are able to piece together something more than a story. These are not guesses based on isolated personal incidences, and these are not conclusions based on quantitative tests. These are methodologies that illuminate and highlight, in various qualitative ways, what children want in technology and what they notice about it.

What Kids Want in Technology

When we compared our data from each of these methods, we came to three overall conclusions about what children want in technology experiences.

Control

The nature of being a child is such that they are dependent on others. Children are empowered when they feel in control of their environment and when they feel they "own" the environment. Our research has shown that children need to make their own decisions about how they spend their technology time, doing what they choose, when they choose it. We saw in both our CI and technology immersion research that when new technology offered children limited paths of interaction, children easily became bored and uninterested. When technology offered options for varied interaction, children spent a considerable amount of time exploring and actively engaged.

Social Experiences

Children naturally want to be with other children. We saw in both our CI and technology immersion research that no matter how much technology children are offered (for example, one computer per person), they will consistently form groups around one piece of technology (a computer, video game, etc.). We saw technology as a bridge and catalyst for children interacting with each other. If children are strangers to each other, technology is the icebreaker. If children already know each other, technology is the means to get to know one another better. Children generally do not create in isolation: they want to share, show, and use technologies with others. We saw, on numerous occasions during technology immersion experiences, older children (11 and older) working with younger children (4 and younger), using technology. We also saw in technology immersion experiences that close relationships can quickly form between children from France and Saudi Arabia, from the United States and India. Thanks to the shared use of technology, cultural differences were replaced with shared interests. In addition, the participatory design results showed numerous examples of technology that multiple users can share. We saw that it was important for children that their tools of the future offer social opportunities.

Expressive Tools

Children like to tell stories, make up games, and build things. We saw this in all three of our research methodologies. Children enjoy many different forms of expression: sound, visuals, movement, and physical appearance. They want all of these and more in the technologies they use. In much of our field research, we saw that children are natural-born artists and writers, architects and philosophers. They are sculptors and poets, dancers and musicians. Children are not waiting to become these in the future; they are all of these things right now. When participating in the design process, children suggest that new technologies should enable them to tell stories, design games, and build futuristic machines. Children are part of teams that propose developing "the story-monster machine," "the eyeball-building computer," or "the brain game" (Druin, Boltman, et al. 1997; Druin and Solomon 1996).

What Children Notice about Technology

CI, technology immersion, and participatory design as research methodologies also enabled us to better understand what children notice about technology.

What's "Cool"

Our research has shown that there is a great deal of peer pressure among children, even at early ages. They want to wear headphones rather than listen to built-in speakers because headphones are "cooler." They want to play the newest video games, not last year's, because last year's are past the "cool prime." They want what their friends have because that is "what's always cool."

"How Easy It Is to Learn"

Children want to be in control of their world as quickly as possible—and that means learning something quickly. If it is a struggle, they will have little patience for something. If it is easy to learn, they will quickly become immersed in the experience. Contrary to what most adults might imagine, children have long attention spans, but only when there is something to do that is meaningful and makes sense. If a tool offers them little control, they will lose interest quickly.

What Things Look Like

Children are sensitive to what they see, much more so than adults would imagine. They care what something looks like just as much as how it works or what it does. They don't want the visual look of things to talk down to them or question their intelligence. They want what adults want—things that look good and respect who they are as users.

How Much Multimedia

Children have become accustomed to "having it all." It used to be that technology could get away without having sound, but thanks to video games, TV, movies, multimedia, and so on, kids want a multisensory experience. Not only do they find it more entertaining, but they also find it a more engaging environment to explore.

3.4 Use of the Research Methodologies

KidPad is an example of what these research methodologies can lead to (Druin, Stewart, et al. 1997; Stewart 1997). This technology was created with the Pad++ software developed by researchers at the University of New Mexico and New York University. Pad++ offers software tools that replace windows with a zooming information environment (Bederson, Hollan, Perlin, et al. 1996; Bederson, Hollan, Druin, et al. 1996). While Pad++ was never meant to be a tool for children, we saw the possibilities for future changes and development appropriate for children.

Taking into account what our research told us from CI, technology immersion, and participatory design, we began development of a tool that enabled children to express themselves, in a social way, with a form of control that would be enjoyable. KidPad enabled children to tell stories by drawing

Figure 3.8

*An example of the KidPad technology used by an
8-year-old child*

and visually connecting their images by zooming through their information (see Figure 3.8 and Figure 3.9 [Color Plate only]). We found that the activity of zooming strongly supported the creation of nonlinear stories. It seemed to be a natural way for children to tell their stories. They enjoyed the freedom of piecing together their thoughts and connecting them in ways they chose by zooming (Druin, Stewart, et al. 1997; Stewart 1997). Zooming gave children a feeling of control in their storytelling and also strongly supported collaboration between children. Many times one child would begin the story by typing or drawing, and another child would add the next part of the story in another part of the KidPad surface. In this way, children would work together endlessly writing, drawing, zooming, and telling their stories.

The drawing/storytelling tools developed for KidPad also offered a new form of control for children. These tools came to be called "local tools" (Bederson, Hollan, Druin, et al. 1996). Instead of traditional floating palettes of tools, KidPad had large, simple tools that sat directly on the surface (see Figure 3.10). They enabled children to be "messy" and to use tools that "didn't live in straight lines." With local tools, children could select a tool (by single-clicking on it), and the cursor would turn into that tool in both size and shape. If children wanted to drop that tool and use another, they would double-click in the place they wanted to drop it and the tool would remain in that place. They could leave tools where they chose to, not where the technology decided. These tools included what the children called a "crayon" to draw with, an "eraser" to delete objects, and an "arrow" to select objects. The arrow was used in combination with the picture scrapbook. This scrapbook

Figure **3.10**

KidPad local tools

consisted of a slider to move through pictures that ranged from green dinosaurs to red hats. When children saw what they wanted, they chose a picture with the arrow and dragged the picture onto the surface (Druin, Stewart, et al. 1997; Stewart 1997).

Another local tool was the "magic wand." When children selected the wand and clicked on the surface, a link was started. The next place that was selected would be the place that was "linked to." These two places could be easily seen because a bright yellow line connected the two selections. When children deselected the magic wand, they could zoom between links by touching a "hot zooming spot" with another tool. In this way children told their zooming stories. In addition to these local tools, there was a "tool box." This box was placed in the lower right corner of the screen. When children clicked on it, all the local tools would zoom back to where they started, lined up along the bottom of the screen. This turned out to be extremely useful when children would zoom around the surface and forget where they left their tools (Druin, Stewart, et al. 1997; Stewart 1997).

In much of our work, we saw children sharing one computer. Many times they were frustrated when they could not agree on who would get to use the mouse to zoom or to draw. We observed that more assertive children would tend to monopolize the use of the computer, frustrating more passive children. Currently, a new version of KidPad is being developed that focuses on the children's social needs by enabling more than one child to use the software by implementing software and hardware support for two mice on one computer (Stewart 1997; Stewart et al. 1998). In this way, a computer might better support the work of two children sharing the same software.

Table **3.1**

Correlation of field research results to KidPad features

Field research results	KidPad features
Control	Zooming
	Magic wand storytelling
	Tool box for cleaning up
	Local tools
Social experience	Collaborative storytelling tools
Expressive tools	Drawing crayons
	Magic storytelling wand
	Scrapbook

3.5 Summary

Our work continues in developing and refining new research methodologies that are inclusive of children. Our work also continues in using the results of our field research in developing new technologies for children. We are trying to understand how we can bring our knowledge from the real world of children into the design world of technology development. The techniques we use in recording what we see with children need to show a direct relationship to what we develop (see Table 3.1 as an example for KidPad).

It is our hope that one day the question "Why did you design this?" won't need to be asked. It will be obvious based on the research results. Until that day, we need to continue to refine the research process with children, for children, because ultimately our goal is simple: to create exciting, meaningful new technologies for children.

Acknowledgments

This research could not have taken place without the countless children that became our design partners, including students at Lowell and Hawthorne Elementary Schools in Albuquerque, New Mexico, as well as CHIkids participants at the annual ACM CHI conferences. This research has been generously supported by the Sony Corporation and the Intel Research Council. In addition, this work has been influenced by Jason Stewart, Jim Hollan, and our Pad++ collaborators at the University of New Mexico and

New York University. This work continues today at the University of Maryland in collaboration with our colleagues in the Human-Computer Interaction Lab (HCIL), *www.cs.umd.edu/HCIL.*

References

Bederson, B., Hollan, J., Druin, A., Stewart, J., Rogers, D., and Proft, D. 1996. Local tools: An alternative to tool palettes. *Proceedings of ACM UIST '96.* New York: ACM Press, 169–170.

Bederson, B., Hollan, J., Perlin, K., Meyer, J., Bacon, D., and Furnas, G. 1996. Pad++: A zoomable graphical sketchpad for exploring alternate interface physics: Advances in the Pad++ zoomable graphics widget. *Journal of Visual Languages and Computing* 7(3): 3–31.

Beyer, H., and Holtzblatt, K. 1997. *Contextual design: Defining customer-centered systems.* San Francisco: Morgan Kaufmann.

Bjerknes, G., Ehn, P., and Kyng, M., eds. 1987. *Computers and democracy: A Scandinavian challenge.* Aldershot, UK: Alebury.

Boltman, A., Druin, A., and Miura, A. 1998. What children can tell us about technology: The CHIkids model of technology immersion. *CHI '98 Tutorial.* Los Angeles: ACM Publications.

Collis, B., and Carleer, G. 1992. Summarizing the case studies of technology-enriched schools. In B. Collis and G. Carleer, eds. *Technology-enriched schools: Nine case studies with reflections.* Eugene, OR: International Society for Technology in Education, 135–143.

Druin, A. 1996a. A place called childhood. *Interactions* 3(1): 17.

Druin, A. 1996b. What I learned at CHIkids. *SIGCHI Bulletin* 28(3): 19.

Druin, A., Badshah, A., Baecker, R., Blume, A., Blume, L., Boy, J., Boy, G., Cortes-Comerer, A., Cortes-Comerer, N., Davenport, J., Davenport, L., Jaffee, B., Leventhal, L., Schofield, A., Schofield, E., Schofield, K., and Schofield, M. 1996. CHIkid voices. *Interactions* 3(5): 10–20.

Druin, A., Boltman, A., Miura, A., Platt, M., Uscher, N., and Knotts-Callahan, D. 1997. Understanding children's technology needs and desires. *Intel Research Council Grant Summary.* University of New Mexico.

Druin, A., and Solomon, C. 1996. *Designing multimedia environments for children: Computers, creativity, and kids.* New York: John Wiley & Sons.

Druin, A., Stewart, J., Proft, D., Bederson, B., and Hollan, J. 1997. KidPad: A design collaboration between children, technologists, and educators. *Proceedings of ACM CHI '97.* New York: ACM Press, 463–470.

Fulton, K. 1997. *Learning in the digital age: Insights into the issues.* Santa Monica, CA: Milken Exchange on Education Technology Publication.

Holtzblatt, K., and Beyer, H. 1997. Getting started on a contextual project. *CHI '97 Tutorial.* New York: ACM Publications.

Holtzblatt, K., and Jones, S. 1992. Contextual design: Using contextual inquiry for system development. *CHI '92 Tutorial.* Monterey, CA: ACM Publications.

Holtzblatt, K., and Jones, S. 1995. Conducting and analyzing a contextual interview (Excerpt). In R. M. Baecker, J. Gudin, W. A. Buxton, and S. Greenberg, eds. *Readings in HCI: Toward the year 2000,* 2nd ed. San Francisco: Morgan Kaufmann, 241–253.

Kay, A. 1996. Revealing the elephant: The use and misuse of computers in education. *Educom Review* 31(4): 22–28.

Müller, M. J. 1991. PICTIVE— An exploration of participatory design. *CHI '91 Conference Proceedings.* New York: ACM Press, 225–231.

Müller, M. J., Wildman, D. M., and White, E. A. 1994. Participatory design through games and other techniques. *CHI '94 Tutorial.* New York: ACM Publications.

Norton, P. 1992. When technology meets subject-matter disciplines in education. Part three: Incorporating the computer as method. *Educational Technology* 32(8): 35–44.

Papert, S. 1980. *Mindstorms: Children, computers and powerful ideas.* New York: Basic Books.

Ringstaff, C., Sterns, M., Hanson, S., and Schneider, S. 1993. *The Cupertino-Freemont model of technology in schools project: Final report.* Cupertino, CA: SRI International.

Stewart, J. 1997. Single display groupware. *Extended Abstracts of ACM CHI '97.* Los Angeles: ACM Press, 71–72.

Stewart, J., Rayborn, E., Bederson, B., and Druin, A. 1998. When two hands are better than one: Enhancing collaboration using single display groupware. *Extended abstracts of ACM CHI '98.* Los Angeles: ACM Press, 102–105.

Tinker, R. F. 1993. Telecommuting as a progressive force in education. *TERC technical report.* Cambridge, MA: TERC Publications.

Chapter Four

The Researcher's Role in the Design of Children's Media and Technology

Debra A. Lieberman

KIDZ Health Software, Inc.

4.1 Introduction

There is an art to designing children's media and there is a science to it, too. Researchers who specialize in children's media can serve an essential role on design teams. They bring the team a clear picture of children as media users. During product development, they can fine-tune that picture through additional study and product testing. To be successful, however, researchers must appreciate the creativity and artistic imagination of the creative staff and, within that context, offer content and format ideas based on sound evidence about youngsters' needs, abilities, and preferences. Their job is to ensure the quality and effectiveness of the product without quashing the creative ideas that can make the product unique and compelling.

Researchers who specialize in children's media and work with product design teams typically bring a combination of academic expertise and an understanding of product development—for print, television, multimedia, Internet, or other technologies. Their academic background may focus on young people's uses of media and the gratifications they gain from such use; children's processes of socialization and learning with various media; emotional and behavioral effects of media on children; or issues related to interface and instructional design. Usually they know a variety of quantitative and qualitative research methods that they can put to use in surveys, laboratory or field experiments, usability testing, or observational studies for their clients. Because of their experience working on media products, they know how and when decisions get made during product development and can plan ahead to be ready with research-based answers when the design team needs them most.

Someone who specializes in children's media research can help ensure that the product will meet its goals with children in a targeted age and demographic group in terms of motivation, engagement, comprehension, entertainment, learning, and development of higher-order thinking skills, to name a few. This chapter shows how research skills can be applied to the results-oriented demands of media production by describing the researcher's potential contributions in seven major aspects of media development for children and adolescents. (The list holds true for the development of media targeted to adults as well.)

- Specifying the product concept and goals

- Designing the product

- Funding the project

- Testing and revising during production

- Measuring outcomes

- Publishing and presenting outcomes

- Helping team members keep up with the field

Some of the larger children's media companies have full-time research or usability staffs, and they also hire, for each product, content experts and instructional designers who specialize in the target age or demographic group. Researchers in these companies usually participate in all seven of the areas listed above.

Smaller companies are rarely able to involve researchers so extensively. Some work with no researchers at all and have no plan to do so. The corporate decision makers have not been convinced that research can add value, or if they agree that research can make a contribution, they feel it is not worth extending the production schedule. Other small companies may want researchers to be involved throughout product development, but budget limitations make that impossible. In these cases, the company may ask a research consultant to do nothing more than an "armchair review," that is, to look at a product before it is completed and recommend changes. The researcher must rely on existing knowledge and experience to assess the product and make recommendations. There is no opportunity to put the product into users' hands. In other cases, small companies may hire a research consultant to participate in just one or two of the activities in the list, most commonly specifying the product concept and goals and testing and revising the product during production.

Even when consultants or full-time staff researchers are available from the start, a company may not allot enough time in the schedule to let them do a thorough job in any of the seven areas listed above. For example, it is all too common to find that the time for product testing and revising is so short that there can be little opportunity to meet with children. Or plans may call for only one iteration of the product, leaving no time before the scheduled release date for the production staff to make substantial revisions. In this case, if usability testing finds a need for major improvements, the production staff will implement them in the next release of the product.

On a few occasions I have been fortunate to work with children's media companies that involved me as a researcher from product start to finish. These experiences have been the most satisfying because I could help set goals and then see them all the way through to product completion and evaluation. When these projects began, I worked with the team, with children, and with content experts to develop a clear set of goals for the product.

Then during development, I made sure the goals were addressed with appropriate content and interface design, based on several iterations of usability testing and revision. When the product was complete, I conducted outcome studies with children in natural settings to make sure the goals had been achieved.

Later in this chapter, I describe my work as a researcher for a children's media product, where I was involved throughout its design, development, and evaluation. But first, I present a more general discussion of the seven areas in which researchers can contribute a great deal to the quality and effectiveness of children's media and technology.

4.2 Specifying the Product Concept and Goals

Media researchers bring to a team special knowledge about children's interests and abilities. They know what different kinds of children—by age or gender, for example—prefer in terms of topics, characters, music, game formats, and other features. They also know how different types of children respond to mediated messages and can suggest design and content presentation strategies that have worked in the past.

There is always more knowledge to acquire. The researcher can search the literature to identify valid studies that have addressed the issues the design team is facing. For example, if the team wants to create a product that appeals to girls, a literature review on girls and media can support or debunk common assumptions about girls' typical media preferences and perhaps provide descriptions of products that have been successful with girls. Another kind of research involves collecting pertinent market data on the target group's media use, such as their access to technology, content and format preferences, need for the proposed product, and ability to pay for it. Parents' and teachers' attitudes about the product category are also useful to know since these individuals are often the decision makers for children's media purchases.

Almost every design team has questions that have never been addressed in prior research. This is certainly true in the case of software targeted to girls, for example. A researcher can observe children from the target user group in various activities and settings to gain insights into features that those particular young people would like in media made especially for them. A researcher can also use this time to conduct preliminary usability studies with paper prototypes to see how children respond to features that are being considered for the product.

After experts' knowledge, the literature review, and new research data are gathered, a researcher can synthesize all this information in a user requirements document (URD), sometimes called a user experience requirements document (UERD). The URD presents a model, or profile, of the target users of the product, including their abilities, behaviors, habits, preferences, media use, and allocation of time during school and leisure. Typically, a URD links the characteristics of the target group to particular types of media uses. For example, if one target segment usually does not like to play fast-paced, competitive games, there are implications for the design of interactive games for that segment. Once the team has a clear idea of the user group's characteristics, it can then develop the product's basic concept and identify specific formats and goals especially for those users.

One company, Purple Moon, was formed to create software for U.S. girls ages 7–12. With R&D money provided by Interval Research, the founding team of researchers spent two and a half years reviewing the research literature and observing girls in this age group (see Laurel 1998). The team spent thousands of hours interviewing children; experts in play, gender differences, and gaming; and teachers, play supervisors, scout leaders, arcade managers, computer game retailers, and camp counselors, all of whom have direct contact with children. With this information, the researchers at Purple Moon developed their URD, a comprehensive profile of girls as media users. They identified the concepts and goals of the software in what they call a new breakthrough segment within the girls' entertainment category— adventures for girls. Only after completing this extensive multiyear process of research and concept development were they ready to establish the company and develop products.

Once the URD is created, the design team can identify strategies for reaching each product goal (intended outcome). They can develop and annotate a model showing connections among theories, design strategies, and goals. A model like this for an asthma education video game appears later in this chapter.

Using mathematics education as an example, if one goal is to teach children how to create graphs, then researchers, instructional designers, and mathematics education experts on the team can develop a theory-based instructional approach that helps children in the target group develop, practice, and apply the required graphing skills. Or if a more general, overarching goal of a children's media product is to encourage appreciation of ethnic and cultural diversity, a design strategy might be to include narrators and characters from a variety of ethnic and cultural groups. This strategy is grounded in theory and research. There are educational and psychological studies that demonstrate a link between portrayals of appealing characters and the development of positive attitudes toward the groups they represent (see, for example, [Bandura 1986] for a discussion of social learning theory).

4.3 Designing the Product

One of the team's most critical tasks is to create a design document that specifies all features of the product, including characters, illustrations, graphic design, animation, plot, settings, text, dialogue, user activities, help system, user control, feedback, navigation, and more. The design document is a blueprint that describes the product completely for the developers who will produce it. Researchers can make sure the product's goals, and design strategies for achieving those goals, are written clearly and accurately in the design document. There should be no ambiguity about the way any aspect of the product is to be created.

When the design document is finished and the developers get to work, a researcher should be on hand to review the product's content and interface as they are implemented. A product feature may be described too vaguely in the document and may turn out in ways that were not intended. Also, new issues always arise once the concept starts to become a reality. It is much easier to keep an eye on the product during production and make fundamental changes early on than to try to patch things up later.

4.4 Funding the Project

The presence of a researcher on a media design team is likely to increase funders' confidence in the product's quality and potential effectiveness. Foundations and other grant-giving agencies tend to look more favorably on children's media projects that include someone with demonstrated expertise in children's media. It is very common for at least one member of the team on federally funded children's media projects to have a Ph.D. in education, communication, or psychology and to have prior experience designing, producing, or evaluating children's media. Some funding agencies require children's media projects to have a media researcher involved.

The team should let potential funders know how research serves as the basis of the product, and a researcher should be responsible for conveying this information in the form of a report or proposal. Grant proposals typically include a review of the research literature that demonstrates a need for the product and supports the theory-based strategies that will be implemented in the product's design. Researchers on the design team should write these proposal sections. They won't have to start from scratch. Their previous work in the field, and the literature review they conducted at the outset of the project, will provide many studies to cite in the proposal.

In meetings with potential funders, researchers can be present to demonstrate that the product has a solid foundation in current research and theory. They can explain the research that has gone into the product's concept, goals, and design, and they can talk about previous observations of children in the target group, children's involvement in the design process, and children's reactions to paper prototypes. Researchers should be available to answer funders' research-related questions during the meeting and afterward.

Potential investors, another important constituency, want evidence that the company and its products will succeed. Involvement of a children's media researcher can reassure them that the products will be appealing and effective with the target user group.

4.5 Testing and Revising during Production

Most large software companies have in-house usability specialists trained in social science research methods and experienced in testing and designing software interfaces (see Chapter 1). These staff members are responsible for testing the product with target users in the lab and in natural settings and for recommending improvements based on their findings. Smaller companies tend to rely mostly on outside contractors to direct an occasional usability study as needed. Larger companies with an in-house usability team may also work with outside contractors during "crunch" times when there is more testing to do than the in-house staff can handle. (For more on usability testing, see [Hanna et al. 1998].)

Some companies ask usability specialists to work on some or all of the seven research areas presented in this chapter, while other companies ask them to focus exclusively on usability testing during product production. Usability specialists who take on various research roles use a full range of methods, such as task analyses, focus groups, ethnographic and observational studies, natural use studies, field experiments, surveys, longitudinal studies, beta tests, and competitive analyses (also known as "bake-offs") that pit competitors' products against the product under development. As a rule, usability specialists will videotape target users as they interact with the product. After a study is finished, a usability specialist may edit the tapes into a highlights tape of key moments during testing, when a participant has done or said something that indicates a problem or when there is a clearly demonstrated success story about some aspect of the product. The usability team can play the highlights tape for others in the company to show where revisions are needed or that the design is working well.

Outside usability contractors are sometimes hired to set up the test procedures and then to return to the project to help with data analysis after the test has been conducted. I have worked this way with several small software companies that wanted to cut costs by doing as much work as possible with in-house staff. After working with the staff to identify the goals of the study, I created the test plan, questionnaires, interviews, and observation sheets. I trained the staff to observe and interview usability test participants. Next, they spent a week conducting sessions with target users and afterward they transferred the data (such as questionnaire or interview results or a tally of user errors) to a spreadsheet. I then rejoined the project to analyze the data statistically, create tables and charts of these analyses, write narrative reports of the quantitative findings, and recommend product revisions. The in-house staff wrote up their qualitative observations of study participants and then combined their report with mine to come up with one seamless document to be read by those responsible for the final version of the product.

4.6 Measuring Outcomes

Outcome studies serve a product's developers and its marketers. When data are collected about usage and impact over time with target users in natural settings, a developer can discover the weaknesses and strengths of the product and learn how to improve it next time. Marketers, on the other hand, are mostly interested in favorable study outcomes because these provide solid evidence that the product achieves its goals. In the next marketing campaign, product packaging and advertisements can boast that the product was scientifically tested and works as intended.

Some large companies that develop children's media products conduct beta tests of the next-to-last iteration of each product. This version must be fully functional so it can be tried out in natural settings. Beta testers are people in the target user category who agree to try out the product in settings where it is typically used. They understand that their job is to provide feedback to the company about the product's pros and cons, including any software bugs or problems. For children's products, parents or teachers are involved in beta testing because researchers need them to report what children are doing with the product at home or school and whether the product is successful.

Researchers may send online questionnaires to beta test participants (or to parents or teachers, in the case of younger participants), and they usually observe participants using the product and conduct face-to-face interviews at that time. Usage data may be collected, especially if the product is on a network and the data can be gathered and entered into a database automatically. A researcher may conduct other forms of research during beta testing, such as an experiment in which beta testers are randomly assigned to use one or the other of two versions of the product to determine which is preferable. Findings from all of these research activities can help the company identify and then correct significant problems and make revisions before releasing the product.

Some companies are satisfied to avoid beta testing and simply collect feedback from users who have purchased version 1.0 of the product. However, children's media companies, especially those developing educational media, benefit greatly when they conduct beta tests. If they wait to see whether version 1.0 sinks or swims in terms of appeal or effectiveness after it is released, it may very well sink. Then it is often too late to convince customers that the company knows what it is doing. There may be no second chance.

Outcome studies often continue after the final version of a product is complete so that developers will continue to receive user feedback. The company uses this information to develop future versions of the product. In other cases, a company may decide to begin another outcome study that uses a new pool of participants and a different research methodology. If the study is an experiment and the control group is not supposed to have access to the product, it would be best to conduct the study before the product is released for sale. This will ensure that those in the treatment group are the only people in the study who see and use the product.

An outcome study could be as simple as putting the product in the target users' environment and observing how often they use it and what they do with it. Or the study could go into greater depth and measure cognitive, learning, social, emotional, or behavioral changes in target users. I directed a field experiment of a diabetes education video game in which target users (children and adolescents with diabetes, ages 8–16) were randomly assigned to take home either the diabetes video game (treatment condition) or another entertainment video game that had no diabetes-related content (control condition). They also received a Super Nintendo system and could play their video game as much or as little as they wished, as long as they followed their family's rules about video game playing. In this experimental design, outcomes were measured after 6 months. When the treatment group improved significantly in certain intended outcomes and the control group did not, we could attribute those outcomes to the children's use of the media product. The study found that the participants who took home the diabetes video game improved in communication with parents about diabetes and in daily self-care behaviors (e.g., remembering to test blood glucose, take insulin, and eat a balanced diet). There was also a 77 percent decrease in their urgent doctor visits for diabetes during the 6-month study period (Brown et al. 1997).

4.7 Publishing and Presenting Outcomes

After an outcome study is completed, researchers are often asked to help communicate the findings. They may write articles for academic or trade journals or for publications geared to the general public. They may also work with the public relations, marketing, and sales departments to create collateral materials, such as brochures, annual reports, and press releases, making sure the research findings are reported accurately. Managers who write business plans, product plans, strategic plans, and other company documents may also need researchers to contribute accurate descriptions of their studies and results. And researchers may write sections of grant proposals that describe the methodology used in previous outcome studies and present their findings as evidence that the company creates media products that are appealing and easy to use and that achieve their stated goals.

Researchers are called on to create the sections of slide presentations that present study findings. They also present research results at professional conferences and participate on panels. Their articles and illustrations of study findings, in charts and tables, can be included in major company presentations to potential customers, investors, and funding agencies.

4.8 Helping Team Members Keep Up with the Field

Media designers and producers are intelligent people who know a lot about their products and about target audiences and user groups. But they are also very busy, and it is difficult for them to find time to keep up with developments in their field. Researchers, whether in-house staff or outside contractors, can collect worthwhile information resources, summarize them in easily accessible formats, and help keep the collection current.

One K–12 educational media company contracted with me to develop a research database. I selected only those resources that used rigorous study designs or that presented valid arguments substantiated with evidence. I entered bibliographic information and wrote a succinct abstract for each book, chapter, report, or journal article I selected. The company's staff could search the abstracts for keywords or text strings, print out selected abstracts or save them to disk, and find the original publications in a nearby bookcase if needed. This database was used most heavily as projects started up and the team was in the stage of specifying the product concept and goals. Another time, when that company asked me to write overviews of current trends in K–12 student assessment, constructivist learning, and mathematics and science education, the research database was the first resource I used.

Other ways researchers have helped their colleagues stay up-to-date include setting up brown-bag lunches with invited speakers, product demos, and group discussions about hot topics in the field. Online, researchers typically have ready resources for other in-house tasks, such as posting notices of conferences and local professional group meetings or emailing field-related articles or Web site addresses.

Table 4.1 presents a list of the researcher's potential tasks and deliverables during the seven phases of product development.

Table **4.1**

Researcher's roles and responsibilities during media product development

Researcher's roles	Tasks	Deliverables
Specifying the product concept and goals	Read research literature that focuses on the content, format, and outcomes that may be of interest to the team. Write a narrative review or annotated bibliography that cites specific research findings.	Literature review
	Observe target group children engaged in similar activities. Similarity could be in the nature of the activity, content, medium, or environment. Interview children, their parents, and their teachers. Talk with experts in child development, content area, and software and interface design.	User requirements document (URD)
	With the design team, identify the product's basic concept and goals.	Part I of design document
	Develop a model showing how the product design will achieve desired outcomes.	Annotated model linking theory and research to product design and to outcomes
Designing the product	Using the documents already written, work with the design team to describe specifically the product's characters, interface, navigation, and other features.	Part II of design document
Funding the project	In meetings with potential funders and investors, present the product concept and goals, showing how they are based on theory and research. Present the theoretical model and the design document to show that the product is focused on specific, achievable goals.	Slides, handouts, and portions of the company's business plan

continued on page 84

Table 4.1 continued

Researcher's roles and responsibilities during media product development

Researcher's roles	Tasks	Deliverables
Funding the project (*continued*)	Write grant proposals to support research and development of the product.	Grant proposals
Testing and revising during production	Work with developers to create a functional prototype of the product. Show prototype to target users, their parents, and their teachers for feedback. Watch children using the prototype and note their usage.	Usability reports with recommended revisions to product
	Show prototype to experts in child development, content area, and software and interface design, and gather feedback.	
	When parts of the product are complete, conduct at least two iterations of usability testing with target users.	Usability reports with recommended product revisions
	Observe children using the product in the intended environment, then interview them.	Field test report with recommended revisions to product
Measuring outcomes	Use educational and social science research methods to test intended outcomes in large-scale beta tests and studies with target users over time.	Research reports
Publishing and presenting outcomes	Publish findings in peer-reviewed academic research journals, trade publications, and the popular press.	Research articles
	Contribute to brochures, ads, and press releases that describe the findings in language that the general public can understand. Also post the information online.	Collateral materials
	Present findings to groups with an interest in the product, such as professionals in related fields, parent education groups, and youth groups.	Slides and handouts
Helping team members keep up with the field	Maintain files of articles with research pertinent to the product's content or format. Circulate emails and Web site addressess to producers who need to stay up-to-date. Hold brown-bag lunch meetings to present research findings and case studies that the team should know about. Invite experts to give presentations on topics related to the product.	Searchable electronic database of references, article abstracts, and notes from research presentations

Figure **4.1**

Asthma education video game, Bronkie the Bronchiasaurus. Bronkie the Bronchiasaurus Video Game © KIDZ Health Software, Inc.

4.9 Designing and Evaluating an Asthma Education Video Game

This section describes how research contributed to an asthma education Super Nintendo video game called Bronkie the Bronchiasaurus (Figure 4.1, [see also Color Plate], and Figure 4.2) and targeted to children with asthma, ages 6–12. I was in charge of the research on Bronkie, and throughout production I was involved in the video game's design, development, and evaluation.

Specifying the Product Concept and Goals

We decided to use the Super Nintendo platform because it was very popular among children in all socioeconomic groups in the United States and was much less expensive than a computer. We also made the game available on CD-ROM. We focused on asthma education because millions of youngsters have this chronic condition. Many experience severe asthma problems that

Figure 4.2

Bronkie the Bronchiasaurus city scene showing Bronkie setting out on his adventure to save his planet. He ultimately travels through cities, lakes, jungle, sky, canyons, and caves.

can be ameliorated or prevented with appropriate self-management. To keep asthma under control, the child must make decisions throughout the day. It is impossible for even the most well-meaning parents to monitor and guide their child every moment. The child must be responsible for taking care of asthma—for instance, by avoiding asthma triggers, recognizing the onset of an asthma episode, and knowing what to do if a problem arises.

To begin this project, we identified characteristics of the Super Nintendo medium, the features children liked about it, and the kinds of games they played. We watched children playing Super Nintendo games in their homes, at video game stores, and in our offices, and we asked them about their favorites. After weeks of observation and interviewing, we concluded that side-scrolling adventure games were by far the most popular, for both boys and girls, on the Super Nintendo platform. We noted that youngsters liked to have control over a main character, immediate action and feedback, and the challenge of succeeding in increasingly difficult situations. We knew our asthma game would need to have these features, too. While there were many other possible formats we could have used in Super Nintendo video games, we felt it was important to stick with the side-scrolling adventure game, a format children already knew and loved. It was enough of a departure to add elements of health education, so keeping other aspects of the video game familiar seemed like a good idea.

We met with children and adolescents who have asthma and asked them what they wanted to see in a video game dealing with this topic. Many liked the idea of controlling a main character who has asthma and of managing that character's asthma well to play optimally in the game. They wanted characters to be cool, capable, and full of energy so their friends would see that asthma need not slow anyone down. They looked forward to playing a video game like this with friends so they could teach them about asthma and use the video game as a springboard for personal discussion.

Drawing on the literature on computers and learning, we saw that video games, like computers, have interactive capabilities that could readily support simulation-based experiential learning. In side-scrolling adventure video games, players control a character that moves through a series of environments, has a goal, confronts obstacles, makes decisions, and experiences the consequences. Consequences can accumulate until the player is forced to take action to improve the character's situation or lose the game. This sequence of action and consequences can be applied to a variety of learning situations, including, we believed, learning asthma self-management skills.

Video games provide opportunities to rehearse new skills in a realistic and interactive simulated environment, and they allow players to see the end results of every choice they make. Most children like this combination of interactivity, entertainment, story line, engaging characters, fantasy, challenge, decision making, feedback, repetition, duration, and privacy (Lepper and Gurtner 1989; Lieberman 1997; Malone and Lepper 1987). Video games also present important content repeatedly. Young people will typically play a video game frequently over several months as they try to complete an increasing number of game levels. Our diabetes study, for example, found that on average participants played for 36 hours in 6 months (Brown et al. 1997). Players have not really conquered a game until they have completed all game levels in sequence, and they continue learning new things throughout this period.

Once we understood what side-scrolling adventure video games were like and why children enjoyed them, we developed a theoretical model showing how a video game could help children improve their asthma-related behaviors and health outcomes (see Figure 4.3). We identified mediating factors that a video game could improve, under the categories of self-concepts, social support, and knowledge. Research has shown that improvements in these factors can improve health-related behaviors and outcomes (Bandura 1986,

Figure 4.3

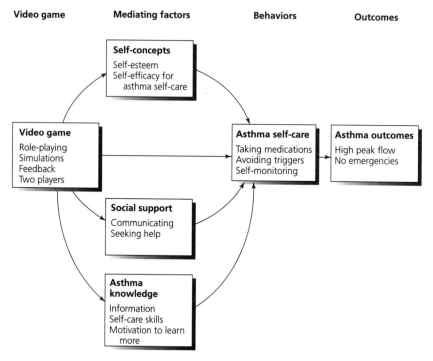

Theory-based model showing asthma video game goals. Video game influences mediating factors that influence behaviors and outcomes.

1990; Maibach and Parrott 1995; Peterson and Stunkard 1989). Arrows indicate the hypothesized direction of influence. (A detailed discussion of this model, with citations of relevant research, appears in [Lieberman and Brown 1995].)

Designing the Product

Our medical director for the asthma video game was physician Dale Umetsu, an expert in pediatric asthma clinical care and research at Stanford University Medical Center. We met with Dr. Umetsu and other caregivers—pediatric asthma physicians, nurses, researchers, and patient educators—to identify the knowledge and skills they felt were most important for young asthma patients to learn. We wanted the educational goals to focus on a few skills and areas of knowledge that we could present repeatedly throughout the game. Our expert advisors concluded that there are just a few basic things that children with asthma need to know, so the game included all of them. Working with these asthma experts, we identified eight areas to address in the asthma Super Nintendo game:

1. Taking medication daily

2. Using an inhaler correctly to take medication

3. Avoiding asthma triggers in the environment

4. Monitoring peak flow (breath strength) with a peak flow meter

5. Recognizing and responding to changes in peak flow

6. Using a sick-day plan appropriately

7. Reviewing a personal daily asthma record

8. Learning basic facts about asthma causes and precautions

We decided to put the video game's main characters into situations where they must deal realistically with these eight asthma issues, within a story line that is pure fantasy adventure. In our game, the main characters—Bronkie, a boy dinosaur, and Trakie, a girl dinosaur—have asthma and must use all eight skills in the list. While on an urgent quest to find missing pieces of a wind machine, needed to save their planet from oncoming lethal dust clouds, they also have to remember to take their daily asthma medication and to avoid environmental triggers. Smoke, dust, pollen, furry animals, and cold viruses (shot through the air by Sneezer characters) are some of the triggers the heroes must watch out for. If one of them comes in contact with triggers too frequently, then peak flow goes down and the character, controlled by the child, must take appropriate action or else lose the game.

We turned to educational theory and previous studies of instructional technology to help us develop video game design strategies that would address the eight skill areas. For instance, asthma caregivers told us that many children have a hard time using an inhaler correctly to take their medication. Even those who remember to take it every day are losing out because much of the medication does not enter their lungs. We used Bronkie and Trakie, the appealing male and female heroes of the asthma game, as role models who took their medication daily. Children saw an animation of one or both of them going through six distinct steps (breathing out, putting inhaler in mouth, pressing down, etc.), along with text describing every step, at the beginning of each of the 18 game levels (Figure 4.4). Our justification for this approach came from social learning theory (Bandura 1986; Larson 1991), which describes how people learn from observing the actions of role models in their immediate environment and via media. The most effective role models are those who have attractive characteristics and who experience rewards for their modeled behaviors.

In addition to addressing the eight asthma goals, we designed the game to improve the mediating factors in the model in Figure 4.3. For example,

Figure 4.4

Bronkie using an inhaler to take daily asthma medicine

we expected that rehearsing asthma self-management skills in the course of playing the game would improve children's self-efficacy regarding their own asthma care. That is, they would feel more capable and efficacious about carrying out asthma self-care in their own lives after learning how to carry out the same activities for the main characters in the video game simulation. Using media to enhance self-efficacy has been done successfully before (Bandura 1990, 1997; Maibach and Cotton 1995), and we concluded that interactive games offer an especially rich learning environment for this purpose (Lieberman 1997).

Figure 4.5 (see also Color Plate) shows Bronkie finding his emergency medications inhaler, which he can use if his peak flow gets low. The Asthma Management screen (Figure 4.6) allows Bronkie and Trakie to test peak flow, use an inhaler during an emergency, follow a sick-day medication plan if one of them catches a cold, or call for help if peak flow gets dangerously low. As children make decisions about Bronkie and Trakie's asthma management, they are rehearsing these activities and, according to our predictions, enhancing their self-efficacy and skills.

Figure 4.5

Bronkie finding an emergency meds inhaler that he can use to improve his peak flow the next time he bumps into too many asthma triggers

In another example of a mediating factor, we expected that offering a two-player option in the video game would enhance players' social support regarding asthma. We knew from our observations of children and from our literature review that video game playing is often a social activity for young people; many of them talk about games even when not playing (Clements 1987; Lieberman 1997; Salomon and Gardner 1986). Children often help each other with video game strategies and enjoy games they can play with others (Lieberman 1985; Malone and Lepper 1987). So we predicted that an asthma education video game in which two players could control cooperative characters would help stimulate players to discuss asthma with friends, family, and caregivers. Importantly, they would be more likely to talk about their own asthma with others instead of trying to hide it. Improvements in social support and reduction in the social stigma of having asthma, we predicted, would also lead to better self-management of asthma when friends were around. If youngsters with asthma feel that friends understand and support their efforts at self-care, then self-care should persist even in the presence of friends.

Figure 4.6

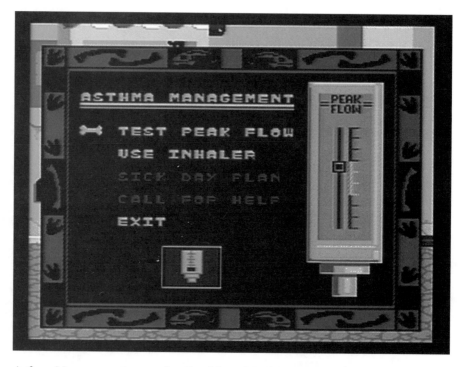

Asthma Management screen that Bronkie and Trakie use when they need to measure peak flow, take emergency or sick-day medication, or call for help in a severe asthma emergency

We addressed other asthma self-management goals and mediating factors with a variety of instructional design strategies, all based on theory and research. Our review of the research literature, observations of youngsters playing Super Nintendo video games, and analysis of the Super Nintendo platform's capabilities helped us create these new approaches. (For a more thorough discussion of the instructional design strategies we developed for Bronkie and other health education video games, see [Lieberman 1997] and [Lieberman and Brown 1995].)

Funding the Product

We wrote two successful grant proposals to the National Institutes of Health to fund research, development, and outcome studies of Bronkie the Bronchiasaurus. Several corporations and asthma research and education organizations invited us to present the design of the asthma education video game so they could consider sponsoring or endorsing it. Our previous research with children, the observational studies we conducted, the literature reviews, and our Bronkie design document were important components of our presentations. We obtained a corporate sponsor, Astra, which supported development of the video game and later gave copies of it to asthma summer camps and clinics. We also attracted several endorsing organizations, including the Asthma and Allergy Foundation of America and the American Academy of Pediatrics, which helped publicize the video game to clinicians, families, and children.

Testing and Revising the Product during Production

During production we tested Bronkie the Bronchiasaurus in a wide range of settings with a variety of children who had asthma. The results helped us improve almost every aspect of the product as it went through several iterations of testing and revision. For example, we learned how to improve the characters' personalities, the animations showing characters using an inhaler to take daily meds, the on-screen status bar, the Asthma Record screen (see Figure 4.7), and the method of awarding points and displaying scores.

Measuring Outcomes

We conducted an outcome study with 50 outpatients at Stanford Medical Center's pediatric asthma clinic. The study showed that playing Bronkie for less than an hour led to significant and immediate improvements in the children's self-efficacy for asthma self-management, in self-efficacy for talking with friends about asthma, and in asthma knowledge. These gains endured in delayed posttest assessments 1 month later. Children who participated in the study also improved in the amount of asthma-related communication and social support during the month after they played the video game. A more extensive study of Bronkie's outcomes is now under way in a long-term randomized clinical trial, supported by a grant from the National Institutes of Health. The results of this trial will help us create enhanced interactive products that improve asthma self-care.

In another study, we placed Bronkie the Bronchiasaurus video game cartridges in the pediatric ward of the hospital at California Pacific Medical Center in San Francisco for 4 weeks. There were six children hospitalized for asthma complications during the study period, and the hospital had video game systems available in hospital rooms on rolling carts. Nurses were asked to observe whether and how children were using the game. When the

Figure 4.7

Asthma Record screen showing Bronkie's previous peak flow highs and lows, and the medications he has taken, in four previous game levels

study period ended, the nurses reported that Bronkie was in constant demand even for pediatric patients who did not have asthma. Children as young as 5 and as old as 18 were avid players. Parents were pleasantly surprised to see a Nintendo game with health education content. According to the nurses, social interaction among all the children increased because they spent a great deal of time talking about the game and playing it together. There was also more social interaction between children and caregivers. The video game provided an informal way for youngsters to interact with their doctors and nurses, and the content in the video game sparked further discussion about asthma.

Publishing and Presenting Outcomes

We have published our video game instructional design strategies and the findings from our outcome studies in several venues, including this chapter and other publications (Brown et al. 1997; Lieberman 1997; Lieberman and Brown 1995). We have presented these results at many professional association conferences in the fields of clinical medicine, education, and the social sciences. Bronkie the Bronchiasaurus has received a great deal of national press coverage because it is so unusual to see a Super Nintendo game intentionally designed with educational and pro-social goals. Also, the press was interested because asthma is a serious problem that affects millions of young people; here is an asthma education product that research has shown is appealing and effective with children and adolescents who have this condition. We would not have had most of these opportunities to publish and present information about Bronkie if we did not also have research findings that substantiate and demonstrate the video game's positive impact on children's asthma self-management.

Helping Team Keep Members Up with the Field

Almost every time we wrote a new proposal or prepared a new presentation, we updated our literature review. It was my responsibility to find current research, and to do this I used online bibliographic search tools. Our field, then and now, moves ahead quickly, so it is extremely important to stay up-to-date.

4.10 Conclusion

This chapter describes many ways a researcher can contribute to children's media design, development, and evaluation. I hope it will encourage undergraduate and graduate students to consider entering this field and will encourage more media producers to integrate research into their product development process.

A colleague suggested that I not use the term "research" to describe what I do because she thinks it sounds bland and vague. She wants me to call it "quality enhancement," "value optimization," or some other name that emphasizes the results-oriented nature of this work. She has a point. While this chapter discusses the process of doing media research, it also provides examples of products that have benefited tremendously from research. Their quality has certainly been enhanced and their value optimized. I hope that—no matter what we call it—research will become more central to the creation of the mediated information, education, and entertainment we provide for our children.

Acknowledgments

I am grateful to my teachers from *Sesame Street* and the Harvard Graduate School of Education in the mid-1970s, producer Sam Gibbon and professors Gerald Lesser and Aimee Dorr, who showed me how researchers can work with creative teams to develop high-quality children's media. I value my research training in the mid-1980s in the Ph.D. program at Stanford University's Department of Communication with professors Don Roberts, Bill Paisley, Steve Chaffee, and Ev Rogers. I also appreciate the opportunity to do research and development for Bronkie and other health education video games in the mid-1990s with Health Hero Network colleagues Steve Brown, Beth Gemeny, Patty Brown, and Aaron Baker and with KIDZ Health Software colleague Alan Miller.

For information about new interactive health education products and those currently in development, send an email to *dlieberman@kidz health.com*.

References

Bandura, A. 1986. *Social foundations of thought and action: A social cognitive theory.* Englewood Cliffs, NJ: Prentice Hall.

Bandura, A. 1990. Self-efficacy mechanism in physiological activation and health-promoting behavior. In J. Madden IV, ed. *Neurobiology of learning, emotion and affect.* New York: Raven.

Bandura, A. 1997. *Self-efficacy: The exercise of control.* New York: W. H. Freeman.

Brown, S. J., Lieberman, D. A., Gemeny, B. A., Fan, Y. C., Wilson, D. M., and Pasta, D. J. 1997. Educational video game for juvenile diabetes self-care: Results of a controlled trial. *Medical Informatics* 21(4): 77–89.

Clements, D. 1987. Computers and young children: A review of research. *Young Children* 43(1): 34–43.

Hanna, L., Risden, K., Czerwinski, M., and Alexander, K. 1998. The role of usability research in designing children's computer products. In A. Druin, ed. *The design of children's technology.* San Francisco: Morgan Kaufmann.

Larson, M. S. 1991. Health-related messages embedded in prime-time television entertainment. *Health Communication* 3: 175–184.

Laurel, B. 1998. Purple Moon research highlights. *www.purple-moon.com/cb/laslink/pm?stat+corp+research_highlights.*

Lepper, M. R., and Gurtner, J. 1989. Children and computers: Approaching the twenty-first century. *American Psychologist* 44(2): 170–178.

Lieberman, D. A. 1985. Research on children and microcomputers: A review of utilization and effects studies. In M. Chen and W. Paisley, eds. *Children and microcomputers: Research on the newest medium.* Beverly Hills, CA: Sage.

Lieberman, D. A. 1997. Interactive video games for health promotion: Effects on knowledge, self-efficacy, social support, and health. In R. L. Street, W. R. Gold, and T. Manning, eds. *Health promotion and interactive technology: Theoretical applications and future directions.* Mahwah, NJ: Lawrence Erlbaum.

Lieberman, D. A., and Brown, S. J. 1995. Designing interactive video games for children's health education. In K. Morgan, R. M. Satava, H. B. Sieburg, R. Matthews, and J. P. Christensen, eds. *Interactive technology and the new paradigm for healthcare.* Amsterdam: IOS Press.

Maibach, E. W., and Cotton, D. 1995. Moving people to behavior change. In E. W. Maibach and R. L. Parrott, eds. *Designing health messages: Approaches from communication theory and public health practice.* Thousand Oaks, CA: Sage.

Maibach, E. W., and Parrott, R. L., eds. 1995. *Designing health messages: Approaches from communication theory and public health practice.* Thousand Oaks, CA: Sage.

Malone, T. W., and Lepper, M. R. 1987. Making learning fun: A taxonomy of intrinsic motivations for learning. In R. E. Snow and M. J. Farr, eds. *Aptitude, learning and instruction III: Conative and affective process analyses.* Hillsdale, NJ: Lawrence Erlbaum.

Peterson, C., and Stunkard, A. J. 1989. Personal control and health promotion. *Social Science and Medicine* 28: 819–828.

Salomon, G., and Gardner, H. 1986. The computer as educator: Lessons from television research. *Educational Researcher* 15: 13–19.

Chapter Five

Designing Collaborative Applications for Classroom Use:

The LiNC Project

Jürgen Koenemann

GMD—German National Research Center for Information Technology

John M. Carroll

Department of Computer Science,
Virginia Polytechnic Institute and State University

Clifford A. Shaffer

Department of Computer Science,
Virginia Polytechnic Institute and State University

Mary Beth Rosson

Department of Computer Science,
Virginia Polytechnic Institute and State University

Marc Abrams

Department of Computer Science,
Virginia Polytechnic Institute and State University

5.1 Introduction

This chapter reports on the design of educational technology for classroom use at the middle school and high school level. The Learning in Networked Communities (LiNC) project is a joint, interdisciplinary endeavor of computer scientists and human-computer interaction specialists from the Virginia Polytechnic Institute and State University (VTech) Department of Computer Science, and educators from the local school system (Montgomery County Public Schools in Virginia).* The project leverages the technological and cultural opportunities of the Blacksburg Electronic Village (BEV), a densely interconnected community in rural southwestern Virginia (Carroll and Rosson 1996). The focus of the project is not on the design of technology per se (even though we do develop advanced systems and interfaces) but on the design of a learning *environment* that includes not only the technology but the human actors (students and teachers) and the situational school "work" context. That is, we actively design "use" in our belief that technology can only be successful if the future use context is reflected in the design itself. Because of this orientation, our design and development work is heavily driven by scenarios of current and envisioned classroom activities that are developed with and by educators in a participatory fashion.

The LiNC project understands itself not only as a design project but as a project *about* design: We have devoted significant energy toward developing and evaluating principled, scenario-based participatory design strategies and methods (Carroll et al. 1997; Chin, Rosson, and Carroll 1997).

The focus of our work is on computer-mediated collaboration of school children. In this chapter, we will describe a Java-based "virtual physical science laboratory" that enables colocated as well as geographically distributed groups of children at the middle school and high school level to collaboratively work on physics problems. The LiNC environment is designed to support longer-term asynchronous group collaboration (for example, shared discussions and report writing) as well as real-time synchronous collaboration (for example, the joint construction, execution, and control of simulations). We will discuss how such technology must fit into real classrooms and be integrated with computer-external activities to create a beneficial learning environment that merges and integrates real and "virtual" (i.e., online) activities and objects.

The remainder of the chapter is organized as follows. We first trace the background and motivation for the LiNC project and discuss the scenario-based participatory design process. We then describe in some detail the

*The work reported here was carried out while the first author was a member of the Department of Computer Science at Virginia Tech and Technical Project Coordinator of the LiNC project.

system we developed along with its technological foundation. The chapter concludes with a discussion of the lessons of our project for the design of the classroom of tomorrow.

5.2 Background

Our motivations for undertaking this project were threefold. First, we wanted to extend our prior education research into the K–12 context. Second, we specifically wanted to extend our prior research on supporting K–12 education with Web-based discussion forums to supporting K–12 classroom activities with a richer and more diverse set of mechanisms for networked communication and collaboration. Third, we wanted to explore and develop methodologies and concepts for "community computing" within the framework of the BEV.

In 1994, some of us had already been working in instructional design for more than a decade. During the 1980s, Carroll, Rosson, and colleagues developed the minimalist instructional model, which was widely applied in the computing industry (Carroll 1990, 1998), and investigated the efficacy of design-based instructional tasks and curricula in the context of Smalltalk programming and object-oriented software design (Koenemann-Belliveau et al. 1994; Rosson and Carroll 1996). The minimalist model has its roots in the educational research of John Dewey (1966), Jerome Bruner (1960, 1967), and Jean Piaget (1963, 1985). We wanted to explore the efficacy of minimalist instruction in the K–12 context and to develop our understanding of instruction by studying and designing for this context. We also wished to apply our prior experience with simulations at the college level to the K–12 level (Carstensen et al. 1993).

Stuart Laughton (1996) had conducted ethnographic studies of participatory design with teachers in which several Web-based, structured, asynchronous discourse applications were developed. We were fortunate to extend these collaborations with public school teachers who had substantial experience with design-based classroom activities and interests in supporting such activities with information technology (Carroll, Mauney, and Rencsok 1997). We wanted to build on the use of relatively low-bandwidth, asynchronous networking mechanisms to investigate the potential of higher-bandwidth, synchronous mechanisms.

Laughton's project and ours were conceived and developed in the context of the BEV (Carroll and Rosson 1996). As early as 1995, more than 40 percent of the Blacksburg community had access to the Internet, and most community groups and local businesses had developed and were maintaining Web sites and were using other network services. T1 lines were being run to the local schools, enabling new opportunities for school activities through Internet connectivity, such as access to community resources. One specific goal of the LiNC project was to investigate the role that this infrastructure could play in facilitating community involvement with schools, in improving access of rural schools to educational opportunities, and in enhancing gender equity in science and mathematics education (Carroll et al. 1997).

These motivations for undertaking the LiNC project align closely both with major currents of educational theory and with significant contemporary challenges to education. For example, the importance of hands-on or "active" learning is taken as a given in contemporary educational theory. Students must be taught to transform, evaluate, and apply information, not merely to store and retrieve it (Bruner 1960; Simon 1980). Such activity stimulates intrinsic motivation to learn (Lepper 1988; Malone and Lepper 1987). Project-based and collaborative activities are particularly valuable (Blumenfeld et al. 1991; Light et al. 1987). Recently, the view of science as a problem-solving process to be learned, rather than a collection of facts to be memorized, has become a prominent part of proposed standards and educational reform documents for science education, including Project 2061 (AAAS 1989) and the Scope, Sequence, and Curriculum Coordination project (NSTA 1990).

Yet many school-based interactions with the World Wide Web consist of passively absorbing multimedia information. The most common Internet activities in middle and high school are open-ended and single-source search projects; the most common collaborative activities are email pen pal interactions (Carnegie Mellon 1994). More generally, the call to develop and deploy laboratory exercises that are investigative and where the responsibility for learning lies with the student has not been accompanied by adequate classroom support:

1. Teachers trained in systemic reform programs are not always provided with active learning materials to implement these reforms in their classrooms (Honey and Henriquez 1993).

2. Hands-on activities often require lengthy setup and takedown times, for which teachers are not supported and which can distract students (Hofstein and Lunetta 1982).

3. Consumable material costs can be significant, even for relatively inexpensive "household item" experiments.

4. The number of students who can interact with an experiment directly must typically be limited.

Ironically, there is some indication that emphasis on engagement in meaningful, real-world tasks has *decreased* in schools over the past decade (Darling-Hammond 1990).

Similarly, there is now great interest in synchronous and higher-bandwidth networked interaction. Most investigations of high-bandwidth collaborations have focused on shared liveboard tools and media spaces in support of small business meetings (Kraut, Egido, and Galegher 1990; Mantei et al. 1991; Tatar, Foster, and Bobrow 1991). A smaller amount of research has addressed teaching and learning situations, generally in lower-bandwidth and asynchronous contexts. For example, Hiltz (1993) studied a virtual classroom situation constituted by asynchronous, text-based interactions and demonstrated improved access to educational activities and improved grades for students using the virtual classroom.

More recent computer-supported collaborative work (CSCW) on education has urged an even stronger focus on constructive student activity (Berger and Luckman 1966). Scardamalia, Bereiter, and Lamon (1994) have carried out extensive classroom development and testing of their CSILE (Computer Supported Intentional Learning Environments) system. CSILE is a database system in which public school students create notes that other students can read and annotate. The system is used with curriculum materials that emphasize open-ended discovery learning. Bellamy, Cooper, and Borovoy (1994) studied CSILE-like collaborations focused on student-created animated graphics. Pea and Gomez (1992) studied collaborations focused on weather data. Early evaluations of these projects have been extremely encouraging.

5.3 The Scenario-Based Participatory Design Process

We assumed from the start that a serious community computing project would itself have to be a thoroughly collaborative endeavor. Our project was established as a participatory design activity with teachers (Laughton 1996; Williams 1994). Teachers can easily be disempowered by instructional technology that displaces their pedagogical role. The typical lack of management in the introduction of technology into the schools causes even teachers with special interests in information technology to be cautious and skeptical. It has not been a trivial matter to create the trust required to have a truly participatory design process, but we have found it essential to have teacher input all the time across a broad front of technical issues (Chin, Rosson, and Carroll 1997).

The LiNC project serves as a testbed for applying and evaluating scenario-based design methods that we have been developing for several years. The

Figure 5.1

> Marissa is a 10th-grade physics student. She is studying gravity and its role in planetary motion. Through the network-viewer client on her personal computer, she accesses the county's virtual shared-laboratory server; she does this by typing "physics lab". The reception area appears. Since she already knows where the gravity room is, she immediately makes her way down the hall (i.e., using her mouse) and "enters" the second room on the left. Two other students, Randy and David, are working with the Alternate Reality Kit (Smith 1987), a Science Object that allows students to alter various physical parameters (such as the universal gravitational constant) and then observe effects in a simulation world. The three students, each of whom is from a different school in the county, discuss possible experiments by typing messages from their respective personal computers. They build and analyze several solar systems, eventually focusing on the question of how comets can disrupt otherwise stable systems. They capture the data from these experiments and display it with several alternative visualization tools. Finally, they write a brief report of these experiments, sending it for comments to Don, a student in Marissa's class, and Ms. Gould, the physics teacher in Randy's school.

Envisionment scenario (November 1994)

Task-Artifact Framework (TAF) (Carroll, Kellogg, and Rosson 1991; Carroll and Rosson 1992) relies on scenarios as a central representation in design, both as a source of analysis (e.g., what is working well or poorly in an existing situation) and as a source of design (e.g., how a situation can be improved through revised or new features). An important feature of scenarios is their ability to communicate design ideas among a variety of stakeholders, making them a natural component of any participatory design approach. We were interested in how TAF methods could be useful in the LiNC setting.

Our original thinking was heavily influenced by the existing MUD/MOO environments. These were mostly text-based, but we recognized that things were in a rapid state of change with the Web and graphics-on-demand over the network. We originally envisioned something along the lines of a 3D virtual world in which students would go and do exploratory activities within the context of a spatial metaphor. In November 1994, we created a scenario (Figure 5.1) that explicated this vision to help guide the development of the project.

Analyzing the Classroom Context

One of our first project activities was to create a rich analysis of the preexisting classroom context for the teachers participating in the research project. We visited two eighth-grade and two high school science classrooms while a wide range of physical science activities with a variety of collaborative activities were under way, observing and taking notes and videotaping both the class as a whole and individual work groups. Afterwards, we interviewed the teachers and a few students from each class who had volunteered to participate.

The videotapes, field notes, learning artifacts, and interviews were analyzed from two perspectives. First, an ethnographic encoding was carried out to identify the predominant themes of the existing classroom practice—for example, characteristics of experiments, of collaboration, of students, and of groups. This analysis in turn prompted the extraction of "interesting" episodes or scenarios from the videotaped experiments. We identified episodes that exercised some of the collaboration and experiment themes we had analyzed from the overall data and documented selected scenarios at two levels: the overall pedagogical activity (e.g., an open-ended exploration session) and the detailed student and group interactions. These scenarios were shared within the project team and have served as a central representation of the preexisting classroom context.

Participatory Analysis

One question we had concerning our scenario-based design methods was the extent to which the *analysis* of learning scenarios could be carried out in a participatory fashion. In TAF, scenarios are analyzed for their consequences for users, either good or bad, using a technique called "claims analysis"—a feature is identified and a set of possible positive and negative consequences are proposed. These consequences may or may not be illustrated in the scenario, so this analysis technique is useful for taking a single concrete scenario and generating a more articulated "design space" that is relevant to the situation under analysis.

We carried out participatory analysis sessions as part of an intensive two-week workshop that involved teachers, technology developers, and researchers (see [Chin, Rosson, and Carroll 1997] for details). A facilitator first summarized a selected scenario to be analyzed and showed snippets of the videotaped classroom activity from which the scenario had been drawn. The group then began an extended process of suggesting interesting features of the learning situation and proposing and discussing positive and negative consequences associated with each feature. An example of a resulting "claim" (i.e., features with associated consequences) appears in Figure 5.2: we observed that up to six students formed a single group and pulled out this feature. Immediately observable were negative consequences: that is, subgroups of students would disengage and become passive bystanders or even initiate off-topic interaction. Claims analysis asks the designer to always consider pros and cons, and we identified positive consequences such

Figure 5.2

Feature: Large group size

Pros
- may provide greater input and knowledge than smaller groups
- may handle more challenging and complex experiments
- requires fewer workstations and equipment
- requires less grading by teacher if group is graded as whole
- may allow teacher to grade in greater depth since there are fewer groups
- is easier for teacher to provide guidance to each group since there are fewer groups

Cons
- not everyone in the group may be engaged (group may be too large to keep everyone interested)
- is easier for the dominant personalities to simply take control of the experiment
- demands greater accessibility to the equipment since the equipment must be shared among a larger number of students
- tends to produce subgroups—one subgroup may simply take control of the experiment while the others idly stand by

Claim for large group size

as reduced burden (grading) on the teacher, dealing with constraints of limited equipment, and enabling the execution of complex tasks that—at least temporarily—required participation by all group members.

As with the original scenarios, these claims have become a central component of our design records, as we have proposed and reasoned about possible changes to the collaborative learning activities used by these teachers.

Technology Exploration

After analyzing the preexisting classroom context, a second major design effort involved the analysis of existing technology *in the classroom context*. Thus, we had available a number of well-known technologies (e.g., email, the Web, videoconferencing), but needed to understand what it would be like to use these in the science activities of the four LiNC teachers.

We worked with the teachers to propose and develop a set of test scenarios: specific learning activities that exercised one or more components of the collaborative technology. Examples included a collaborative pooling of data from a simulation collected at two different high schools and a mentoring activity in which high school students guided middle school teams through an interesting physical science demonstration. In the mentoring activity, a shared whiteboard and videoconferencing were used for communication.

The high school mentors guided middle school students by means of verbal instructions, comprehension questions, and explanations. The video channel was mainly used to communicate relevant parts of the physical world rather than faces: video images showed the "correct" setup of apparatus, and high school students monitored progress remotely through the use of video. Furthermore, snapshots of the situational context were pasted to a shared whiteboard, and experts annotated the video snapshots—for example, by superimposing force vectors to explain the observed phenomena—thus creating a mixed media space.

These scenarios were realized in the classrooms and analyzed (using both informal ethnographic techniques and claims analysis) to better understand the opportunities and challenges of the available technology. An important focus at this point was on the pragmatics of the real-world classroom setting—for example, the difficulties in scheduling truly synchronous activities across different school organizations, the problems of managing limited physical space and a limited number of computers, and the "social grounding" time (off-task time to establish a minimum of personal rapport) required for effective remote collaboration (Carroll et al. 1997).

Activity Design

In parallel with technology exploration, the team began to develop a new vision of science learning. The teachers were encouraged to take active control of this technology design process rather than to adapt their teaching plans to existing technology. As they did so, what emerged was a set of activities that was customizable to each educator's teaching style. All teachers decided to focus on an extended project-based collaborative learning activity in their one-year science curriculum. However, the degree to which this activity was prestructured, guided, or open-ended varied considerably among the four teachers.

Initially, textual narratives were developed (see Figure 5.3) that captured essential aspects of envisioned activity. This activity envisionment was guided by the scenarios and claims developed to this point, as well as by the cumulative experience gained by all participants through technology exploration and the software development of the virtual school environment. For example, the importance of student-generated research questions came mainly from our claims analysis; shared telepointers were an available technology in our shared whiteboard tool. (A *telepointer* is an image of the mouse cursor visible to a collaborator at another computer.) These envisionment scenarios were then used as a starting point for participatory design sessions in which the teachers (and subsequently a small number of

Figure 5.3

Maynard and Ethel (middle school students from Auburn) form a project group with Felicity and Mertyl (middle schoolers from Blacksburg) to study the Mars Pathfinder mission. They meet using videoconferencing when both classes are in session.

They first brainstorm questions to address. As questions emerge, group members add them to the shared work area. They negotiate a final set of questions, then divide the questions among individuals.

Maynard volunteers to research "What is the Pathfinder lunar vehicle and how does it work?" He searches the Web and finds text passages and images describing Pathfinder at the main NASA Web site. He copies these onto the work area.

Maynard also looks for simulations in the Virtual School. He finds a Mars landing simulation, copies it into the work area, and executes it. The simulation allows students to land the Lander spacecraft and to navigate Pathfinder off its dock and onto Martian terrain.

To organize his findings, Maynard marks the original question as a "question" and the resources he has found as "answers." He draws lines from the question to each answer to identify relationships among the research items he has collected. He notifies his group of his findings with an email message and proceeds to another research question.

Later the group meets over the computer to review each other's findings in detail and to negotiate which research items should go into the final project report. Maynard describes his Pathfinder findings, using a telepointer to point at and discuss the items he has placed in the work area. He also demonstrates the Pathfinder simulation. Felicity and Mertyl annotate his comments and try out the simulation themselves.

Scenario envisioning project-based activity

students) worked with other LiNC team members to build low-tech prototypes of the virtual school, using paper, markers, mocked-up user interface elements, and Post-It notes. Teachers typically focused on specific pieces of the design, and we as user interface experts synthesized from this teacher input the overarching, organizing principles of the interface. In the next iteration, our design was again presented to the teachers for comments. These paper-and-marker prototypes or storyboards were turned into a Macromind Director prototype version of the system that served as the primary design envisionment for the virtual school development team.

5.4   The LiNC Environment

This section describes the LiNC environment that was developed using the design process outlined above. We begin with an overview followed by a detailed description of its individual functional components and a discussion of the underlying technical architecture.

Toward an Extensible Environment for Collaborative, Project-Based Learning

The LiNC system is designed to support group projects carried out by students. These projects can cross classroom and school boundaries; that is, small groups of students from different classes and different schools may collaborate on a project. By "project" we mean a sustained, goal-oriented activity that may or may not be prestructured by a teacher. Projects often go through phases such as topic definition, outline, information gathering, experiments, analysis, and presentation of results. Students are typically required to produce artifacts such as written reports or verbal presentations as part of a project to document the process or a learning outcome. LiNC provides an electronic lab notebook to support these activities. Phases of active work (e.g., running a simulation or analyzing data) are interleaved with reflective work (e.g., writing a lab report section in a notebook). Students typically work in groups that remain more or less stable throughout a project, but not all project-related work need be carried out as a group. Students often collect information, perform calculations, or write report sections individually before sharing them with the group and integrating their results with those of other group members. Coordination and coexecution require extensive communication between participants.

Both individual and group work is supported. A student can log on from home, thereby working individually on his or her private electronic lab notebook, or a student can log on as part of a group at school, working on a group notebook. Artifacts created by students can be tagged as individually or group-owned. LiNC provides a range of communication mechanisms, both synchronous (text chat, a shared workbench that supports annotations) and asynchronous (email, notes in notebooks).

Rather than focusing solely on collaboration of individuals in a virtual environment, we needed to integrate the LiNC software environment (called the "virtual school") with activities in the physical school environment. Our goal was to develop a mixed media space in which virtual collaboration and virtual experiments could coexist with unmediated collaboration and interaction with the physical world. Along with the physical school environment come its real constraints on resources (e.g., available hardware and software per classroom) and rather rigid time constraints. For example, meaningful units of activity must be completed within a single class period. Since different schools rarely have overlapping class periods, there may be limited time for synchronous collaboration among students during school hours. This requires a system in which groups of colocated students can work together on a single terminal. A student must be able to quickly restore the state of the virtual school to where he or she last left off working.

LiNC supports synchronous and asynchronous collaboration and a smooth transition between them as students log on and off. Cues in the form of iconic representations for users and groups, representing users that are present (online), are used to give an awareness of whether to collaborate synchronously or asynchronously.

Instead of designing the virtual school as a monolithic environment in which we program all applications, we view the LiNC environment as a framework. We can include our custom applications (e.g., special simulations) as well as standard commercial applications (e.g., email, Web browser, videoconferencing, word processing, spreadsheet). In addition, third-party Java simulations and visualization applets can be made to support collaboration (see "System Architecture" later in this section).

Using the LiNC Virtual School Environment

This section describes the set of interconnected components that comprise the LiNC environment:

1. A *task bar* for launching internal components and external applications and for initiating communication actions

2. A *chat tool* for synchronous, text-based communication

3. A sectioned *notebook* for all project-related information (ranging from the assignment and collected data to final reports)

4. A *workbench* that serves as an extensible modularized visualization and whiteboard environment

In addition, LiNC provides a special *login mechanism* and a *resource finder* tool, along with some administrative tools to extend and personalize the environment.

Login

Students can log in from any networked computer in their school, public library, or home. A student can log in either as an individual or as a group member by supplying an individual login identifier or a group name. A student can be a member of many groups throughout the school year, depending on the teacher's philosophy. In the case of a group login, the user completing the login screen on behalf of the group supplies his or her individual password. A subsequent window lists the names of all group members known to be logged in at other computers and asks the user to click on checkboxes to specify who else is seated (physically colocated) at his or her computer.

Task Bar

Following this login process, students enter a *workspace*. A task bar is displayed on top of the screen (Figure 5.4, [see also Color Plate]).

The left side of the task bar contains a customizable set of icons representing tasks that can be performed. Teachers can populate the task bar with items appropriate for the day's classroom activities. Clicking on a task icon launches either an internal component that was written as part of the virtual school or an external application. Internal components currently available are the notebook, workbench, resource browser, and text chat client. Any external application, from commercial Web browsers to spreadsheet programs, can be added to the task bar. Currently, this customization occurs manually,

Figure 5.4

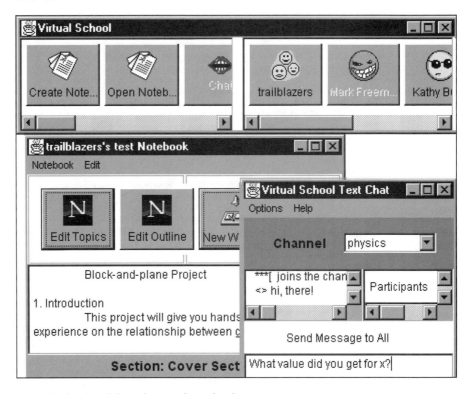

Virtual school task bar, chat, and notebook

but in the future it will be part of the administrative functionalities that will be offered.

The right-hand area of the task bar contains iconic representations of the group and each of its members. Colored icons signify members who are currently online. If the student clicks on one of these icons, a menu pops up listing possible tasks such as sending mail to the named group or individual or, if the targeted user is currently online, initiating a text chat session. If mail is selected, a mail client of the user's choice is launched, with the "to:" field of the mail message set to an address of that student kept on file by the virtual school. Or, if a student selects "chat," then a window will pop up on the targeted user's computer asking if a chat session will be accepted. If accepted, a text chat window appears on each computer and students can now converse using the usual text chat facilities (group chat, whisper, etc.).

Resource Finder

The "Find People" task icon provides access to the resource finder. One of the default views, a window containing icons (either gray or colored to indicate online presence) of registered LiNC users, is displayed. A variety of search criteria can be specified, such as to sort students by class or by school. Searches can be performed for other registered resources such as labs and notebooks.

Notebook

The task bar typically contains icons labeled "Create Notebook" and "Open Notebook" that provide access to associated *projects*. For example, a class might start a new project investigating gravity, and hence a student will click "Create Notebook" and enter a notebook name (such as "gravity"). If students log in as a group, the "gravity" notebook is group-owned. Later, other members of the group at another school can click "Open Notebook", see a list of group-owned notebooks in a traditional directory file structure, and select one for opening. Initially, students selecting the same notebook at different locations would have a copy of the same notebook opened in read-only mode.

A notebook contains one or more sections. Subgroups of students may each create their own section and work independently by writing information to their own section. Group members can also create their own private sections to record their individual reflections.

Students may jointly write sections of a lab report. Members of the group deal with writing access by using a *floor control mechanism* built into the notebook. Included in the notebook interface is a traffic light icon. When a student clicks on the traffic light, that student gains exclusive write privilege to the current notebook section. After writing, another student can take control by clicking on the traffic light. At this point, all students will have their window updated to show the latest contents of the notebook section. Collaborators may "pass the pen" back and forth to alternately contribute to a section. At all times, a persistent copy of the latest version is kept on a network file server.

Teachers can create prototype notebooks for their students, typically with existing sections related to project tasks. For example, a teacher can populate the notebook with an assignment sheet giving instructions to the students, other predefined sections required by the project (e.g., "References"), and worksheets for students to complete as they collect data. Student groups copy these prototypes into their shared workspace.

In addition to creating content in notebooks, students can interact with Web pages viewed through an external Web browser launched from a task bar in the notebook. In Figure 5.4, the notebook shows tasks labeled "Edit Topics" and "Edit Outline." These tasks were created by a standard Web page creation program to support standard tasks in a lab science course. Teachers can ask students to select a topic within a larger project to explore in detail. Using text chat, the workbench, or an external video teleconferencing application, the students can negotiate with group members at other computers to choose a topic. An "Add Topic" button on the form allows addition of a new topic. Similarly, the "Edit Outline" task can be used to negotiate a project outline.

Future elements planned for the notebook include a contents page that contains hypertext links to the proper section of a notebook, integration of a Web browser within a notebook page, a collaborative calendar for students and teachers to plan deadlines, and the ability for a teacher to place a transparent annotation layer over a notebook page.

Workbench

The notebook also provides access to the workbench (Figure 5.5 [see p. 117 and Color Plate]). The workbench is a shared Modular Visualization Environment (MVE) that allows users to link together data-generating tools, data-filtering tools, and data-visualizing tools. For example, simulations or external sensors generate data that are filtered by a filter object whose output flows into an applet with limited graphing capabilities. Users can create data flow diagrams that start with a simulation and pass the resulting data to a visualization in a flexible way. Keep in mind that this is taking place in a shared environment that supports synchronous collaboration. Thus, multiple students, at distant locations, can be actively working together on an experiment. For example, students can hook their respective simulation runs to the same graphing unit to compare results, or they can all watch the same simulation.

To further support collaboration, both synchronous and asynchronous, the workbench has many of the features commonly available in a shared whiteboard system. Users may place notes and various graphical objects in the workspace to help describe what is going on. The workbench includes explicit user support for synchronous collaboration through the use of telepointers. A telepointer is an image of the mouse cursor for a collaborator at another computer. Each telepointer is given a color associated with the respective user. Thus, students can get some indication where their collaborators are focused and what they are doing by observing the telepointers.

The second piece of user support for collaboration is the RadarView window, a small-scale overview of the entire workbench that contains iconic representations of the various components currently within the work area. The RadarView can be used to move around a work area that is too large to view all at once on the screen. The RadarView also directly supports collaboration by promoting awareness of other users' likely focus of attention. Superimposed on the RadarView are colored rectangles, one for each collaborator, indicating what part of the workspace is presently shown on that collaborator's computer screen (Gutwin, Greenberg, and Roseman 1996).

Administrative Functions

The final component of the system performs administrative functions. For students, these include selecting which tasks go into the group's workspace task bar, whether a notebook is readable by other groups, the iconic and color representation of each group member, and so on. For teachers, administrative functions include creating user accounts, creating groups, specifying rules for notebook sharing (e.g., to prevent students from glancing at other student notebooks), and prepopulating student workspace task bars with only those tasks needed for a particular project.

System Architecture

Our system design has been heavily influenced by the emerging technology of JavaBeans, a technology that didn't exist when we first conceived the project. This choice was made for the following reasons:

1. Java facilitates the implementation of synchronous collaboration mechanisms.

2. Java increases (but does not yet entirely achieve) portability among platforms in the classroom.

3. Java simplifies extensibility (e.g., new simulations can be plugged into the work-bench—see below).

4. Java allows a person anywhere in the world to run the virtual school through a Java 1.1–enabled Web browser without first downloading the school as an application to be installed on their computer.

JavaBeans technology allows components, called "Beans," to communicate with each other, allowing complex applications to be constructed by binding together existing components in simple ways. LiNC makes use of the Beans' underlying communication technology both to support synchronous collaboration through replicated copies of the Beans at each user's workbench and to implement the data flow mechanism that connects simulations to visualizers.

When building a collaborative system, we can choose between a *centralized* or a *replicated* system (for a detailed discussion of this issue and related literature, see [Begole et al. 1997]). In a centralized system, there is a single copy of the application, and various collaborators see copies of the application state. Typically, this is done through an approach called *display broadcasting*, in which each user receives a copy of the application's display state. Users may think that they are manipulating the application in the usual way (pushing on buttons, etc.). In reality, primitive interface actions such as mouse button presses are sent to the central copy, and the result of the action is rebroadcast to all users. The cost to this approach is increased network traffic as the graphical display is distributed to all users. Its advantage is relative simplicity of implementation.

In contrast, in a distributed or replicated architecture, each user in the collaboration runs his or her own copy of the application. To synchronize the copies, user interface events such as button presses are distributed to each user's computer, an approach known as *event broadcasting*. An event-broadcasting architecture might send messages directly between all of the collaborators, or it might rely on a centralized broker to handle potential conflicts in the various interface events generated by the multiple users. The advantage of event broadcasting is the potential for greatly reduced network traffic. The disadvantage is that implementation is more complicated, depending on the underlying system architecture. However, the Java runtime model tends to favor a replicated approach. A replicated approach is also being adopted by many of the current online gaming systems, partly because it reduces network bandwidth requirements and partly because it reduces computational burden on the centralized server since the applications are running on the users' machines.

We chose a replicated approach for the LiNC environment. This approach minimizes information passed through the network, allows use from home over modem lines, allows the system to support more users by minimizing load on a central server, and provides an easy way to distribute our software to the computers of end users. Furthermore, a replicated approach allows us to gradually move toward a situation where one client can run on its own even when the server is down, provided no server services (e.g., for opening a new notebook) are required. We are especially concerned about such reliability because breakdowns are often disastrous in an educational setting. Teachers quickly lose confidence in unreliable technology, crashes waste precious classroom time, and recovery of lost work is difficult.

The LiNC virtual school environment is a distributed system implemented in Java. The virtual school runs on students' computers (in the classroom or at home) and interacts with other copies of the virtual school through a central machine (currently located at Virginia Tech). A copy of the virtual school initially connects to the server for logon/logoff. The virtual school contacts a chat server when users initiate a chat. The virtual school launches external applications and opens notebooks when requested.

The *profile server* stores information about users and groups (e.g., accounts and passwords). It keeps track of state information, such as who's logged on where, and answers queries about resources. The profile server also keeps track of user profiles (student class, teacher, school, etc.). The *chat server* listens for requests from users to connect to other users or channels. The *notebook server* provides persistent storage through the JavaFileSystem. It satisfies requests by notebook users to open notebooks and manages floor control for shared sections. Notebook updates are sent to all other users of shared sections.

The LiNC workbench is a version of Sieve—our advanced platform for synchronous collaborative data manipulation, analysis, and visualization (Isenhour et al. 1997). Sieve blends a number of old and new technologies in a unique way. Sieve is written entirely in Java and follows the JavaBeans specification.

Sieve allows users to run any Java application as part of the virtual school. However, not all Java applications can take full advantage of Sieve's capabilities for linking together various pieces into a greater whole. We identify three levels of support. At the first level, an arbitrary Java applet can be run within the workbench. This gives users access to the whole world of Java software, but does not always allow the user to connect any applet to other applets. However, standard functionalities like cut and paste can be used to share data. Arbitrary Java applets must rely on *transparent collaboration* techniques to be used collaboratively (Begole, Struble, and Shaffer 1997). The goal of a transparent collaboration system is to support use of existing applications, written for single users, within a synchronous collaboration environment. The advantages to this approach are that a body of software becomes available with no additional work, and users are able to use their old, familiar applications. The disadvantages are the inherent difficulty of supporting single-use applications in a collaborative environment and the lack of navigation and orientation tools in such applications, which may make synchronous collaborative work more difficult.

At the second level of collaboration support, Java applications that conform to the JavaBeans specification can be connected in all the normal ways supported by that technology. The workbench can be viewed as a collaborative bean box, where a "bean box" is the term used for any runtime system that supports the JavaBeans specification. The highest level of Sieve conformity is used by our own applets. A special communications library is used to communicate through a data flow network that supports the creation of data visualization and analysis, as shown in Figure 5.5.

Figure 5.5

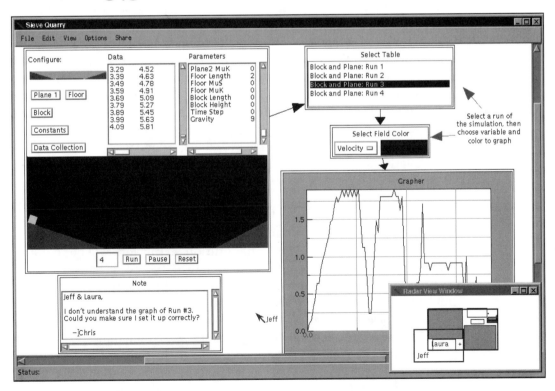

Virtual school workbench

5.5   Designing for the Classroom of Tomorrow

The participatory element of the LiNC project has clearly been a success: the teachers have been intensively involved in all aspects of the design process, from the initial classroom studies up to the design of project-based science activities that could leverage the technology provided by a virtual school. We also believe that the scenario-based methods have been successful in creating and maintaining a sharable design vision. However, our process has been a tedious one, requiring the authoring and maintenance of many narratives and associated analyses. We are exploring ways in which the benefits of scenario-based analysis and envisionment can be realized without commitment to a comprehensive process of scenario documentation and analysis.

The availability of teacher training will be a crucial parameter in the adoption process for this new technology. Teachers need to reach a level of confidence in the use of the new technology that allows them to present the technology to the students and to focus on the delivery of the lesson content rather than worrying about troubleshooting equipment and software glitches. A high level of experience and sophistication is needed to respond to student problems in the use of technology in real time while keeping the class as a whole on task. We provided technical support during the execution of most of the technology-enhanced activities to address these problems, but a more generalizable solution must be developed. We see this as a general problem for the increasing reliance on technology in the classroom as teachers are forced to take on the dual roles of educators and technical staff.

Similarly, the new technology creates new logistic tasks that schools are ill-equipped to carry out. For example, we had to overcome a number of logistic problems in setting up individual mail accounts with personalized passwords for all students. At least until mechanisms and procedures are developed to manage such administrative tasks and until schoolwide standards allow a centralized, one-time solution, extra work will be required from teachers that may impact the availability of the new technology.

Another problem that became evident in the process was the coordination between teachers from various schools. Last-minute schedule changes by the school administration, differences in course content and sequencing, and differences in teaching philosophies prevented ongoing synchronous collaboration. This may be, in part, an artifact of the project's limited participant base. Use throughout the United States (and beyond) would make it more likely to find collaboration partners with congruent philosophies and curricula. On the other hand, different class times, schedules, time zones, state requirements, and so on make it even less likely that long-term partnerships for synchronous collaboration can be established. We conclude that a more likely scenario is the primary use of asynchronous technology (such as email and asynchronous shared writing) interspersed with short-term, synchronous activities.

The LiNC project is under way, but it still has not achieved one of its most significant objectives. A particularly important horizon for us is the objective of school-community integration, leveraging the BEV. One direction for this is an activity we call the "virtual science fair" (VSF). Our vision of the VSF is not that it replace existing fairs, but rather that it supplement or enrich the normal experience. For example, a science project might now have multiple components engineered by students in different age groups or disciplines, with an integrative structure provided by an online project plan and a presentation that might include multimedia displays or other artifacts that can be shared with peers, parents, or community members over the Web. The scientific methods proposed and implemented by students might now be annotated and refined through collaborations with mentors from the community—for example, retirees who are experts in the field of study. Our work on the VSF is using a participatory design approach similar to that used for the virtual school to realize this vision.

The LiNC project continues and will provide us with many more lessons—undoubtedly unexpected and painful ones among them. Change in education comes slowly, especially if measured against the speed of technological advancement. Providing the appropriate technological tools is not enough; we need to become (as researchers and as parents) engaged participants in the educational arena to promote the changes that are so urgently needed.

Acknowledgments

Many people have contributed significantly to this ongoing project; our thanks and appreciation goes to them all. We especially thank the teachers and students of the Montgomery County Public School System who allowed us into their world. This research was partially supported by the National Science Foundation, under awards RED-9454803 and REC-9554206 from the Networking Infrastructure for Education program. Jürgen Koenemann was supported under NSF CISE Postdoctoral Research Associate Award 9625577.

References

American Association for the Advancement of Science. 1989. *Project 2061: Science for all Americans.* Washington, DC: AAAS.

Begole, J. M. A., Struble, C. A., and Shaffer, C. A. 1997. Leveraging Java applets: Toward collaboration transparency in Java. *IEEE Internet Computing* 1(2): 57–64.

Begole, J. M. A., Struble, C. A., Shaffer, C. A., and Smith, R. B. 1997. Transparent sharing of Java applications: A replicated approach. In *Proceedings of UIST '97*. New York: ACM Press, 55–64.

Bellamy, R. K. E., Cooper, E. B. W., and Borovoy, R. D. 1994. Supporting collaborative learning through the use of electronic conversational props. In J. Gotnostaev, ed. *Proceedings of the East-West HCI '92: The St. Petersburg International Workshop on ICSTI*. Moscow.

Berger, P., and Luckman, T. 1966. *The social construction of reality*. New York: Doubleday.

Blumenfeld, P. C., Soloway, E., Marx, R. W., Krajcik, J. S., Guzdial, M., and Palincsar, A. 1991. Motivating project-based learning: Sustaining the doing, supporting the learning. *Educational Psychologists* 26(3–4): 369–398.

Bruner, J. 1960. *The process of education*. Cambridge, MA: Harvard University Press.

Bruner, J. 1967. *Towards a theory of instruction*. Cambridge, MA: Belknap Press/ Harvard University Press.

Carnegie Mellon University. 1994. *The Internet in K–12 education*. Heinz School of Public Policy and Management. Pittsburgh, PA: Carnegie Mellon University.

Carroll, J. M. 1990. *The Nürnberg funnel. Designing minimalist instruction for practical computer skill*. Cambridge, MA: MIT Press.

Carroll, J. M., ed. 1998. *Minimalism beyond the Nürnberg funnel*. Cambridge, MA: MIT Press.

Carroll, J. M., Kellogg, W. A., and Rosson, M. B. 1991. The task-artifact cycle. In J. M. Carroll, ed. *Designing interaction: Psychology at the human-computer interface*. New York: Cambridge University Press, 74–102.

Carroll, J. M., Mauney, S. M., and Rencsok, C. F. 1997. Learning by design. Paper presented at the Design Education Workshop, Georgia Tech, Atlanta, GA, September 8–9.

Carroll, J. M., and Rosson, M. B. 1992. Getting around the task-artifact framework: How to make claims and design by scenario. *ACM Transactions on Information Systems* 10(2): 181–212.

Carroll, J. M., and Rosson, M. B. 1996. Developing the Blacksburg Electronic Village. *Communications of the ACM* 39(12): 69–74.

Carroll, J. M., Rosson, M. B., Chin, G., and Koenemann, J. 1997. Requirements development: Stages of opportunity for collaborative needs discovery. *Proceedings of DIS '97: Second ACM Symposium on Designing Interactive Systems*. New York: ACM Press/Addison-Wesley, 55–64.

Carstensen, L. W., Jr., Shaffer, C. A., Morrill, R. W., and Fox, E. A. 1993. GeoSim: A GIS-based simulation laboratory for introductory geography. *Journal of Geography* 92(5): 217–222.

Chin, G., Rosson, M. B., and Carroll, J. M. 1997. Participatory analysis: Shared development of requirements from scenarios. In S. Pemberton, ed. *Proceedings of Human Factors in Computing Systems Conference (CHI '97)*. New York: ACM Press/Addison-Wesley, 162–169.

Darling-Hammond, L. 1990. Achieving our goals: Superficial or structural reforms. *Phi Delta Kappan* 72(4): 286–295.

Dewey, J. 1966. *Democracy and education: An introduction to the philosophy of education*. New York: Free Press.

Gutwin, C., Greenberg, S., and Roseman, M. 1996. Workspace awareness in real-time distributed groupware: Framework, widgets, and evaluation. In M. A. Sasse, R. J. Cunningham, and R. L. Winder, eds. *People and Computers. XI: Proceedings of HCI '96*. London: Springer, 281–298.

Hiltz, S. R. 1993. Correlates of learning in a virtual classroom. *International Journal of Man-Machine Studies* 39: 71–98.

Hofstein, A., and Lunetta, V. 1982. The role of the laboratory in science teaching: Neglected aspects of research. *Review of Educational Research* 52: 201–217.

Honey, M., and Henriquez, A. 1993. *Telecommunications and K–12 Educators: Findings from a national survey*. Center for Technology in Education, Bank Street College of Education, New York.

Isenhour, P. L., Begole, J. M. A., Heagy, W. S., and Shaffer, C. A. 1997. Sieve: A Java-based collaborative visualization environment. In *IEEE Visualization '97*. Los Alamitos, CA: Computer Society Press.

Koenemann-Belliveau, J., Carroll, J. M., Rosson, M. B., and Singley, M. K. 1994. Comparative usability evaluation: Critical incidents and critical threads. In *Proceedings of Human Factors in Computing Systems Conference (CHI '94)*. New York: ACM Press/Addison-Wesley, 245–251.

Kraut, R. E., Egido, C., and Galegher, J. 1990. Patterns of contact and communication in scientific research collaboration. In J. Galegher, R. E. Kraut, and C. Egido, eds. *Intellectual teamwork*. Hillsdale, NJ: Lawrence Erlbaum, 149–171.

Laughton, S. 1996. *The design and use of Internet-mediated communication applications in education: An ethnographic study*. Ph.D. dissertation (unpublished), Virginia Polytechnic Institute and State University.

Lepper, M. R. 1988. Motivational considerations in the study of instruction. *Cognition and Instruction* 5: 289–309.

Light, P., Foot, T., Colbourn, C., and McClelland, I. 1987. Collaborative interactions at the microcomputer keyboard. *Educational Psychology* 7: 13–21.

Malone, T. W., and Lepper, M. R. 1987. Making learning fun: A taxonomy of intrinsic motivations for learning. In R. Snow, and M. Farr, eds. *Aptitude, learning, and instruction: Conative and affective process analyses*, vol. 3. Hillsdale, NJ: Lawrence Erlbaum, 223–253.

Mantei, M. M., Baecker, R. M., Sellen, A. J., Buxton, W. A. S., and Mulligan, T. 1991. Experiences in the use of a media space. In *Proceedings of Human Factors in Computing Systems Conference (CHI '91)*. New York: ACM Press, 203–208.

National Science Teachers Association. 1990. *Scope, sequence, and coordination of secondary school science.* Washington, DC: NSTA.

Pea, R. D., and Gomez, L. M. 1992. The collaborative visualization project: Shared technology learning environments for science learning. In *Proceedings of SPIE '92: Enabling technologies for high-bandwidth applications* 1785: 253–264.

Piaget, J. 1963. *The origins of intelligence in children.* New York: W. W. Norton.

Piaget, J. 1985. *The equilibration of cognitive structures: The central problem of intellectual development.* Chicago: Chicago University Press.

Piaget, J., and Inhelder, B. 1969. *The psychology of the child.* New York: Basic Books.

Rosson, M. B., and Carroll, J. M. 1996. Scaffolded examples for learning object-oriented design. *Communications of the ACM* 39(4): 46–47.

Scardamalia, M., Bereiter, C., and Lamon, M. 1994. The CSILE project: Trying to bring the classroom into World 3. In K. McGilly, ed. *Classroom lessons: Integrating cognitive theory and classroom practice.* Cambridge, MA: MIT Press, 201–228.

Simon, H. A. 1980. Problem solving and education. In D. T. Tuma and F. Reif, eds. *Problem solving and education: Issues in teaching and research.* Hillsdale, NJ: Lawrence Erlbaum, 81–96.

Smith, R. B. 1987. The alternate reality kit: An example of the tension between literalism and magic. In J. M. Carroll and P. P. Tanner, eds. *Proceedings of CHI+GI '87: Conference on human factors in computing systems and graphical interfaces.* New York: ACM Press.

Tatar, D. G., Foster, G., and Bobrow, D. G. 1991. Design for conversation: Lessons from Cognoter. *International Journal of Man-Machine Studies* 34(2): 185–209.

Williams, M. 1994. Enabling schoolteachers to participate in the design of educational software. In R. Trigg, S. J. Anderson, and E. Dykstra-Erickson, eds. *Proceedings of PDC '94.* Palo Alto, CA: Computer Professionals for Social Responsibility, 153–157.

Children as Designers, Testers, and Evaluators of Educational Software

Yasmin B. Kafai

UCLA Graduate School of Education & Information Studies

6.1 Introduction

Consider Andrew, 11 years old, who designed and programmed a science simulation game to help younger children in his school to learn about ocean life by emulating the food behavior of different fish. After the project ended, I interviewed him about various aspects of his game design experiences and asked, "You mentioned user-friendliness before, what does that mean to you?" He answered:

> I think that this game is kinda hard because it's over the head with some people and it's a bit too easy for others. I think that some people wouldn't understand it. For example, you have to type in "alewife" when the following question appears on the screen, "What am I?" but some people wouldn't understand what's going on here. I think I need to put a little more instruction on the bottom about what to do. I already have the button to push, but I'm talking about something like "Think about, maybe you are an alewife" or to have a picture of an alewife on the screen. When you do something, it would understand what you are doing and move toward it. But unfortunately, that would mess up the rest of my game. I'm trying to think about how to redo that. I mean, more user-friendly would mean instead of just leaving the person to play the game, you would have more tips on how to help them. For instance, later in the game you could have a type flash "Think about what other fish you ate." If an alewife ate a crab, for instance, it would say "Watch it, that fish is too big for you." If then you came upon an otter, you would realize, "That otter is much bigger than a crab," and you probably wouldn't go after it again. I think tips like that would make the game a lot better: "Remember what happened last time" or "Think about what happened last time you tried to get a crab" or "Think about all of the other choices." If you decided to eat a flounder, then you know that's too big and then you see a small clam and maybe you'll take a chance on that instead. I'm also thinking of making sort of a character, inventing a character, and maybe give them chances in a friendly way, especially for the smaller kids.

We could easily dismiss Andrew's evaluation of his own software as an exceptional case, as someone who is above and beyond what children understand about software and how they evaluate it. But with children's increasing use of commercial software and access to the Internet, a generation is growing up that is more savvy and knowledgeable about what to expect of software. If we are interested in designing for children, how can we make use of children's knowledge and include it in the process of designing software?

There are many discussions in the HCI community of how users should be included in the design process (Allen et al. 1993). Approaches have assigned users different places in the design process (user-centered design, informant design, and participatory design) and assumed different perspectives on who the users are (users or learners). User-centered system design places users and their needs at the center of the design process by identifying their task demands and including their evaluations of systems in the software development process (Norman and Draper 1986). On the other end of the spectrum is participatory design, which sees users more as partners than reactants to a system in development (Schuler and Mamoika 1993; see also Chapter 3). In the participatory design approach, users often work together with the designers to develop systems that fit their needs. More recently, informant design has been proposed as the middle ground between user-centered and participatory design approaches. Informant design describes situations and interactions in which the user provides input at different stages of the design process using various methodologies such as scenarios, interface evaluations, task specifications, and usability testing (see Chapter 2).

In all these approaches, the user has been invited to the design table in some form or other, but it is unclear to what extent these approaches can apply to children or young learners, who by definition are different from traditional users in several ways:

1. *Motivation:* Users are motivated; learners are not necessarily.

2. *Knowledge:* Users know the domain; learners might not.

3. *Diversity:* Users are a homogenous group; learners vary in many aspects.

4. *Growth:* Efficiency is the main goal for users; learners are supposed to grow intellectually.

A system design that takes into account that users are a moving target whose needs, interests, and skills are constantly changing has been called *learner-centered design* (Soloway, Guzdial, and Hay 1994). Learner-centered design assumes that eventually everyone—not just students and children—is a learner when it comes to learning new software or new skills. In its current instantiation, learner-centered design focuses on the interface design of representations and manipulations in educational software that deal with the issues of adapting to the various interests, knowledge, and styles of learners using the software (Soloway et al. 1997). By taking into consideration the various demands and needs of children, learner-centered design is a step in the right direction. But very much in the same spirit as the other approaches, the learner-centered system designer controls the features to be included in the software, assuming that learners will use and benefit from these interactions in the intended ways.

In this chapter, I will argue for a different approach, the learner as designer, thus breaking the traditional barriers between end users and system designers. Although I do not expect end users to become designers of commercial systems, I propose this as an extension to the existing approaches for identifying users' needs and demands. In this approach, end users become learner-centered designers themselves based on the assumption that the end goal of learner-centered design is to make users/learners smarter. I agree with that end goal, but I think that it can be accomplished in a different way by making users the actual designers of software. In this particular case, I have educational software in mind, which intends to help the learner acquire specific knowledge and skills in particular domains. By turning the tables, I place the learner in the role of thinking like an educational designer and conducting inquiries about the subject or skill domain by creating representations that teach and help prospective learners. I see this as a privileged way for children, in particular, to learn about various subject matters (Kafai, Ching, and Marshall 1997).

One thing we might learn through this "learner-as-designer" approach is how learners think about educational software. With the increasing proliferation of interactive technologies into work, schools, and homes, children have multiple opportunities to interact with systems—particularly the current generation, which is the first truly digital generation growing up with expectations for interactive technologies formed in their early years. Many observations of children's interactions with technologies seem to point to levels of proficiency that reach beyond those of many adults. Examples include the programming of VCRs or the playing of video games, which demonstrate children's abilities to interact with and navigate through complex multilayered systems. Based on these many experiences, children have built preconceived notions about software. It is important to understand these preconceptions, and the potential limitations or benefits that they might entail, if children are to be involved in the design process.

Another thing we might learn reaches far beyond the boundaries of traditional HCI research concerned with creating better system design. Professionals engaged in HCI research learn a lot about the domain they are studying, the tasks and routines involved, and what people have to understand and accomplish at their workplaces. I see this as an ideal learning situation. In traditional human-computer interaction, the learning experience ultimately benefits the system; in the learner-as-designer approach to system design, I see the learner benefiting from these inquiries. For that reason, I suggest having end users such as children act in the role of interface and system designers in the very same way professional designers would undertake the task of designing software and interfaces.

To assess the feasibility of the learner-as-designer design approach, I conducted a study with a class of 29 students between the ages of 10 and 11. For a period of 3 months, the students were engaged in software teams to design and implement educational software to teach younger children in their school about the ocean environment. None of the students had programming experience before the beginning of the project. They learned programming features and concepts of the multimedia design environment called Microworlds (which incorporates Logo) as they went along in their software design. During the software production process, the student designers met twice (4 weeks and 8 weeks into the project) with their prospective users for usability testing. Furthermore, I asked students in pre- and posttests to evaluate different educational screens designed by other students in a previous design project. In the following sections, I describe the assessment methods and present and discuss the results.

6.2 Background

For many years now, children have been engaged in programming software. Initially, children wrote small programs for the purposes of learning programming concepts. The most prominent case in point is probably the use of Logo in schools (Papert 1980). Children's problems in learning more sophisticated programming concepts or transferring problem-solving knowledge into other domains have been documented in the research literature (Pea and Kurland 1986). One way to deal with these issues has been in the design of end user programming environments that make use of direct manipulation and graphical rewrite rules (Cypher and Smith 1995; Repenning and Ambach 1996). As analyses have indicated, young children are capable of using systems such as KidSim/Cocoa or AgentSheets to program explanations of scientific phenomena (see Chapter 9). Other researchers noticed, however, that children's failure to grasp certain essential features of the software's functionality limited their creation of more sophisticated representations (Rader, Brand, and Lewis 1997).

More recent approaches to using programming in schools have done so under the heading of learning by designing educational software (Harel 1991; Kafai 1995). In this view, programming educational software is seen as more than the mere production of code; children designers are also concerned with creating interfaces for their software, thinking about representations that teach, and conducting user evaluation sessions as part of their design enterprise. The idea that the learners engage not only in the design but also in the evaluation and testing is key to the process. These three elements of the software design cycle are essential features:

- Designing educational software is crucial because it places children in the teaching situation and forces them to shift their perspective between being a teacher and being a learner.

- Testing is included because children designers need to meet the prospective learners they are designing the software for.

- Evaluating other software designs is essential because students can apply the insights gained from their own design process.

When Harel asked children designers (age 10) to analyze different features of instructional software designed to teach fractions to younger students, she found that the instructional design strategies employed by children could be grouped into two categories: (1) appeal and users' attitude considerations, such as "They [the learners] will pay attention to the colors and parts" and (2) instructional and learning considerations, such as "My introduction is important because you have to explain to them [the users] what to do and how" (Harel 1991). Although all students had incorporated features such as providing feedback and help functions, basing the progress in their software on the learner's answer, most of them did not have features such as options for restarting, time limits, or paging capacities. This was some preliminary evidence that children designers could show a variety of considerations for their users.

In an analysis of educational games to teach mathematics designed by 10-year-old students over a period of 6 months, I found that many students took the idea of an educational game to mean drill-and-practice software (Kafai 1995). This implementation feature revealed that many children think about teaching as asking questions and learning as giving answers—probably not too far from the classroom reality many students experience every day. These are important preconceptions that professional designers need to take into account as they are designing new educational software.

Other, albeit sparse, research supplements children's design perspective from another side (Smith and Keep 1986). By asking children to articulate their criteria for evaluating educational software, Smith and Keep documented a whole set of categories with both positive and negative expressions, such as excitement (having challenges, variety, and feedback), audio-visual features (positive or negative feedback), interface issues (dealing in particular with keyboarding problems), learning experiences (reflecting on the narrow use of computers only for subjects such as English or mathematics), and so on. Many of these features confirmed those identified by Malone as motivating features of software use (Malone 1981). Although this study was conducted over 10 years ago, many of those opinions might still hold true since the use of computers in schools has not changed dramatically. It appears that students' perspective on educational software is mostly impacted through their experiences with software in schools.

These few studies provide an important background to draw upon in the following analyses: children can be active and discriminative participants in evaluating and designing software, and students can implement many of these features even if they are beginning programmers. Although in the past the major focus has been on children's programming performance, the current analysis will focus more on software design experience—how children incorporate various interface and multimedia features in their software, what they focus on and learn from usability sessions, and how they apply their criteria to the evaluation of educational software. The general purpose is to assess in which ways children can be learner-centered designers and how this understanding can help us in using this methodology in designing for children.

6.3 Method

To assess students' software design, I chose three perspectives that encompass different aspects of the software design cycle: design, testing, and evaluation.

- *Software design.* I analyzed the final educational software programs created by the student teams by categorizing the content of developed screen pages and the extent to which they contained instructional interactive representations.

- *Usability testing.* At different times in the project, I asked students to evaluate their software in progress with their prospective users. I first asked students to list questions they would present to their potential users. After the evaluation session, I asked students to articulate what they had learned from their users and how they would incorporate these suggestions and insight into their own software.

- *Evaluation.* To assess students' interface evaluations, a questionnaire with a series of comparative screen assessments was developed using sample screen shots designed by students in a previous software project (Kafai, Ching, and Marshall 1997). I selected three pairs of different screen types. Each pair focused on a different topic (solar/lunar eclipses, planet navigation, and planet information) and represented the information and purposes in different ways. It is debatable whether screens designed by novice designers are appropriate evaluation material for other students to consider. On the one hand, these screens are not perfect examples of good software design, and consequently it might be more difficult to detect principles in the clutter of information. On the other hand, students of this age do not have experience talking about interface design; they do not know the pertinent vocabulary. The point of the activity was not to see whether students knew those principles but what criteria they would employ in judging the value and purpose of the presented screens. This assessment was given as a pretest before the design project and as a posttest after all the students had completed their software design projects. For the analysis and summary of data, I collected all criteria used by children in their choices and evaluated which criteria were used most often.

6.4 Results

In the following sections, I present the results of our analyses for each aspect of students' involvement in the software design cycle.

Children's Software Designs

All the student teams finished a software product with the goal to teach younger students about the ocean environment. Each software piece consisted of a set of interrelated pages that were linked together with the help of buttons or objects that could be activated through a mouse click. An

Table 6.1

Distribution of different screen pages

Group	Simulations	Animations	Informational/ navigational	Graphics	Written content	Total screens
1	0	0	3	3	4	10
2	2	2	2	4	3	13
3	2	1	3	1	8	15
4	2	4	5	5	7	23
5	4	0	1	0	4	9
6	2	2	3	10	3	20
7	0	0	3	0	6	9

Figure **6.1**

Example of simulation design

overview of all the pages designed in each project and their use of multimedia features is provided in Table 6.1. There was quite a variation in number of pages among the students' projects. This scoring, however, is not a good indicator of the quality of the pages. Those teams with fewer pages tended to dedicate more effort to incorporating multimedia pages with animations. For that reason, the final product was analyzed in terms of the page functionality. I defined five categories of screen pages:

- *Simulations:* Simulations are animated pages or series of pages that show the user the workings of a particular ocean phenomenon, usually involving more than one interacting element (e.g., several ocean life forms moving around in a coral reef, the effects of pollution on fish, etc.). Figure 6.1 (see also Color Plate) shows an example of simulation design.

- *Animations:* Animations differ from simulations in that they may not show relationships or complex phenomena, but they use movement nonetheless (e.g., a shark swimming across the page or a scuba diver jumping off his boat). Figure 6.2 shows an example of animation design.

- *Informational/navigational:* These kinds of pages make navigating through the software easier (e.g., a table of contents or pages announcing the next topic area) or serve as a platform for the designers to directly address the users (e.g., a page

Figure **6.2**

Example of animation design

Figure **6.3**

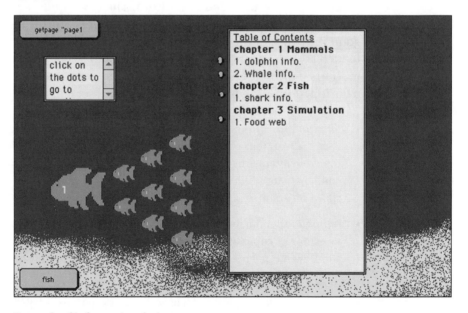

Example of information design

Figure 6.4

Example of graphics design

saying, "We hope you enjoyed our software!"). Figure 6.3 (see also Color Plate) shows an example of information design.

- *Graphics:* In these pages, the primary means of conveying information is through pictures, which have either been cut and pasted from other sources (e.g., photographs of actual marine life forms) or created in Microworlds (e.g., drawings by the students). These graphics may be accompanied by minimal text, such as "This is a lamprey," or they can stand alone. Figure 6.4 shows an example of graphics design.

- *Written (or spoken) content:* Here the primary means of conveying information is through words, which can be either spoken, written, or both. An example is a page that includes many written details about pinnipeds: their average life span, reproduction cycle, where they live, the function of their flippers, and so on. These pages may contain graphics to complement the information, but the focus is mainly on what is written. Figure 6.5 shows an example of written content design.

Table 6.1 shows the distribution of different screen types for each team. The most interesting and also the most complex screen pages were the ones containing the simulations. Two teams did not include any of these features in their software; other groups made extensive use of simulations (even more so than simple animations) to explain educational aspects for their

Figure 6.5

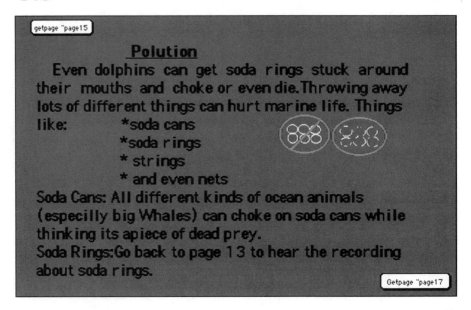

Example of written content design

users/learners. A hierarchy of programming and content complexity in creating content for these pages would have the following levels:

- Level 0: text and static graphics

- Level 1: animations

- Level 2: simple simulations that involve more than one element

- Level 3: complex simulations that involve several elements

- Level 4: interactive simulations that allow the user to regulate variables

Although all teams have information represented on Level 0 and Level 1, the majority of simulations are on Level 2 (e.g., simulation of a person throwing trash into a sewer; the aluminum can moves through the sewer and ends up in the ocean, where a fish tries to eat it and dies) and Level 3 (e.g., food chain simulation in which each life form gets eaten by the one higher above it on the food chain, such as plankton, anchovy, jellyfish, or rockfish; the user can click on each life form individually to see it eat whichever is its prey). Only one of the teams designed a simulation on Level 4: a cleanup scene where the user is shown a very messy beach and must use the mouse to drag all the various pieces of trash (aluminum cans, potato chip bags, syringes, empty bottles) to the garbage can.

It is evident from these results that students had a rich library of different screen types that they employed in their software for conveying particular information. They also showed that they were able to consider other perspectives in their design. Interactive aspects, which would allow players to manipulate software on their own, were the least prominent feature in these designs. Given the limited programming and software design experience of these students, these results are hardly surprising, but they do need to be taken into consideration when asking children to design software. The absence of interactive simulations might not be an indicator of lack of interest but a lack of programming ability.

Children's Usability Testing

During the project, I asked students to conduct a usability session of their software in progress with their prospective users. First I asked students to outline questions that they would ask their learners to assess usability issues. Although each student had the opportunity to ask more than one question and not all of them prepared questions, I found that the questions were divided fairly equally among learning questions ($n = 7$), general impression questions ($n = 10$), and design suggestion questions ($n = 12$). Table 6.2 provides a detailed listing of different categories within each question type.

For example, in learning questions, a few students asked rather generic questions such as "Did you learn anything?" or "Did you understand it?" But the majority of students developed questions asking for responses about specific learning features of the software—feedback that would be more useful for further development. Examples here were "What did you think

Table 6.2

Nature of usability questions

	Learning questions	General impressions	Design suggestions
General	3	4	2 (existing) 4 (future)
Specific	3	6	
Content-related			6
Other	1		
Total	7	10	12

this simulation was about?" or "Was this a good way of explaining what happens?"

Among the general impression questions, many questions were of a general nature such as "Do you think that our software is interesting?" or "Ask if they like the stack." Other questions were asking about specific features that were liked or disliked such as "What did you like best?" or "What was interesting?"

In the design suggestions, some students were asking for suggestions about existing features of the product such as "What should we change?" Others were asking for suggestions for things to make that are new such as "What should we add to make our software more complete?" But the majority asked for suggestions about what content to include: "What do you want to know about the ocean?" or "Do you want to know about sea animals?"

If anything, students' questions revealed a large set of issues they hoped to address in their usability session. Each student team conducted their session with two younger students. Some had a difficult time letting their user "use" the software; they understood testing as demonstrating. In contrast, other teams developed strategies in which they separated their two users and tested the usability with each of them individually.

After the evaluation session was over, I asked students to articulate what they learned from their interactions with their users. Only one student said that he learned "nothing" from the usability session. The majority reported that they learned something about who the third-graders are and came back with a listing of specific features to include in their further software development. They listed features such as more multimedia, more information, more interactivity, more realism, more animations, and *less* reading. The last feature was a direct consideration of the younger users' slower reading abilities. Many of them translated the usability impressions directly into ideas for their further software design, usually articulating them as specific content such as "more information about sharks" or "have a diver go to different levels of the ocean." Some of them articulated those ideas in terms of graphical components to be added to different pages such as "put a starfish at the bottom," "make bubbles in water," or "more seaweed," responding obviously to the demand for more detail and realism.

To sum up, students were covering a wide range of design and learning interests in their questions and were considerate of their users' suggestions. But students had problems in assessing particular needs of their users. This result is not surprising given the incomplete state of their software. Furthermore, it might have been a problem that students were testing their own software instead of software designed by other classmates.

Children's Software Evaluations

When students were asked to evaluate contrasting pairs of screens, their choices shifted between pretest and posttest. In the case of the first topic, eclipses, screen A (Figure 6.6) showed an animation of either solar or lunar eclipses by having the earth or moon rotate in pertinent ways; screen B (Figure 6.7) showed a static diagrammatic representation of the solar eclipse and a view from the earth but did not include animation features. Table 6.3 summarizes the choices of students for either screen A or B.

Several students decided to switch from screen A, which was by far the more popular screen choice in the pretest, to screen B. What rationales did students employ for their choices, in particular those students who decided to switch from A to B? Many students in the beginning were interested in the animation features because they "liked animations, [to] see things move," they thought it was "neater" or "for looks," or because of "realism"; the students who switched focused more on how the represented content explained what it was supposed to teach, had more information and detail, and was better organized. Many students also commented that screen B had labels, a feature that was missing in screen A.

For the second topic, planet navigation, screen A (Figure 6.8) showed a view of different planets revolving around the sun; screen B (Figure 6.9)

Figure 6.6

Content screen (animation)

Figure 6.7

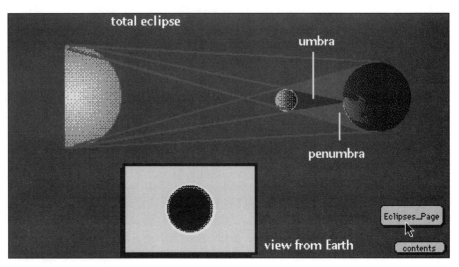

Content screen (schematic representation)

Table 6.3

Content screen (animation vs. schematic representation)

	Pretest	Posttest
Screen A (animation)	20	14
Screen B (schematic representation)	10	13

showed several buttons with names of planets on it that would lead to different pages. The majority chose screen A because it provided greater detail and realism (see Table 6.4). The few students who chose screen B did so for its "ease of use" and "better setup."

In the case of a third comparison, screen A showed an image of Saturn with additional information about the planet in text; screen B was a page with text only. The vast majority of students preferred screen A (see Table 6.5), which combined text and graphics. The overwhelming rationale was that they preferred to have a combination of text and graphics. Not one student commented on the aspect that the text content itself was presented in very different ways: while screen A listed a number of different facts in no particular order, screen B contained a more narrative form of the same content. It is worth noting that students were not only evaluating screen features but also the content described in each screen. Some students pointed out that in the text-only version of the screen (B) one major aspect was missing: there was no mention of Saturn's rings.

The general impression from these software screen evaluations is that students develop a wide range of criteria. The students went from "media

Figure 6.8

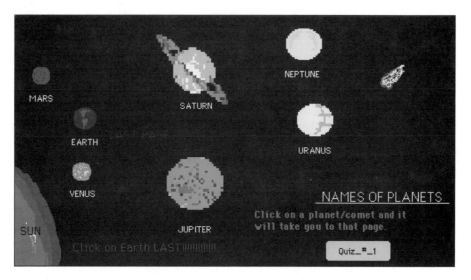

Navigational screen (content organization)

Figure 6.9

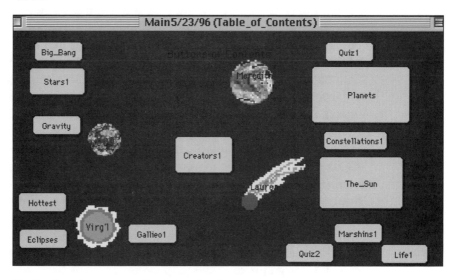

Navigational screen (random organization)

Table 6.4

Navigational screen (content organization vs. random organization)

	Pretest	Posttest
Screen A (content organization)	24	23
Screen B (random organization)	2	5

Table 6.5

Content screen (combined text/graphics vs. text only)

	Pretest	Posttest
Screen A (combined text/graphics)	22	25
Screen B (text only)	4	1

enthusiasts" to "information enthusiasts" in their main evaluation rationales, although many of these criteria were present from the beginning of the study.

6.5 Discussion

The initial intention of this study was to examine whether learners could become designers and what we could learn about their understanding of educational software in this process. For that reason, I examined the results of a study in which seven teams of students were engaged in designing educational software to teach younger children in their school about the ocean environment. I collected data about the quality of students' final software screens as one indicator of how they included and distributed different functionalities. Furthermore, I assessed what kind of questions children developed to conduct usability sessions with their software and what their insights from the experience were. I also studied students' educational screen comparisons and examined their rationales for preferring one screen over another. Taken together, the results presented in the preceding sections painted a rich picture of children as software designers. Based on these results, the following discussion addresses two questions: Can children become learner-centered designers? And can children become partners in the software design process?

Can Children Become Learner-Centered Designers?

In most learner-centered design efforts, professional designers concentrate on defining and constraining interface features for the learner with the hope that the given interactions and representations will guide and motivate the learner in the right direction. In the current study, I asked the learners themselves to be the designers. One way to answer the question is to apply the principles of learner-centered design listed in the introductory section. I found the following:

- Designing (and not just using) educational software is motivating for learners despite the extended time frame of the classroom activity.

- All students know something about software and content that they can use as the beginning point for their designs.

- The educational software provided different entrance points for interests of individual learners. In particular, the simulations designed by each team varied considerably in their focus and content. Although there were a few overlaps, most teams succeeded in finding a unique topic. All seven software products created by the teams presented a rich array of simulation examples.

- Software design is adaptable to learners' various skills, as students could participate in this activity by either creating simple educational screens or more complex simulations.

These results point out that students can become learner-centered designers. As the analysis of the testing and evaluations pointed out, students were concerned with their "users" as they were designing software. Very much like professional software designers, they were trying to balance the multiple demands involved in software design: content issues and users' motivations and needs. Although this chapter does not address the topic of learning, from research conducted over the past six years that engaged children in designing educational games and simulations in mathematics and science, we have seen that students as software designers significantly increased both their understanding of the subject domains and their programming skills (Harel 1991; Kafai 1995).

Can Children Become Partners in the Design Process?

Previous approaches limited children's involvement in the design process. For example, Scaiffe and Rogers have suggested the "informant design" approach for design collaboration with children (see Chapter 2). One of their main arguments for making children informants rather than partners or users is that children cannot design their own learning goals or define the needs of interactive systems. According to our interpretation of students' software designs, the children designers were well able to set their own learning goals for the educational software they had to design. The only requirement set out in the beginning of the project was that students design ocean environment simulations; how they would go about it and what kind of topics they would choose were left to them.

I found further support that students can become more refined in the evaluation of educational representations in software in the screen comparisons. In their criteria for evaluating software, students switched from "media enthusiasts" to "information enthusiasts." According to my criteria, this would represent a more sophisticated view of software and interface features, as students are no longer bound to just focus on the form of expression but also to judge the content in relation to form. This result is just one indicator that students are able to see beyond the multimedia "bells and whistles." Children can be more than informant designers; they obviously have the ability to become participants in the design process.

Considering the increasing use of interactive technologies by children, this is an important discovery. Research efforts in interface design have not matched this interest; there is little known about what kind of interface features work best for what age groups (Brouwser-Janse et al. 1997; Frye and Soloway 1986). Knowing that children can become partners in the design process is an important stepping-stone in changing this situation.

6.6 Next Steps

These results have several implications for designing technology with and for children. The benefit of using children as informants in the system design process has already been indicated by the work of Druin and Solomon (1996; see also Chapter 3) and Scaiffe and Rogers (see Chapter 2). Inclusion at various stages of the system design process and design with different materials can help designers to learn about children's ideas and knowledge. Although not a focus of this study but of previous research (e.g., Kafai 1996), the interface and software designs generated by children also provide rich source material for the gender differences found between girls and boys of that age. As HCI research talks about tailoring interfaces and manipulation modalities to individual user's needs and demands, these are important aspects to consider. One of the next steps should be to conduct studies with larger groups of children to gain more systematic information.

The current study pointed out that it might be meaningful to have children not just to design their ideas on paper but also to implement them on the computer. Although the generative ability of children was clear, the examined simulations were different from software previously generated by children (e.g., Kafai 1995; Kafai, Ching, and Marshall 1997). Most often, when asked to design educational software, children use the "drill and practice" format by posing questions for the user to answer. This reflects a stereotypical understanding of the teaching situation: teaching is posing questions and learning is giving answers. In the current study, students were explicitly asked to design instructional simulations. For any designer who wants to use this "learner as designer" methodology for collecting information from children, careful phrasing of the software specifications is required.

But the current study also points to a need for more and better authoring and programming systems for children to express themselves in the technological domain. A student like Andrew quoted in the introductory section of this chapter had considerable experience with designing and implementing software through his participation in the software design projects. The work described in the second part of this book provides multiple examples of what forms such design systems for children could take (see Chapters 7 through 11). These expressive technologies can be of help when designers are creating software for children or learners to use. But they also will help children to participate in technological design. Ultimately, the design of any system has a goal of making the end user/learner "smarter"—more efficient and knowledgeable. Children can become part of this process as they are designing, testing, and evaluating software and as they develop more sophisticated criteria for understanding and making technology.

Acknowledgments

The research reported in this chapter has been supported by a grant from the National Science Foundation, Applications of Advanced Technologies, and a grant from the Urban Education Studies Center at UCLA. We thank the teacher, Cathie Galas, and the students of the upper elementary grade at the Corinne Seeds University Elementary School for their participation. Also many thanks to Ken Daniszewski, Cynthia Carter Ching, and Sue Marshall for their help in collecting and analyzing the data.

References

Allen, D., Ballman, D., Miller-Jacobs, H., Muller, M., Nielsen, J., and Spool, J. 1993. User involvement in the design process: Why, when and how? In *INTERCHI '93 Proceedings.* New York: ACM Press, 251–254.

Brouwser-Janse, M. D., Sari, J. F., Yawitz, M., de Vries, G., Fozard, J. L., and Coleman, R. 1997. User interfaces for the young and old. *Interactions* 3/4: 34–46.

Cypher, A., and Smith, D. 1995. KidSim: End-user programming of simulations. In *Proceedings of CHI '95 Conference.* New York: ACM Press, 27–34.

Druin, A., and Solomon, C. 1996. *Designing multimedia environments for children: Computers, creativity, and kids.* New York: John Wiley & Sons.

Frye, D., and Soloway, E. 1986. *Interface design: A neglected issue in educational software.* Technical report. Cognition and Programming Project, Yale University, Department of Computer Science, New Haven, CT.

Harel, I. 1991. *Children designers: Interdisciplinary constructions for learning and knowing mathematics in a computer-rich school.* Norwood, NJ: Ablex.

Kafai, Y. B. 1995. *Minds in play: Computer game design as a context for children's learning.* Hillsdale, NJ: Lawrence Erlbaum.

Kafai, Y. B. 1996. Gender differences in children's construction of video games. In P. M. Greenfield and R. R. Cocking, eds., *Interacting with video.* Norwood, NJ: Ablex, 39–66.

Kafai, Y. B., Ching, C. C., and Marshall, S. 1997. Children as educational multimedia designers. *Computers & Education* 29(2–3): 117–126.

Kafai, Y. B., and Resnick, M., eds. 1996. *Constructionism in practice: Designing, thinking and learning in a digital world.* Mahwah, NJ: Lawrence Erlbaum.

Malone, T. W. 1981. What makes computer games fun? *Byte* 17(10): 258–277.

Norman, D. A., and Draper, S. W., eds. 1986. *User-centered system design.* Hillsdale, NJ: Lawrence Erlbaum.

Papert, S. 1980. *Mindstorms.* New York: Basic Books.

Pea, R. D., and Kurland, D. M. 1986. On the cognitive effects of learning computer programming. In R. D. Pea and K. Sheingold, eds., *Mirrors of mind: Patterns of experience in educational computing.* Norwood, NJ: Ablex, 147–177.

Rader, C., Brand, C., and Lewis, C. 1997. Degrees of comprehension: Children's understanding of a visual programming environment. In *Proceedings of the CHI '97 Conference.* New York: ACM Press.

Repenning, A., and Ambach, J. 1996. Tactile programming: A unified manipulation paradigm supporting program comprehension, composition and sharing. In *Proceedings of the 1996 IEEE Symposium on Visual Languages.* Los Alamitos, CA: IEEE Computer Society Press.

Schuler, D., and Mamoika, A., eds. 1993. *Participatory design: Principles and practices.* Hillsdale, NJ: Lawrence Erlbaum.

Smith, D., and Keep, R. 1986. Children's opinion of educational software. *Educational Research* 28(2): 83–88.

Soloway, E., Guzdial, M., and Hay, K. 1994. Learner-centered design: The challenge for HCI in the 21st century. *Interactions* 1(2): 36–48.

Soloway, E., Jackson, S., Klein, J., Quintana, C., Reed, J., Spitulnik, J., Stratford, S., Studer, S., Jul, S., Eng, J., and Scala, N. 1997. Learning theory in practice: Case studies of learner-centered design. In *Proceedings of the CHI '97 Conference.* New York: ACM Press.

Part II

The Technology
of Children

Chapter Seven

Constructional Design:

Creating New Construction Kits for Kids

Mitchel Resnick
MIT Media Laboratory

Amy Bruckman
Georgia Institute of Technology

Fred Martin
MIT Media Laboratory

7.1 Introduction

Would you rather that your children learn to play the piano or learn to play the stereo? The stereo has many attractions: it is easier to play and it provides immediate access to a wide range of music. But ease of use should not be the only criterion. Playing the piano can be a much richer experience. By learning to play the piano, you can become a creator, not just a consumer, of music, expressing yourself musically in ever-more complex ways. As a result, you can develop a much deeper relationship with, and deeper understanding of, music.

So too with computers. In the field of educational technology, there has been too much emphasis on the equivalent of stereos and CDs and not enough emphasis on computational pianos. We are developing a new generation of "computational construction kits" that, like pianos, enable people to express themselves in ever-more complex ways, deepening their relationships with new domains of knowledge.

To guide the development of these computational construction kits, we are developing a theory of *constructional design*. The traditional field of instructional design focuses on strategies and materials to help teachers instruct, but our theory of constructional design focuses on strategies and materials to help students construct and learn. Constructional design is a type of metadesign: it involves the design of new tools and activities to support students in their own design activities. In short, constructional design involves designing for designers (Resnick 1996b).

In recent years, a growing number of researchers and educators have argued that design projects provide rich opportunities for learning (e.g., Harel 1991; Lehrer 1993; Soloway, Guzdial, and Hay 1994). In particular, Papert (1993) has argued for a "constructionist" approach to learning. There are many reasons for this interest in design-based learning. Design activities engage people as active participants, giving them a greater sense of control over, and personal involvement in, the learning process. Moreover, the things that people design—be they sand castles, computer programs, LEGO constructions, or musical compositions—serve as external shadows of the designer's internal mental models. These external creations provide an opportunity for people to reflect upon, and then revise and extend, their internal models of the world.

Of course, not all design experiences, nor all construction kits, are created equal. Some provide richer learning opportunities than others. What criteria should guide the design of new construction kits and activities? The concept of learning-by-doing has been around for a long time. But the literature on the subject tends to describe specific activities and gives little attention to the general principles governing what kinds of "doing" are most conducive to learning. From our experiences, we have developed two general principles to guide the design of new construction kits and activities. These constructional design principles involve two different types of "connections":

- *Personal connections:* Construction kits and activities should connect to users' interests, passions, and experiences. The point is not simply to make the activities more motivating (though that, of course, is important). When activities involve objects and actions that are familiar, users can leverage their previous knowledge, connecting new ideas to their preexisting intuitions.

- *Epistemological connections:* Construction kits and activities should connect to important domains of knowledge—especially "high-leverage knowledge" that helps learners acquire even more knowledge. Kits should encourage new ways of thinking—and even new ways of thinking about thinking. A well-designed construction kit makes certain ideas and ways of thinking particularly salient so that users are likely to connect with those ideas in a very natural way in the process of designing and creating.

The challenge of constructional design—and it is a very significant challenge—is to create construction kits with both types of connections (e.g., Wilensky 1993). Many learning materials and activities offer one type of connection but not the other. In this chapter, we discuss three of our computational construction kits. In each case, we discuss how the kit facilitates both personal and epistemological connections—and, as a result, supports rich learning experiences.

7.2   Programmable Bricks

Traditional construction kits enable children to build structures like bridges and buildings. Contemporary construction kits (e.g., LEGO Technic) add power and motion, enabling kids to build motorized cars, Ferris wheels, and other battery-powered machines. The MIT Programmable Brick adds a third level—sensing and control. Children can not only build machines that move around but systems that have behaviors and respond to their environment (Martin 1994, 1996; Resnick 1993).

The Programmable Brick is a tiny computer embedded inside a LEGO brick. Children can build Programmable Bricks directly into their LEGO constructions and then write programs to make their creations react, behave, and collect data.

About the size of a child's juice box, the Programmable Brick can be seen as a "very personal computer." To use the Brick, children write programs on a "regular" computer, then download the programs to the Brick via a cable. After that, they can disconnect the Brick and take it (or put it) anywhere—the programs remain stored in the Brick. The Brick can control four motors at a time, receive inputs from six sensors, and communicate with other electronic devices via infrared communications.

We have used the Programmable Brick with children in a variety of settings, including after-school clubs, weekend museum classes, and as part of the school-day curriculum. Working with elementary school teachers, we wanted a framework that would appeal to young children and to both genders and collectively decided on a theme we called the "Robotic Park." In the Robotic Park activity, students selected an animal, researched the animal and its habitat, and then implemented LEGO models of these animals, including sensors, actuators, and control programs.

In one Robotic Park activity, fifth-grade students created a LEGO dinosaur (Figure 7.1 [see also Color Plate]) that was attracted to flashes of light from the headlights of a motorized Jeep (also built by the same team). Inspired by the dinosaurs in *Jurassic Park,* this project had a clear connection to popular culture. But it also had a direct connection to scientific culture. To make the dinosaur move toward the light, the students needed to understand basic ideas about feedback and control. Their program caused the dinosaur to spin in a circle, looking for the Jeep's lights. When the reading from the dinosaur's light sensor crossed a certain threshold, the dino started driving straight ahead. If the light sensor reading fell, the dino would start spinning again.

Figure 7.1

Three fifth-grade students show off their LEGO dinosaur, including a knapsack to carry its Programmable Brick

This algorithm—designed by the students themselves—is an example of a classic feedback strategy that typically is not taught until university-level courses. But with the right tools, fifth-graders were able to explore these ideas.

Other students have used Programmable Bricks to augment their surroundings. For example, a pair of students created a "smart room." They wanted to use a Brick to automatically turn on the lights in a room whenever anyone entered and turn them off again when the room was empty. They built a contraption, controlled by a LEGO motor and mounted on top of the standard wall light switch, that could be driven from the Brick to turn the lights on and off.

The more difficult challenge was determining when there were people in the room. The students began by equipping the door itself with a sensor, so their program could know when the door was opened. But they quickly realized they wouldn't know whether people were entering or leaving the room just by monitoring the door. So they added a sensor to the inner door handle. If the door was opened and the door handle was turned, their program decided someone was leaving the room. But if the door was opened and the handle wasn't turned, it must be someone entering from the outside. The students realized their program would be fooled if someone entered the room at the same time as someone exited, but at this point they had thought through many of the issues involved in what initially seemed like a simple problem.

Through projects like these, students gain a sense of how the pervasive technology around them actually operates. Rather than being passive users of technology, students can actively construct their own models of computation affecting the world around them. For many students, it is an empowering experience to have their program control real activity in the world. Students come to understand "embodied computation"—something far different than Web pages coming through a modem or video games projected through a television screen.

At a vocational high school in our project, students have used Programmable Bricks to prepare robots for competitive performance events. In one such challenge, students had the problem of programming their robot to follow along a curved black line on the robot playing field.

A canonical solution to the problem is shown in Figure 7.2. Using just one light sensor to detect the line, this approach makes the robot weave back and forth across the line. When the robot crosses completely over the line, it changes direction to go back across it again. As long as the robot is making forward progress while weaving back and forth, the approach is successful. Many students find this solution counterintuitive, though, since the robot never drives straight ahead: in their minds, when the robot is directly over the line, it should simply drive straight ahead.

Figure 7.2

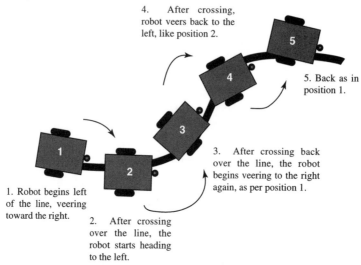

4. After crossing, robot veers back to the left, like position 2.

5. Back as in position 1.

3. After crossing back over the line, the robot begins veering to the right again, as per position 1.

1. Robot begins left of the line, veering toward the right.

2. After crossing over the line, the robot starts heading to the left.

Canonical line-following algorithm. In this algorithm, the robot uses a single sensor in a front center position. The robot starts on one side of the line and begins moving so as to cross the line while moving forward. After crossing all the way over the line so that the line sensor sees the table, the robot changes direction and veers back across the line. This process repeats, giving the robot the appearance of waddling back and forth across the line. Note that when using this algorithm, the robot never drives straight forward; it is always turning across the line in one direction or the other.

We did not present the canonical answer to the students, preferring them to struggle with the problem themselves. One student in particular, Djonnie, took a special interest in the problem and devised the following solution (depicted in Figure 7.3):

1. If the robot is on the line, it should drive straight ahead.

2. After falling off the line, the robot turns left, looking for the line. If it finds the line within 2 seconds, it goes back to step 1 (driving forward on the line).

3. If the robot does not find the line within 2 seconds, then it assumes that the line headed off to the right, spins right for 4 seconds, and then continues back at step 1.

There are several things worth noting about Djonnie's solution. First, it works. It is not as symmetrical as the canonical approach, but it is efficient in its own way. The robot makes fine progress when driving straight and when the line bears to the left (its preferred direction). The corrective action that the robot takes when the line bears to the right is often amusing.

Figure 7.3

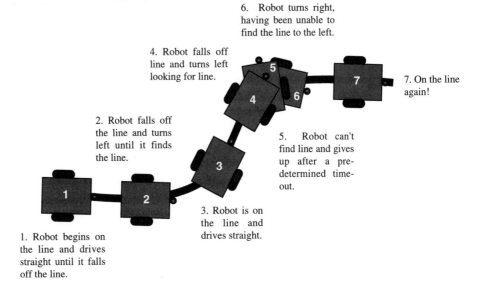

6. Robot turns right, having been unable to find the line to the left.

4. Robot falls off line and turns left looking for line.

2. Robot falls off the line and turns left until it finds the line.

5. Robot can't find line and gives up after a pre-determined time-out.

7. On the line again!

3. Robot is on the line and drives straight.

1. Robot begins on the line and drives straight until it falls off the line.

Djonnie's line-following algorithm. This algorithm uses the same robot configuration as the canonical follower, but is based more on personal intuition. If the robot is on the line, it drives straight ahead until it falls off the line. After leaving the line, the robot attempts to find the line by turning left. If this succeeds, the robot starts driving straight again. If it fails, after a certain amount of time, then the robot assumes that the line turned the "wrong" way and spins to the right for twice as long as it tried to turn to the left.

More importantly, Djonnie used what Papert calls *body syntonic thinking* in developing his approach (Papert 1980). That is, he thought about how he would solve the problem if he were the robot. As a student who is not particularly academically minded, Djonnie made the connection between the robot as a physical entity and how he would use his own body to solve the problem and leveraged this understanding to create the solution.

Projects with the Programmable Brick, like this robotic line-follower, often make strong personal connections to children's lives. Children frequently treat their robotic creations like pets—cradling them gently, cussing them for undesirable behavior, and getting excited when they perform well. Toys in general, and LEGO building materials in particular, are part of children's culture. When Programmable Bricks are added to the bin of LEGO building parts, computation becomes part of children's culture, too.

At the same time, Programmable Brick projects encourage strong epistemological connections. When students build and program robotic creatures, for example, they often wonder about the similarities and differences between animals and machines. Are their LEGO creatures like animals? Or like machines? They compare their robots' sensors to animal senses, and they discuss whether real animals have "programs" like their robots.

The Programmable Brick project is part of a larger Media Lab initiative known as Things That Think, and it relates to a field of research sometimes called "ubiquitous computing" (Weiser 1991, 1993). The overarching goal in this research is to embed computational capabilities in everyday objects like furniture, shoes, and toys—mixing together bits and atoms.

The Programmable Brick fits within this initiative—but with an important twist. In our research, we are interested in Things That Think not because they might accomplish particular tasks more cheaply or easily or intelligently but because they might enable people to think about things in new ways. That is, Things That Think are most interesting to us when they also act as Things To Think With. We believe that Programmable Bricks act in just that way: by enabling children to build their own Things That Think (like the light-seeking dinosaur), Programmable Bricks engage children in new types of thinking.

In our latest work, we have created a spin-off of the Programmable Brick—an even tinier computer (the size of a 9-volt battery) that we call the Cricket. But Crickets are more than just small Programmable Bricks: in addition to connecting to motors and sensors, Crickets can communicate with each other via infrared light.

With Crickets, we are encouraging children to think about not just one "smart brick" but systems of communicating entities. Children can have three or four—or even a dozen—Crickets in a given project, all communicating with one another. In doing so, children can explore the behaviors that arise from all of their interactions. In one of our example projects, two

Figure 7.4

Dancing Crickets

little Cricket creatures perform a coordinated dance (Figure 7.4 [see also Color Plate]). Each one takes a step and then electronically "chats" with the other, asking the other to take its turn. After the second dancer goes, control passes back to the first one. With playful examples like these, children begin to understand and then create their own examples of distributed control systems—systems much like the most sophisticated engineered technology all around us.

7.3 StarLogo

Programmable Bricks enable students to embed computers in the world; StarLogo enables them to construct worlds in the computer.

In particular, StarLogo is designed to help students model and explore the behaviors of *decentralized systems,* such as ant colonies, traffic jams, market economies, immune systems, and computer networks. In these systems, orderly patterns arise without centralized control. In ant colonies, for example, trail patterns are determined not by the dictates of the queen ant but by local interactions among the worker ants. In market economies, patterns arise from interactions among millions of buyers and sellers in distributed marketplaces.

Decentralized systems are important throughout the sciences and social sciences, but most people have difficulty understanding the workings of such systems. People seem to have strong attachments to centralized ways of thinking. When people see patterns in the world (like the foraging patterns of an ant colony), they generally assume that there is some type of centralized control (a queen ant). According to this way of thinking, a pattern can exist only if someone (or something) creates and orchestrates the pattern.

StarLogo is designed to help students make a fundamental epistemological shift, to move beyond the "centralized mind-set" to more decentralized ways of thinking (Resnick 1994, 1996a). With StarLogo, students construct and experiment with decentralized systems. In traditional versions of Logo (Papert 1980), students program the motion of a graphic "turtle" on the computer screen. As students "teach" the turtle to draw different geometric shapes, they learn important mathematical ideas. StarLogo is a massively parallel version of Logo: it includes *thousands* of turtles that can all execute instructions in parallel. And while the traditional Logo turtle is primarily a "drawing turtle," the StarLogo turtles are "behavioral turtles," with built-in "senses" for interacting with other turtles and with the world around them. With StarLogo, students can write simple rules for thousands of turtles, then observe the patterns that arise from all of the interactions. Students have used StarLogo to model everything from bird flocks to predator–prey ecosystems to marketplace interactions.

In one project, two high school students used StarLogo to model the formation of traffic jams on the highway. Since the students had recently received their drivers' licenses, this topic was of great interest for them. Traditional studies of traffic flow rely on sophisticated analytic techniques (from fields like queuing theory). But many of the same traffic phenomena can be explored with simple StarLogo programs. To get started, the two students, Ari and Fadhil, decided to create a one-lane highway. (Later, they experimented with multiple lanes.) Ari suggested adding a police radar trap somewhere along the road to catch cars going above the speed limit. But he also wanted each car to have its own radar detector so that cars would know to slow down when they approached the radar trap.

After some discussion, Ari and Fadhil decided that each StarLogo turtle/car should follow three basic rules:

- If there is a car close ahead of you, slow down.
- If there are not any cars close ahead of you, speed up.
- If you detect a radar trap, slow down.

Ari and Fadhil implemented these rules in StarLogo. They expected that a traffic jam would form behind the radar trap, and indeed it did (Figure 7.5). After a few dozen iterations of the StarLogo program, a line of cars started to form to the left of the radar trap. The cars moved slowly through

Figure 7.5

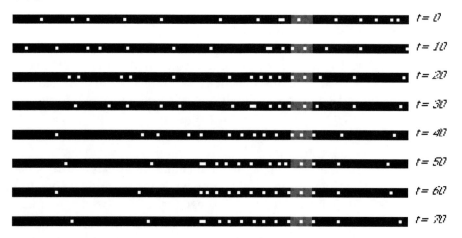

Traffic jam caused by radar trap (shaded area). Cars move left to right.

Figure 7.6

Traffic jam without radar trap. Cars move left to right, but jam moves right to left.

the trap, then sped away as soon as they passed it. Ari explained: "First one car slows down for the radar trap, then the one behind it slows down, then the one behind that one, and then you've got a traffic jam."

We asked Ari and Fadhil what would happen if only *some* of the cars had radar detectors. Ari predicted that only some of the cars would slow down for the radar trap. Fadhil had a different idea: "The ones that have radar detectors will slow down, which will cause the other ones to slow down." Fadhil was right. The students modified the StarLogo program so that only 25 percent of the cars had radar detectors. The result: the traffic flow looked exactly the same as when all of the cars had radar detectors.

What if *none* of the cars had radar detectors—or, equivalently, if the radar trap were removed entirely? With no radar trap, the cars would be controlled by just two simple rules: if you see another car close ahead, slow down; if not, speed up. The rules could not be much simpler. Fadhil predicted that the traffic flow would become uniform: cars would be evenly spaced, traveling at a constant speed. Without the radar trap, he reasoned, what could cause a jam? But when the students ran the program, a traffic jam formed (Figure 7.6). Along parts of the road, the cars were tightly packed and moving slowly. Elsewhere, they were spread out and moving at the speed limit.

Ari and Fadhil were surprised. And when we showed Ari and Fadhil's program to other high school students, they too were surprised. In general, the students expected the cars to end up evenly spaced along the highway, separated by equal distances; no one expected a traffic jam to form. Some of their predictions:

Emily: "[The cars will] just speed along, just keep going along . . . They will end up staggered, in intervals."

Frank: "Nothing will be wrong with it. Cars will just go . . . There's no obstacles. The cars will just keep going, and that's it."

Ramesh: "They will probably adjust themselves to a uniform distance from each other."

When we ran the simulation and traffic jams began to form, the students were shocked. In their comments, most students revealed a strong commitment to the idea that some type of "seed" (like an accident or a broken bridge) is needed to start a traffic jam. Perhaps Frank expressed it best: "I didn't think there would be any problem, since there was nothing there." If there is nothing there—if there is no seed—there should not be a traffic jam. Traffic jams do not just happen; they must have localizable causes. And the cause must come from outside the system (not from the cars themselves).

Fadhil suggested that the jams were caused by differences in the initial speeds of the cars. So the students changed the StarLogo program, starting all of the cars at the exact same speed. But the jams still formed. Fadhil quickly understood. He noted that their program had initially placed the cars at random positions on the road, so the cars started with uneven spacing between them. The uneven spacing, he said, could also provide the seed from which a traffic jam could form. If a few cars, by chance, happened to be near one another, they slowed down, which, in turn, made it likely that even more cars behind them would have to slow down, leading to a jam. By continuing to modify and play with their StarLogo program, Ari and Fadhil began to build an understanding of how a traffic jam can form without an accident, radar trap, or broken bridge. More generally, they began to understand how patterns can form without centralized control.

Traditionally, students do not study the behaviors of dynamic systems (such as the patterns of traffic on a highway) until the university level, using differential equations and other advanced mathematical techniques. StarLogo makes these ideas accessible to younger students by providing them with a stronger personal connection to the underlying models. Traditional differential equation approaches are impersonal in two ways. The first is obvious: they rely on abstract symbol manipulation. The second is more subtle: they deal in aggregate quantities. In the traffic example, differential equations would describe how the density of cars evolves over time. There are now some very good computer modeling tools—such as Stella (Roberts et al. 1983) and Model-It (Jackson et al. 1996)—based on differential equations. These tools eliminate the need to manipulate symbols, focusing on more qualitative and graphical descriptions. But they still rely on aggregate quantities.

In StarLogo, by contrast, students think about the actions and interactions of individual objects. StarLogo is not simply a computerization of a traditional mathematical model; it supports what we call "computational models"—models that wouldn't make sense without a computer. In the traffic example, students think not about aggregate quantities but about individual cars. They can imagine themselves as cars and think about what they might do. In this way, StarLogo enables learners to dive into the model, making a more personal connection. Future versions of StarLogo will enable users to zoom in and out, making it easier for users to shift back and forth in perspective from the individual level to the group level.

7.4   MOOSE Crossing

While StarLogo users typically build new worlds on their own or in pairs, MOOSE Crossing provides a way for large numbers of children to build virtual worlds together, as part of an online community.

MOOSE Crossing is a text-based virtual world on the Internet (a MUD) built and inhabited by children (Bruckman 1994). On MOOSE Crossing, children not only "talk" with one another online but also collaboratively construct (with words and computer programs) the virtual world in which they interact (Figure 7.7). MOOSE Crossing is similar to existing MUD environments (Curtis 1992), but it includes a new programming language (MOOSE) and new client interfaces (MacMOOSE and JavaMOOSE) designed to make it easier for kids to learn to program. For each object that kids create, they write a combination of text and computer code to describe the properties and behaviors of the object. For example, one 12-year-old girl made a baby penguin that is always hungry. It responds differently when you offer it different kinds of food, and it won't eat certain foods if it is on a diet. A 9-year-old girl made a magical room at the end of the rainbow— answer the riddle correctly and you can take the pot of gold. Children help one another with their projects and share them with others excitedly. MOOSE Crossing places construction activities in a community context.

MOOSE Crossing is immediately appealing to many children because it draws on their personal connection to computer games, to elements of popular culture, and to socializing with each other. The environment has the feel of a text-based adventure game (and historically has its roots in such games), but it opens up greater intellectual challenges: you not only

Figure 7.7

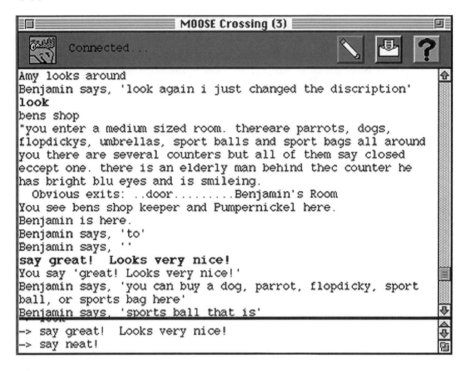

Sample interactions on MOOSE Crossing

experience the world but also build it. Children often choose popular culture as the subject of their conversations and as inspiration for their creations: for example, one afternoon, two 12-year-old girls started talking about *Star Trek* and then decided to build themselves spaceships. Commercial culture is also a popular starting point for projects. One 11-year-old girl first made a vacation resort called Paradise Island, next made a travel agency to sell people trips there, and lastly added a car rental agency.

Some cultural scholars (Postman 1985) argue that popular culture, especially television, stifles children's learning and creativity. But Henry Jenkins (1992) documents how television and other popular media can function not to stifle individual creativity but to stimulate it. Television fans make videos and write stories and folk songs about their favorite characters, taking the stories further and making them more personally relevant. The community of fans serves as an audience for these creations. Similarly, children on MOOSE Crossing use elements of popular culture as starting points for their creative projects, and the other children online function as an appreciative audience. Popular culture is not a force to be struggled against, but rather one to be leveraged for children's educational benefit.

Having an appreciative audience is an essential element in encouraging people to undertake creative projects (Bruckman 1998). One 13-year-old girl writes (we have left her spelling and punctuation unchanged):

> Another thing about moose-crossing is that I feel as if I can really help some-
> one. I like learning and doing stuff on my own, but the real reason I come to
> moose-crossing is that I feel needed, and wanted. While programing is a lot
> of fun, I don't think I'd do it, if there wasn't anyone who would apprecitate it.

Another natural interest of children is talking to one another. Educators inspired by the work of Lev Vygotsky increasingly recognize the centrality of interpersonal relations to learning (Newman et al. 1989). However, most often, this takes the form of designing collaborative work activities in the classroom. Still not adequately recognized is the fact that social activity is also central to learning. In their interactions on MOOSE Crossing, children talk not just about their writing and programming projects but also about their friends, their families, their favorite sports teams, and what they ate for lunch. They talk about everything kids talk about. Some might view these more socially oriented conversations as a waste of time. We disagree. At the simplest level, these conversations are useful because the children are expressing themselves in words, practicing using the written word as a means of communication. More fundamentally, the social bonds that are formed between children support the learning that takes place.

When children help one another on MOOSE Crossing, they are supporting friends, not strangers. Getting help from a stranger or an authority figure is very different from getting help from a friend you've shared your best elephant jokes with. Most educational research that strives to acknowledge the social nature of learning has children working in groups on traditional schoolwork. If an electronic network is used, children are told to use the network to discuss the current officially selected curriculum material; discussion of popular culture, friendships, or elephant jokes would be considered bad behavior. MOOSE Crossing deliberately blurs the boundaries between work and play. The friendships and general spirit of fun that emerge not only support the learning that takes place, they also deepen it. Forced, dry school lessons are often forgotten. Knowledge gained while having fun with friends, working on a personally meaningful project, is more relevant and more lasting.

Children on MOOSE Crossing create things to show off to one another and also spend a significant amount of time teaching and helping others.

Even new members take pleasure in teaching; they enjoy showing off what they've just learned. Participants tend to form strong social bonds with others who helped them when they were new. Completed projects are enthusiastically shown off to online friends and give the creator a kind of social capital. Social activity is a strong motivating force behind children's creative endeavors.

Another kind of personal connection is free choice as to whether or not to participate in the activity at all. MOOSE Crossing was originally designed to be a free-time activity, used either from home or from after-school programs. It is increasingly being used as an in-school activity. However, in an informal comparison of five classrooms using MOOSE Crossing as an in-school activity, we found significant advantages to the setting in which children could freely choose to use either MOOSE Crossing or some other activity. Three-quarters of the children in that class voluntarily chose to use MOOSE Crossing over other available computer activities. All the children in that class knew that they were participating because they wanted to; many other appealing options were available. Children in another class where the activity was mandated were less engaged and less happy (Bruckman and De Bonte 1997). Although we would not go so far as some critics who argue that all educational activities should be voluntary (Falbel 1989), personal choice to participate is a motivating factor that could be used more effectively in schools.

Freedom to choose to participate or not both helps children form stronger personal connections to an intellectually valuable activity and helps form new epistemological connections. Children learn not just *how* to read, write, and program but also *why* they might want to choose to make use of these skills.

MOOSE Crossing leverages children's natural interests to engage them in these intellectually valuable activities. Children establish a new relationship to reading, writing, and programming, beginning to see these activities not just as something they are forced to do in school but as expressive media through which they can make personally significant meanings. In other words, they establish a new epistemological relationship to these ways of understanding the world and expressing themselves.

MOOSE Crossing also establishes new connections between different ways of knowing that are often separated and isolated in school activities. Making a successful MOOSE object is equal parts creative writing and computer programming. For children who have a greater initial strength in one area, it helps them develop greater confidence and competence in the other. One 9-year-old girl who says she hates math and mathlike activities loves programming on MOOSE Crossing because she sees it as a form of writing. Asked if she likes to write, she replied yes: in school she's writing stories about imaginary people; on MOOSE Crossing, she's writing programs. The only difference between these two kinds of writing is that with "programming it everything has to be right so the thing you're making can work." She is bridging from her strong verbal skills to develop greater interest and skill in more analytic activities.

Most research on constructionist learning focuses on individual children working on independent projects. MOOSE Crossing situates those projects in a supportive community context, emphasizing learning as a collaborative process. It's worth noting that most projects on MOOSE Crossing are in fact individual. A group of children worked together to build a zoo and a mall, and one class built an ocean liner that sinks. But these are notable exceptions; most projects are done by individual children. In what sense, then, can it be considered a "collaborative" learning environment? First, children help one another with their projects; few projects are completed without help and constructive feedback from others. Even the most accomplished writers and programmers often solicit input from others and revise their work accordingly. Second, children learn from one another's projects. As you walk around the virtual world, you can see who made each object and how it is put together. Younger children often choose to learn from projects made by older children whom they have met online and look up to. The virtual world is filled with both project models and role models, and those two kinds of models are interconnected. Younger children see not only the finished projects of older children but also works in progress. They have the opportunity to observe not just finished products but also the process of their creation. They learn not only what is possible but also what is involved in creating something.

Seymour Papert has written about the epistemological value of debugging (Papert 1980):

> The question to ask about the program is not whether it is right or wrong, but if it is fixable. If this way of looking at intellectual products were generalized to how the larger culture thinks about knowledge, we all might be less intimidated by our fears of "being wrong." This potential influence of the computer on changing our notion of a black and white version of our successes and failure is an example of using the computer as an "object-to-think-with."

On MOOSE Crossing, children not only debug their own programs, but also get to watch others engaged in that process. Perhaps the most valuable part of this lesson is the knowledge that everyone makes mistakes, even the experts. Success is a matter of persistence.

The children participating in MOOSE Crossing are mostly 9 to 13 years old; a few children are as young as 7. Adults may apply to be "rangers."

While we originally expected rangers to help children with their projects, in practice it more often works the other way around. Children have much more time to devote to MOOSE Crossing and generally understand how things work better than the adults. Assisting an adult with a technical question is a thrill for many kids and challenges some of their basic assumptions about learning. On MOOSE Crossing, everyone is playing, teaching, and learning all at the same time, rather like Seymour Papert's vision of activity in a "technological samba school" (Papert 1980). Knowledge is not passed from teachers to students, but is developed by everyone through their activities and interactions with one another.

7.5 Emergent Learning Experiences

Programmable Bricks, StarLogo, and MOOSE Crossing are three very different types of computational construction kits. The first involves interaction with the physical world, the second involves the construction of virtual collaborations, and the third involves collaboration on virtual constructions. What unites these three diverse environments is their attempt to provide both personal and epistemological connections. Each of these kits connects to student interests and experiences while also connecting to important intellectual ideas.

But the process of constructional design is not a simple matter of "programming in" the right types of connections. As students have used Programmable Bricks, StarLogo, and MOOSE Crossing, their learning experiences have been somewhat different than we (as developers) expected. This unpredictability is characteristic of constructional design. Developers of design-oriented learning environments need to adopt a relaxed sense of control. Educational designers cannot (and should not) control exactly what (or when or how) students will learn. The point is not to make a precise blueprint. Rather, practitioners of constructional design can only create "spaces" of possible activities and experiences. What we can do as constructional designers is to try to make those spaces dense with personal and epistemological connections, making it more likely for learners to find regions that are both engaging and intellectually interesting.

In some ways, the design of a new learning environment is like the design of a StarLogo simulation. In creating StarLogo simulations, users write simple rules for individual objects, then observe the large-scale patterns that emerge. Users do not program the patterns directly. So too with constructional design. Developers of design-oriented learning environments cannot "program" learning experiences directly. The challenge, instead, is to create frameworks from which strong connections—and rich learning experiences—are likely to emerge.

Acknowledgments

Portions of this chapter have appeared previously (Resnick, Bruckman, and Martin 1996). Many members of the Epistemology and Learning Group at the MIT Media Laboratory have contributed to the ideas and projects described in this chapter. In particular, Brian Silverman, Randy Sargent, and Andy Begel played central roles in the development of the Programmable Brick and StarLogo. Many of the ideas in this chapter were inspired by conversations with Seymour Papert, Alan Kay, and Mike Eisenberg. Financial support for this research has been provided by the National Science Foundation (9153719-MDR and 9358519-RED), the LEGO Group, and the Media Lab research consortia Things That Think, News in the Future, and Digital Life.

References

Bruckman, A. 1994. MOOSE Crossing: Creating a learning culture. Ph.D. dissertation proposal, MIT Media Laboratory, Cambridge, MA. Available as *ftp://ftp.media.mit.edu/pub/asb/papers/moose-crossing-proposal.{ps,rtf,txt}.*

Bruckman, A. 1998. Community support for constructionist learning. St. Augustin, Germany: *CSCW* (in press).

Bruckman, A., and De Bonte, A. 1997. MOOSE goes to school: A comparison of three classrooms using a CSCL environment. In *Proceedings of CSCL Conference* (Dec.). *www.cc.gatech.edu/~asb/papers/cscl97.html.*

Curtis, P. 1992. Mudding: Social phenomena in text-based virtual realities. In *Proceedings of DIAC '92.* Computer Professionals for Social Responsibility.

Falbel, A. 1989. Friskolen 70: An ethnographically informed inquiry into the social context of learning. Ph.D. dissertation, MIT Media Laboratory, Cambridge, MA.

Harel, I. 1991. *Children designers.* Norwood, NJ: Ablex.

Jackson, S., Stratford, S., Krajcik, J., and Soloway, E. 1996. A learner-centered tool for students building models. *Communications of the ACM* 39(4): 48–49.

Jenkins, H. 1992. *Textual poachers: Television fans and participatory culture.* New York: Routledge.

Lehrer, R. 1993. Authors of knowledge: Patterns of hypermedia design. In S. Lajoie and S. Derry, eds. *Computers as cognitive tools.* Hillsdale, NJ: Lawrence Erlbaum.

Martin, F. 1994. Circuits to control: Learning engineering by designing LEGO robots. Ph.D dissertation, MIT Media Laboratory.

Martin, F. 1996. Ideal and real systems: A study of notions of control in undergraduates who design robots. In Y. Kafai and M. Resnick, eds. *Constructionism in practice.* Hillsdale, NJ: Lawrence Erlbaum.

Newman, D., Griffin, P., and Cole, M. 1989. *The construction zone: Working for cognitive change in school.* Cambridge, England: Cambridge University Press.

Papert, S. 1980. *Mindstorms.* New York: Basic Books.

Papert, S. 1993. *The children's machine.* New York: Basic Books.

Postman, N. 1985. *Amusing ourselves to death: Public discourse in the age of show business.* New York: Viking.

Resnick, M. 1993. Behavior construction kits. *Communications of the ACM* 36(7): 64–71.

Resnick, M. 1994. *Turtles, termites, and traffic jams.* Cambridge, MA: MIT Press.

Resnick, M. 1996a. Beyond the centralized mindset. *Journal of the Learning Sciences* 5(1): 1–22.

Resnick, M. 1996b. Towards a practice of constructional design. In L. Schauble and R. Glaser, eds. *Innovations in learning: New environments for education.* Mahwah, NJ: Lawrence Erlbaum.

Resnick, M., Bruckman, A., and Martin, F. 1996. Pianos not stereos: Creating computational construction kits. *Interactions* 3(6): 41–50.

Roberts, N., Anderson, D., Deal, R., Garet, M., and Shaffer, W. 1983. *Introduction to computer simulation: A system dynamics modeling approach.* Reading, MA: Addison-Wesley.

Soloway, E., Guzdial, M., and Hay, K. 1994. Learner-centered design. *Interactions* 1(2): 36–48.

Weiser, M. 1991. The computer for the 21st century. *Scientific American* 265(3): 94–104.

Weiser, M. 1993. Some computer science issues in ubiquitous computing. *Communications of the ACM* 36(7): 75–84.

Wilensky, U. 1993. Connected mathematics: Building concrete relationships with mathematical knowledge. Ph.D. dissertation, MIT Media Lab, Cambridge, MA.

Color Plates

A screen shot of the "patterns" activity in My Personal Tutor Preschool Workshop *(© 1997 Microsoft Corporation), showing final "return" and "levels" icons (on the bottom of the screen) after iterative testing*

Figure 1.8

A child playing with Actimates Interactive Barney (© 1997 Microsoft Corporation; © 1997 Lyons Partnership, L. P.)

Figure **2.4**

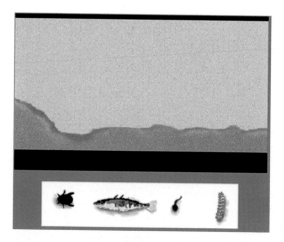

Pond background and creature cutouts used in low-tech prototyping sessions (cutouts not to scale)

Figure **2.6**

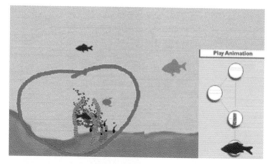

Snapshot taken from "bloodbath" animation, in which the weed eats the fish. The child has deliberately placed the fish and the weed in the wrong places in the food web diagram, resulting in a reversal of normal eating behavior. Chomping sounds recorded from children accompany the animation. The fish also shrinks until it eventually disappears with a loud burp.

Figure **3.4**

A Technology Immersion experience at CHIkids '96

Figure **3.6**

A "low-tech prototype" from an example Participatory Design session at ACM's CHI '94 conference

Figure **3.9**

An early version of KidPad: a zooming storytelling tool, first developed at the University of New Mexico, which continues to be developed at the University of Maryland

Figure **4.1**

Asthma education video game, Bronkie the Bronchiasaurus. Bronkie the Bronchi-asaurus Video Game ©KIDZ Health Software, Inc.

Figure **4.5**

Bronkie finding an emergency meds inhaler that he can use to improve his peak flow the next time he bumps into too many asthma triggers

Figure **5.4**

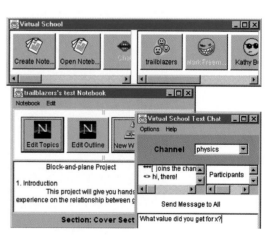

Virtual school task bar, chat, and notebook

Figure **5.5**

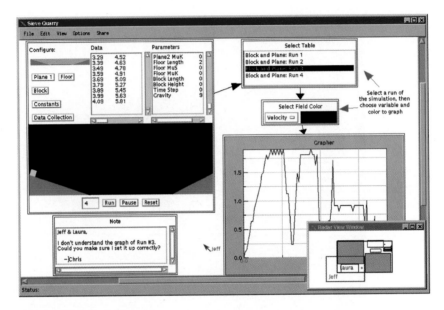

Virtual school workbench

Figure **6.1**

Example of simulation design

Figure **7.1**

Figure **6.3**

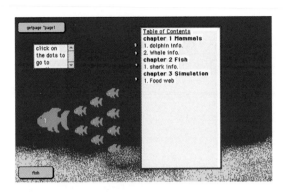

Example of information design

Three fifth-grade students show off their LEGO dinosaur, including a knapsack to carry its Programmable Brick

Figure **7.4**

Dancing Crickets

Figure **8.1**

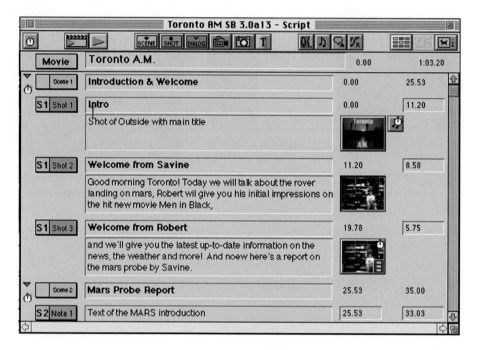

A MAD script view. The first scene of the Toronto AM *movie is composed of three shots, an "Introduction" and two "Welcome" sections. The script text located in the center column has a field for the title of each movie segment and a field for narration, dialogue, and director's notes. MAD supports a hierarchic structure in which movies can be composed of shots inside scenes inside acts. These are displayed in the left column. The right column contains the media elements: graphical images, poster frames depicting video sequences, and icons indicating the presence of narration, dialogue, music, and sound effects. This column also contains timing information—the start time and duration of each segment. Above the script, a control bar provides easy access to commonly used commands.©1998 University of Toronto. Used with permission.*

Figure **8.2**

A MAD storyboard view. Successive shots from Toronto AM appear in this view. As with all MAD views, components of the movie can be added, removed, and rearranged, and the view can be tailored to suit the circumstances. For example, we can request smaller poster frames in order to see a larger number of shots. ©1998 University of Toronto. Used with permission.

Figure **9.1**

Olivia Owl, created by a 10-year-old girl. You control the owl and try to catch mice under the snow. The owl flaps its wings, the mouse turns around if it sees you coming, and the owl burps when it eats its meal.

Figure **9.2**

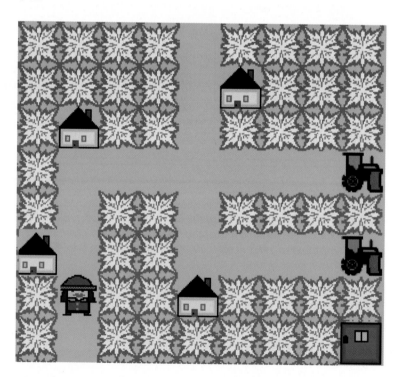

Too much snow, created by an 11-year-old girl. You wait for the snow plows to finish plowing and then move Jessi through the town until she finds the house with the snow shovel. Then shovel through the snowflakes to get to the door.

Figure **10.1**

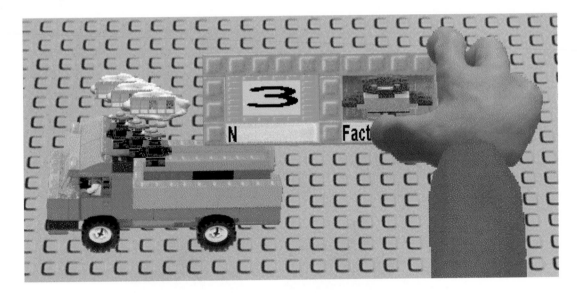

A truck being loaded

Figure **10.2**

The injured alien introducing the fourth puzzle

Figure **11.3**

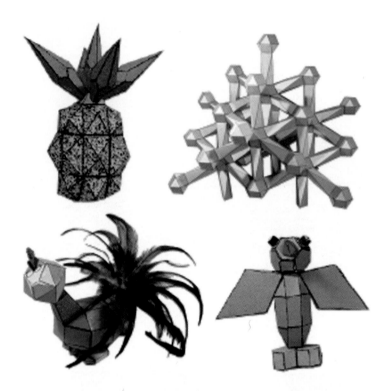

HyperGami constructions. Upper left: *a HyperGami "pineapplehedron";* upper right: *a lattice figure composed of cuboctahedra (as nodes) and antiprisms (as struts);* lower left: *a polyhedral sculpture of a rooster by a middle school student;* lower right: *a duck with "radioactive green feet" by a fifth grader.*

Figure **11.7**

A Cricket-operated color display. Light shines through three water tanks filled (via pumps) with blue-, red-, and yellow-tinted water. The pumps are operated by Crickets, causing the water tanks to fill and empty in programmable patterns.

Chapter Eight

Children as Digital Motion Picture Authors

Ronald Baecker

Collaborative Multimedia Research Group,
Dynamic Graphics Project Laboratory,
Department of Computer Science and
Knowledge Media Design Institute,
University of Toronto

Ilona Posner

Collaborative Multimedia Research Group,
Dynamic Graphics Project Laboratory,
Department of Computer Science and
Knowledge Media Design Institute,
University of Toronto

8.1 Introduction

When left to themselves, most children engage in make-believe fantasies, transport themselves to imaginary worlds through television and movies, play games and sports, chat and gossip, and just hang out. When guided by adults, as in school, they read and write, listen to lectures, do research, answer questions, solve mathematics problems, and engage in artistic pursuits. Unfortunately, only in ideal circumstances do they engage in and carry out projects that are meaningful to them.

The personal computer revolution of the last two decades has enhanced the speed and flexibility with which children can write and edit papers and with which they can do research and structure the knowledge developed in group projects (Scardamalia and Bereiter 1993). Yet many students in many schools are not motivated by the activities that adults and teachers think are valuable. Is there a way to harness the passions of youth so that they can engage in projects that have clear educational benefits and that are also engaging to them?

The premise of this chapter is that authoring and creating motion pictures is compelling to children and educationally valuable in a wide variety of ways. Until recently, the process and technology of motion picture creation was too difficult and too expensive to allow access to any but the most dedicated, such as the young Steven Spielberg. Yet recent advances in computer-based multimedia have allowed for the possibility that many children could have physical, cognitive, and economic access to filmmaking.

We begin with a brief account of filmmaking and digital media creation by children. We then summarize our user-centered, iterative design and development over the past 6 years of the novel Movie Authoring and Design (MAD) system.* We report on MAD's use in two multimedia summer camps in which groups of seventh graders made movies with the support of high school counselors and our research staff. Impacts on the campers are described in the children's own voices. We conclude by extrapolating from these experiences to a vision of significant, educationally valuable, project-based digital filmmaking activities by children, working individually in homes and schools and working collaboratively with others located throughout the world.

---

*The Movie Authoring and Design System described in this chapter is in the process of being commercialized. For information, write *rmb@dgp.toronto.edu* or see *www.dgp.utoronto.ca/CMRG/Projects/MADhp.html* or *www.expresto.com*. The commercial system looks slightly different from what is portrayed in this chapter.

8.2 History and Theory

Children today spend significantly more time watching TV and movies than they do reading. Yet students are not learning to express themselves in the dominant media (Reilly 1996):

> The essential medium of expression in the classrooms is no longer print. It's a hybrid of print, video, audio and video games, but unless we provide access to the tools to compose in this medium, we will be training students to be readers but not writers. And if all they do is read these multimedia texts, not only will they have sore eyes, they will be missing out on an important part of what it means to be literate.

There is very little literature describing studies of children creating media (but see [Buckingham 1990; Paley 1995]). An exception is Reilly (1994, 1996), who documents innovative uses of multimedia authoring at several California high schools as a part of the Apple Classrooms of Tomorrow program. The students create video essays, music videos, and public service announcements, using conventional text-editing software and video-editing equipment.

The conventional filmmaking process is very complex. It is typically a linear flow from pre-production (idea development, script writing, and location and set design), to production (shooting the film or video material), through to post-production (editing and the addition of music, special effects, titles, and credits). It involves a variety of technologies and specialized techniques that deal with disparate media—text, still images, sound, and moving images. It is expensive and difficult for a single individual to master and control. It is hard for those who are not Spielbergs to envision the result until they are near the end of the long process.

Filmmaking has therefore been a boutique item in the school system, expensive, rarely available, and rarely used. We set out to change this because, as we shall illustrate in this chapter, we believe that filmmaking can satisfy our goals of engagement and educational value.

Our MAD system was designed to assist hierarchical development and organization of movie ideas and components such as scripts, pictures, audio, and video; to support their manipulation in a unified manner that is easy to learn and use; and to aid visualization of the ultimate result (Baecker et al. 1996; Cohen et al. 1996; Friedlander et al. 1996; Posner, Baecker, and Homer 1997; Rosenthal and Baecker 1994; Rosenthal 1995). It is therefore useful for both experienced and novice filmmakers, including, in our experience, children as young as 7 years old.

We assert, as does Reilly, that children benefit by being able to express their ideas in movies and that digital media can provide rapid learning opportunities and access to filmmaking tools previously reserved for experts. The idea development, organizational structuring, and visualization capabilities of MAD provide benefits above and beyond those present in conventional consumer digital video editing. MAD is a tool that fits Papert's description of constructionism (Papert 1991, 1):

> ConstructioNism—the N word as opposed to the V word—shares constructiVism's connotation of learning as "building knowledge structures" irrespective of the circumstances of the learning. It then adds the idea that this happens especially felicitously in a context where the learner is consciously engaged in constructing a public entity, whether it's a sand castle on the beach or a theory of the universe.

We wanted to study and test these hypotheses in a controlled but realistic setting. Before presenting the results of our study of the use of MAD in two multimedia summer camps, we shall describe the technology and our design process in more detail.

8.3 Technology and Design Process

MAD introduces a paradigm shift in the making of motion pictures. It allows the easy intermingling of pre-production, production, and post-production. It allows film concepts to be made tangible, demonstrable, and accessible in a way not possible with traditional technologies. It encourages tight artistic control by an "author" over all aspects of a production—words, images, and music. It also encourages the interaction by members of a creative team through an artifact representing the planned production in a way not possible with traditional technologies, in which words, music, still images, and moving pictures appear in separate media.

Technology

In short, MAD is the first system that allows the design and management of words, images, sounds, and video for visualization during the pre-production, production, and post-production phases of motion picture development. Key design goals were

Figure **8.1**

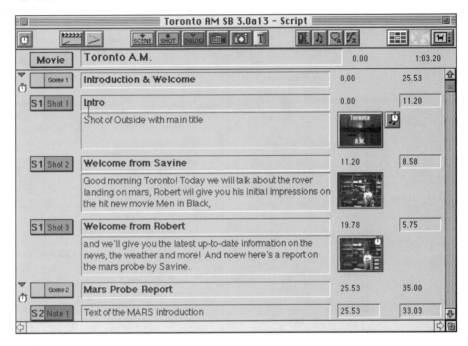

A MAD script view. The first scene of the Toronto AM *movie is composed of three shots, an "Introduction" and two "Welcome" sections. The script text located in the center column has a field for the title of each movie segment and a field for narration, dialogue, and director's notes. MAD supports a hierarchic structure in which movies can be composed of shots inside scenes inside acts. These are displayed in the left column. The right column contains the media elements: graphical images, poster frames depicting video sequences, and icons indicating the presence of narration, dialogue, music, and sound effects. This column also contains timing information— the start time and duration of each segment. Above the script, a control bar provides easy access to commonly used commands. ©1998 University of Toronto. Used with permission.*

- *Ease of learning and ease of use:* The ability to start working productively within a few minutes and to be proficient without the need for a manual or ongoing help from an expert

- *Hierarchic idea structuring:* The ability to develop movie ideas both top-down and bottom-up, to modify the structure with ease as new ideas arise, and to work at various levels of detail

- *Multimedia support:* The integrated handling of scripts (Figure 8.1 [see also Color Plate]), dialogue or narration, music, sound effects, storyboards (Figure 8.2 [see also Color Plate]), and video, and of commentaries on these elements, all

Figure 8.2

A MAD storyboard view. Successive shots from Toronto AM *appear in this view. As with all MAD views, components of the movie can be added, removed, and rearranged, and the view can be tailored to suit the circumstances. For example, we can request smaller poster frames in order to see a larger number of shots. ©1998 University of Toronto. Used with permission.*

accessible through appropriate representations and specialized editors (for example, script and storyboard editors) and all linked to the underlying hierarchic film structure and to a common multimedia database

- *Visualization:* The inclusion of aids to visualizing the film—for example, being able to request a real-time preview of the movie (Figure 8.3) or the best approximation to it at any stage in the film development process

- *Interchange representations:* The provision of mechanisms for importing, exporting, and sharing movies and parts of movies, to allow individuals to communicate to others about their work and to collaborate with others on projects

Figure 8.3

A MAD playback view. Visuals from Toronto AM *appear on the left; narration, dialogue, and director's notes are shown on the right. In this picture we see one of the images downloaded from the Web by the students. We can play back the movie, scan forward and backward in time, or jump from shot to shot much as we would flip through the chapters of a book. The controls at the top right provide users fast access to other views.* ©1998 University of Toronto. Used with permission.

MAD differs from other pre-production filmmaking tools such as script-writing software by including multimedia support and visualization capabilities. It differs from multimedia authoring tools in providing strong support for film narrative and dialogue structure (Baecker et al. 1996).

Design Process

Because MAD enables fundamental changes in the ways films can be made, we had to build and refine a working and functional (not "smoke and mirrors") prototype in order to convey the concept before we could make good use of domain expertise and user feedback. We therefore adopted a user testing methodology (McGrath 1995) that eschewed the internal validity of standardized designed tasks in favor of the external validity of mostly qualitative observations of free-form exploration by users working on real films. We have employed a variety of interview and observational techniques to study and learn from our users' experiences. Adults, university students, and children have used MAD in over sixty 1- to 20-minute filmmaking projects; most of our work has been done with 12- to 14-year-old children.

Our development has gone through three major stages:

1.   Design and construction in the C programming language of a working bare-bones prototype of the concept. Carried out as an M.Sc. thesis project (Rosenthal and Baecker 1994; Rosenthal 1995), MAD 1 allowed us to create a few short movies and to understand both the strengths and weaknesses of our initial approach (Baecker et al. 1996).

2.   Design and construction in the C++ programming language of a more elaborate production prototype. Carried out by part-time professional programmers and students, MAD 2 was robust enough to enable the creation of several dozen short movies in our lab and in two multimedia camps that we ran at the University of Toronto Schools in the summers of 1996 and 1997 (Baecker et al. 1996; Posner, Baecker, and Homer 1997). Careful observation of work in these projects brought significant new understandings in key areas of the design.

3.   Design and construction in the Java programming language of a production version of the concept. Carried out by professional programmers and students, MAD 3 is currently undergoing beta testing pursuant to its becoming a commercial product.

In carrying out these developments, we have constructed dozens of screen prototypes with Adobe Photoshop, Macromedia Director, and other prototyping media. We have given hundreds of demonstrations to educators, film and video professionals, and individuals interested in media, and then listened carefully to their reactions. We have administered questionnaires to most of our users, interviewed them, watched them work, videotaped them, and worked closely with them. We have transcribed and analyzed hours of interview and video data about product and process. (Further details about our methods of data collection and analysis appear later in this chapter.)

The two multimedia summer camps were therefore particularly suggestive sources of insight about the potential of digital video authoring in the classroom. In this chapter we shall focus primarily on qualitative results from both camps.

8.4 Use of Technology

In the summers of 1996 and 1997, seventh-grade students from Scarborough, a Toronto suburb, were selected by lottery to come to the multimedia summer camp for 1 week. At the camp they learned about computers and filmmaking and produced short movies (Figure 8.4).

The students came from different schools and had diverse educational and cultural backgrounds. Their computer experience ranged from none at all to having grown up using computers. The counselors were high school students from the host school who learned the software and the technology just prior to the camp. Three counselors were present both summers.

Camp Process

Each summer camp ran for 2 weeks. Twelve campers aged 13 years old attended each week, 5.5 hours per day. Campers were divided into four groups. We controlled for computer experience and gender and tried to ensure that group members were from different schools.

The first summer we conducted a controlled experiment to evaluate the effect of multimedia tools on the filmmaking process. Groups used two different systems—MAD and conventional digital video-editing software—to create two movies, each one using a different system. Following the completion of their first movie, the campers previewed the movies for their peers and listened to a lecture by a professional filmmaker addressing some of the problems encountered in their moviemaking. Midweek they switched software and created a second movie.

Analysis of the quantitative and qualitative data (see below) yielded interesting results (Posner, Baecker, and Homer 1997). For example, we discovered that children quickly learned moviemaking, regardless of their technical skills and computer background, and brought great imagination and creativity to the task. Their skill and the quality of their creations improved markedly from their first to their second films and were significantly impacted by the work of their counselors. Additional work done in the idea generation and script-writing phase resulted in films of higher quality. MAD proved to be both useful and usable and was preferred by the children over the conventional digital video-editing solution.

After examining these results, we decided to modify our approach. Carrying out the controlled experiment had forced us to give only minimal feedback to the students, with an attendant cost to the quality of the students' experience and the movies they produced. In the second camp, therefore, we gave the campers more time and more in-depth feedback during their work, and we did qualitative, ethnographic observations only. Each group made one movie during the week. We gave constructive criticism to the groups at various stages of their work.

Figure **8.4**

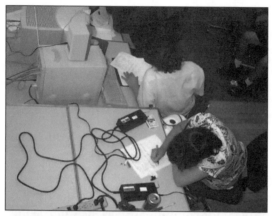

Kids at work. Seventh-grade students at the multimedia summer camp, writing their scripts, digitizing video segments, and presenting their movies to their peers. ©1998 University of Toronto. Used with permission.

Data Collection and Analysis

More specifically, we collected in both camps large amounts of qualitative data using questionnaires, audio and video journals, digital records, paper artifacts, and group discussions:

- *Background questionnaires:* We asked about campers' experience with technology (e.g., video games, VCRs, video cameras), computers, moviemaking, other interests, and group work experience. Knowledge about filmmaking was assessed before, during, and after the camp.

- *Daily questionnaires:* At the end of each day the students filled out questionnaires describing the day's activities, what they learned that day, and the activities they enjoyed most and least.

- *Interactive feedback sessions:* A teacher and a researcher met with each group several times during the week to discuss movie topics, review the groups' progress, stimulate critical thinking and discussion, and suggest possible improvements.

- *Final questionnaires and group debriefings:* At the end of the week all campers filled out a questionnaire describing their experience, evaluating the software, and providing feedback. A group discussion and debriefing session was also held with each group at the end of camp.

In the first camp we also collected quantitative product and process data (Posner, Baecker, and Homer 1997):

- *Analysis of movies and artifacts produced during movie creation:* We kept the campers' paper artifacts, including rough notes of brainstorming ideas, storyboards, and scripts, as well as original film footage and copies of all final films. All digital records and files were saved (approximately 600 MB/movie), including scripts, digitized video segments, and versions of the movies. We analyzed movie and script structure using a detailed quantitative evaluation form. Movie quality was rated by three "experts"—one filmmaker and two avid movie viewers.

- *Process data:* The counselors kept records of their groups' work using paper activity calendars and audio journals. We collected video journals of the first 2 hours of work on each movie, six of which were analyzed (Posner, Baecker, and Homer 1997). We visualized the process information by combining data from calendars, audio journal transcripts, observers' notes, and digital timestamps on files to produce activity plots with categories such as brainstorming, script writing, filming, digitizing and compressing, editing, and Internet searching.

Campers' Accomplishments

The majority of the campers had never made a movie before and had little computer experience. After a short time and with modest support, they were able to produce creative and interesting films that they were very proud to show. They quickly learned about scripts, storyboards, locations, sound, camera angles, directing, editing, and getting video from the Internet.

They used these new skills to create interesting, and in some cases even insightful and educational, movies:

- A variety of fiction thrillers about man-haunting monsters, robots taking over the earth, and kids getting sucked into video games

- A music video countdown show

- A magazine format show about Toronto (Figure 8.5)

- A public service announcement about treating and preventing choking

- A talk show debating cars versus public transit

- A parody of the television show *The X-Files* (Figure 8.6)

- An advertisement

- A film introducing the school in which the camp was being held (Figure 8.7)

- A movie about a bomb blowing up in a school and the value of freedom

Figure 8.5

Toronto AM. *A magazine format program featuring news, weather, sports, entertainment, and advertising.* ©1998 University of Toronto. Used with permission.

Figure **8.6**

The Z-Files. *A science fiction spoof of the popular* X-Files *series. ©1998 University of Toronto. Used with permission.*

Figure **8.7**

UTS: A Journey. *A walking tour and historical look at the school. ©1998 University of Toronto. Used with permission.*

8.5 Impact of Technology

The children were engaged and exhibited lots of creativity. They learned many new computer, filmmaking, and group skills. They provided evidence of the educational value of filmmaking and evidence that MAD's basic concepts are powerful and appropriate.

Engagement and Creativity

For example, the movie entitled *UTS: A Journey* (Figure 8.7) described the history of the host school. The campers visited the school Web pages and gathered background information. They then interviewed the school principal and asked him pointed questions about his job and "about why girls were introduced so late at this school."

Another camper whose parents were refugees from Sri Lanka drew on his family's experience to create a movie dealing with the value of freedom. He described his parents' reaction:

> **Ragif:**   "Well, I just told them [parents] it was about freedom and they said it was a good topic to pick. It is a good movie to make because it is showing you some qualities and telling you how the other world is true. People here don't take freedom seriously and it is a shame to see that people here don't take it seriously here in Canada because there is no war. They don't think about the other side of life."

(Please note that the students' names have been changed to preserve anonymity; however, gender differences were preserved.)

No matter what the theme was, the campers showed great creativity in its execution. They interviewed people in the school and people in the street. They brought reference material, props, and costumes from home. They drew maps and figures. Although the software provided did not support any special effects such as wipes or dissolves, the campers' movies included special visual effects such as an earthquake, many kids coming out of one locker, and people disappearing off the screen. Their movie titles were spoken on camera, filmed chalk drawing on the board, typeset video-recorded text, and scrolling hand-drawn titles set to music.

Writing in Film Authoring

The majority of our seventh-graders admitted that they dislike writing essays:

> **Instructor:**   "Does anyone dislike writing papers here?" [All three raise their hands.]
>
> **Tony:**   "Yes . . . Writing essays is boring."
>
> **Ragif:**   "Yeah. Because it [moviemaking] is more interesting. When the teachers tell us to write an essay, the kids are bored. When they introduce something new, it makes them want to do more stuff."

Yet all the campers' movies included a script component. The students did not complain when they had to write these scripts.

Motivation and Dedication

Despite the fact that the students spent an entire week working on their movies, they all felt that the time went quickly and that moviemaking was fun:

David: "It went by faster here [compared to school] . . . It was more fun. It wasn't 'Sit down, here is this work, do it.' It was 'Go out and have fun.'"

Campers were very enthusiastic about their projects. One group worked on their script at camp, then without prompting went home and further refined it. They were very dedicated to their work and tried very hard even without the threat of marks.

Chris: "I think we tried really hard on this one, just as if we were getting marked, but I think if we had more time we would have done better . . . It was hard work, but it was hard work in a fun way."

Groups were extremely motivated to succeed in their projects. Their daily work was very focused and task driven:

A counselor: "They focused quite well. We didn't even have breaks sometimes. This guy stayed until five one day doing clips. On the whole they were interested because it was new to them. Except for the digitizing and the compressing [when the computer is unusable], sometimes they would go play with the camera, but besides that, they were focused 99 percent of the time."

Novelty

Children like playing with new technology "toys," and if they can create something to show their family and friends, then they are even more motivated. When asked, "If you had access to this technology, would you use it?" they replied:

David: "I would be using it every day . . . Anything [any project] that I had the chance to do."

Victor: "You would feel like doing it more. If you were home, and you had this stuff, you wouldn't be sitting around doing nothing . . . instead of watching TV for two hours."

Although we may be observing a Hawthorne effect—anything new is exciting for a while—there is some evidence that, given the opportunity, children would be active moviemakers instead of passive viewers and television consumers.

Movies as School Projects

Several students were under the impression that they would receive higher marks if they submitted a movie project for school than if they used some other presentation method:

> **Chris**: "I think that if I did a movie, my teacher would give me a higher mark, because anybody can write an essay, and how many students do a movie for their project?"

According to the campers, marks were not the only motivation for contemplating a movie project for school. Several campers felt that viewers would learn more from a movie than from another presentation:

> **Ahmed**: "It might take longer, but when you think about it, you are going to get marks for it. It takes longer but it is worth it for the marks."
>
> **Instructor**: "So you think you would get more marks for doing it?"
>
> **Ahmed**: "Yeah."
>
> **Instructor**: "But if you really couldn't get extra marks, would you still want to do it?"
>
> **Ahmed**: "Yeah, I think it is fun. And the audience could learn more about it than just the essay."

Learning

The campers learned about multimedia and MAD; Internet searching and downloading; moviemaking skills such as camera operation, choice of camera angles, and use of sound; digitizing and editing digital video footage; and project management and organization techniques:

> **David**: "Everything was new. How to film and put it on the computer. I never made a movie before or used a video camera or the Internet. I learned how to do research on the Internet."
>
> **Deborah**: "I learned the importance of organization."

How They Learned

The campers learned from their counselors, the camp staff, and especially from one another. In most schools, the computer-to-student ratio often compels sharing, which in many cases allows students to learn from each other and gain comfort to venture out on their own. There are, however, situations where dominant individuals deny access to technology:

> **Tammy** [in response to question, "Have you ever surfed the Internet before?"]: "Not really. Not by myself. I would usually have a friend with me and she would use it. I would sit there and watch."

The counselors encouraged equal participation by all group members, enabling Tammy to get hands-on experience:

Tammy: "It [the Internet] is fun. You can learn a lot from it!"

By grouping together students from different schools, we tried to avoid biases that students have toward their classmates and to allow everyone equal opportunity to interact with the technology.

Learning about Filmmaking

In the span of 1 week, working on one or two short movies, the campers learned much about filmmaking, filming, and editing and became more discriminating movie viewers.

Most campers had never made a video and many of them had never used a video camera before the camp. At the end of the week, they were comfortable with using a camera:

Mark: "Things I learned were how to use a camcorder; I never knew. I thought they were high tech and crazy things and I didn't know how to use them. Now I know how to use them. I always wondered how in the movie they always did the graphics and all the different overhead shots and camera angles, and I learned them this week."

The campers started out as average movie viewers, who seldom notice technical aspects of movies such as shot compositions, camera angles, lighting changes, and background sounds. In the second camp, after initial work on the movies, we conducted an in-depth analysis of one short segment of a popular movie. The campers were then able to work more professionally and view their own movies more critically:

Chris: "Well, you know how you showed us the Batman movie. I never looked at it like that. I watched the movie and I didn't really look how they had so many cameras. I went home, I was watching movies, and I noticed them now."

Tommy: "We started breaking the filming up into different segments . . . We filmed the guy coming out of the subway station, we didn't watch him cross the road and put the camera down. We stopped and did each thing a couple of times to get it right. We mixed a couple of parts. If the first part of one segment was good, and the last part of the second, we'd mix the two."

After making their movie, the campers gained a profound appreciation of moviemaking. They learned how long it takes to make a movie; how many takes are required to perfect a shot; and how to recognize problems with camera work, lighting, sets, and sound:

> **Andrew:** "Usually when you go out for a movie, you just go, but you don't know how many times they have to take that little thing over again. It may just be a cat walking by, but then they have to take it so many times because they want the cat to walk the right way . . . Usually you just sit down and watch the movie."

> **Ahmed:** "I used to think movies were just camera shooting, but now I found out that you can put it on the computer and do special effects on it."

> **Raymond:** "[Moviemaking is] hard. More than it is cracked up to be. [More] work."

Group Work

Campers learned about both the advantages and disadvantages of group work and developed effective approaches to the distribution of the work. In general, they grew to appreciate the need for team effort in filmmaking, a complex task involving many different kinds of activities.

Advantages and Disadvantages

Campers encountered many advantages and some disadvantages of group work. They appreciated the ability to share the workload, to develop new friendships, and to increase the number of ideas:

> **Andrew:** "There were three minds so it is better than one!"

Yet some students dislike group work because of the difficulty in reaching consensus:

> **Alfred:** "It is easier to work alone than with other people because you can agree on everything."

Others minded not having their ideas used and disliked arguments. However, the main opposition to group work resulted from varied levels of commitment among participants:

> **Chris:** "I don't usually like working in groups. I like to work by myself, unless there is somebody that I know who would work really hard with me. I have

been in groups before and nobody would work, and I would be the only person. They would put everything on me and I would be so angry."

Work Distribution

We observed several approaches to the distribution of group work. In most groups we witnessed campers taking turns on most activities. One group developed a rotating system:

> **David**: "We all took rotations. We had three different chairs. Every time we edited one scene, we would switch."

In some cases the counselors would assign tasks, trying to ensure equal division of labor. Individuals' expertise and preferences were also taken into account in dividing the work. For example, some campers who felt uncomfortable in front of the camera became camera operators.

Group Work in Filmmaking

The campers quickly came to appreciate the complexity of the moviemaking process and the varied roles that are required for a successful production. When asked if they would choose to work on another movie either alone or in a group, all but one said they'd prefer group work—including those who earlier expressed a dislike of group work.

The Educational Value of Moviemaking

Moviemaking is a generic tool for expression and communication. It can be used for school projects in English, drama, history, geography, and science. Campers expressed an interest in using moviemaking for their schoolwork:

> **Paul**: "An information project. If we had to tell a lower grade about something."

> **Victor**: "If you are doing a book report, you can put in little movie clips to act out what you are saying, so people can see it."

Moviemaking has educational value, providing an alternative method for creative and informative expression. Students can become authors in the media they consume constantly.

More Interesting and Memorable Presentations

Students felt that their peers would better attend to video presentations and take them more seriously:

> **Samantha:**   "With this you just have to show it and people will learn more because it is visual and it is easier to learn than just reading . . . because it is more interesting to look at a video than hearing."

> **Victor:**   "[Compared to writing] if you are filming and editing, it would take longer to film but it would come out much better."

Campers were asked, "Who finds it interesting, the author or the audience?"

> **Andrew:**   "Both of us [are more interested] . . . I think it is fun. And the audience could learn more about it than just the essay. . . If you have it digitized, you can show your project, and it is even better because you can see and experience it."

Many campers felt that they would learn better from a video presentation than from an aural one.

> **Samantha:**   "You have to write it up on a science board and present it, but if you had this software at school, you could just do a video and then show it to the class, and people would listen better and learn better."

Ability to Perfect a Presentation

Perfectionists with high quality standards expressed interest in creating movie presentations for school projects:

> **Tommy:**   "If we had the camera, we could fix all the stuff we did wrong and do it over again until we get it right."

Some students felt movie presentations would help them ensure that all group members, especially those with immature tendencies to be silly in class, could be allowed to perform properly:

> **Chris:**   "It depends on who the people are. If they can't act appropriately in front of people, it is better to do it on camera because if they goof up or act stupid, we can just take it out and do it over again."

Improved Self-Expression

Many individuals in society do not have an opportunity to present their best image because their behaviors are inhibited by having an audience. Removing the live audience at the time of the performance can reduce these inhibitions. Individuals can use the privacy of the electronic environment to prepare their presentations without embarrassment and to refine them until the desired result is reached. They have complete freedom and control to create the script, refine and rewrite it, act it out, and produce the final presentation.

> **Ragif**: "And the good thing about this is that you can come up with your own ideas instead of someone thinking for you and then you just acting . . . Because it is good to act what you believe in."

Many students shy of presenting in front of their peers said they preferred to use movies instead of live performances:

> **Alfred**: "I would try to use it [movies] on ones that I would have to present in front of people . . ."

> **Instructor**: "So, even if it takes you more time to prepare, if you had a choice of presenting in front of your class or doing a movie, which would you do?"

> **Alfred**: "I would do a movie."

Exploiting and Recognizing Different Talents

Filmmaking is a task generally done in groups. There are many roles in moviemaking; various talents, abilities, preferences, and technical expertise can contribute to a successful collaborative project. The campers utilized their different talents during moviemaking:

> **David**: "We used her artistic abilities for the pop cans [creating movie props], and Marta was pretty fast at typing, so she did most of the typing."

Team Building

The majority of the campers enjoyed working in groups. Creating a movie in a group was a rewarding experience:

> **David**: "I wouldn't like to make a movie by myself. It would be boring because there would be only one character, and I would have to change my clothes every time."

Smooth moviemaking depends on good group work:

> **Gabriel:** "[I would work with a group] because when you are filming you have to work together."

Although our campers started out as strangers, working in groups helped develop friendships:

> **Kimberly:** "Yeah, it is too short. As you become friends with people, it is the last day, and as soon you get to know people, you have to leave."

Despite the different roles played by various campers, they typically felt that all group members had contributed equally to the movie:

> **Mark:** "I think everybody did the same, even though Christa wasn't in the movie, she was videotaping it all. That is just as important as acting."

In one case, however, where one male camper dominated most of the group activity, two female members did not want to work on another movie with the same group.

Deglamourizing Hollywood

Campers left with a new appreciation of camera, sound, and editing techniques, and work in and behind the scenes. Their 1-week experience moved them somewhat from being passive consumers, absorbing media and its messages, toward becoming informed and discerning viewers.

Evaluation of MAD

The campers' impressions of the MAD software were mostly positive. They found the software easy to use and the script helpful for organizing their multimedia documents, despite some discouraging moments dealing with the technical difficulties inherent in experimental software.

MAD Is Easy to Learn and Use

The campers' feedback suggested that we succeeded in our goal of making MAD easy for novices to learn and use:

> **Chris:** "I don't have a computer at home and we don't use it much at our school that much. For my first time using it, I thought it was pretty cool and easy."

The Script View Is Powerful

During moviemaking, the campers worked primarily in the script view. They wrote scripts, attached video segments, or shots, to elements of the script, previewed the result, and rearranged the elements. They found the layout of the script very helpful.

Samantha: "It is easier to do the script rather than doing it in [my normal word processor]. It is a lot easier to read off of . . ."

Raymond: "Everything is there right in front of you . . ."

Ahmed: "It is better with the pictures there because the script goes with the pictures . . ."

MAD Helps with Organization and Navigation

MAD's structured approach to movie authoring allows novices to get a grasp of all related media and to be able to organize various components into a whole:

Tammy: "It was easier to organize things in MAD because there are places to put everything. Those places to write in, and the space to put the videos and pictures."

Gabriel: "I think it is neat that you can do item by item instead of just going from one camera shot angle to the next one so it is not bunched together. You can do them one at a time."

Breaking up large problems into smaller manageable ones is a skill that the campers can use in many other situations.

The structured organization also facilitates navigation through the movie and access to its segments:

Andrew: "I like the fact that, if you make a movie, you have to look at the whole movie to check a little thing, but if you know the mistake is in MAD, you just go to that one and click on it, and it will preview it for you. You can know that is the one with the mistake and you can fast-forward to that part and fix the mistake in it."

Samantha: "Rather than having to type everything up and figure out where your part is, it is a lot easier to go straight to where you are. It is easy to organize audio and video clips and to edit it."

MAD Supports Creativity

MAD aids users in manipulating all aspects of the movie, encouraging experimentation and refinement and thereby improving quality. One camper who had previous experience with video editing found the digital video much easier to work with:

> **Paul**: "It was really easy to edit. All you had to do was find out where you wanted to cut out. Put the cursor there, hold shift, and drag it to the other part . . . Compared to put it on the other screen [as in videotape editing]. Having two different screens and having to coordinate where it is."

The flexibility provided by the digital representation and the ease of changing the script at any time allowed the campers to evolve their movies and adjust to their audience feedback.

> **Mark**: "We added a couple things. We didn't write them in the script, but when we watched the movie it looked kind of boring, so we added a couple musical numbers and some pictures . . . You could write down your ideas, so you have the general idea, but you don't have to be limited."

Another group wrote a script but as they worked on the movie they "totally changed it around."

> **Victor**: "It makes it more interesting and it brings out the real thing."

8.6 Summary, Issues, Opportunities, and Future Directions

The two multimedia summer camps and our other work with MAD strongly suggest that digital video authoring can be an important new kind of children's technology. We shall support this assertion by summarizing the chapter, presenting current issues in the design, development, and use of MAD, and describing new directions for future work.

Summary

Digital video authoring enables students to learn about research, writing, organization, computers, the Internet, moviemaking, filming techniques, and editing. Students develop group work skills, an appreciation for the amount of work involved, and an understanding that movies are not "real." MAD is easy to use for first film projects and helpful in organizing and managing the movie's structure and constituent media elements. The digital representation allows easy experimentation and manipulation of the elements and facilitates creative expression.

The students are able to produce meaningful and educational movies, and they feel these would be taken more seriously by their peers than other types of presentations. Movies allow individuals to perfect their presentations and to avoid live performances if they are shy. The accessibility and flexibility of this creative medium and the camaraderie of group work increases motivation for filmmaking and results in great dedication to the task despite any technical difficulties that are encountered. Moviemaking and multimedia authoring can enhance self-expression and seduce students who normally hate writing into writing scripts without complaints. The students find these experiences extremely exciting and rewarding— "one week is not enough!"

Issues and Problems to Be Solved

Yet digital video authoring will only achieve its potential in the classroom if a number of problems are solved: overcoming technical glitches with complex multimedia software; providing sufficient resources; enabling a movie to be authored in just a few hours; and developing the culture of criticism, patience, and hard work required to produce films of sufficient quality to reflect the students' potential to achieve quality.

Students Must Achieve Proficiency and Overcome Technical Problems

Campers with little technical knowledge found the experience challenging:

> **Experimenter**: "Did you find it easy to use, especially considering your [lack of] experience?"

> **David**: "So so, because I don't use computers. At first it was really hard."

With time they became more comfortable and successfully completed their projects.

The MAD software used at the camps was a pre-alpha version with many bugs. The campers were frustrated by system crashes and other technical difficulties. Some features that they wanted to use, such as special effects and transitions, were not yet available.

As the complexity of a task increases, so does the number of possible problems. Moviemaking on the computer involves a lot of technology, and there were times when some of it would not function properly. Counselors' inexperience also led to a couple of problems that could have been resolved with more extensive and focused training.

Adequate Resources Must Be Available

Because access to technology can be a bottleneck, it is best if each group or movie has a separate machine. Disk space is a major concern, especially if several groups share one machine. Students are painfully aware of the shortages of technology in their schools:

> **Paul** [when asked if he would use MAD in school]: "It would be full and I would never get to use it because everyone else would use it."

Moviemaking Is Time-Consuming

The campers spent a week to create 5-minute movie presentations.

> **Gabriel**: "If the teacher is only going to give you two days, I would write it out because I wouldn't have enough time to put a presentation together. This one is only four minutes and it took us five days to do it. I wouldn't be able to do a ten-minute presentation in two days."

Although we believe that work can go two to four times faster with software that is stable and that possesses more functionality, the time available for school projects does constrain how filmmaking can be used in school:

> **Tony**: "At school I am always begging the teachers for more time, but they never gave us any. There is only a certain amount of time you can spend on a project because there is much other stuff that we have to do."
>
> **Samantha**: "It is time-consuming to do this."
>
> **Instructor**: "Would it still be worth it?"
>
> **Samantha**: "Yes, if the teacher gave us that much time."

Since multimedia projects often require extended amounts of time, it is hard to fit the work into short one-period segments. Schools must be organized to allow project work to be completed. Some of our students expressed a willingness to work after school to finish their movies.

> **Richard**: "You would probably have to do it after hours at school."

Moviemaking Is Harder Than Essay Writing

Moviemaking requires new skills that students don't normally have:

Ragif: "The acting part is hard. If something that is funny, that is going on, you have to control yourself."

Marlene: "It would be easier to write an essay [than to make a movie]."

One counselor explained why moviemaking is difficult:

Counselor: "But I think that is because there has been so much emphasis on you have to write an essay that people have got so much practice with it. They are so comfortable with it. And since very few people have made movies before, it is new, and it is harder."

Achieving Quality Requires Skill and Persistence

The time factor is especially critical when a group has high standards for the quality of their movie. At the camp we witnessed two extremes.

One group refused to refilm their video footage although they were unhappy with its quality.

Ahmed: "The thing is, I heard that you have to do every scene over and over again, but here, it is for fun, so you don't have to do it over again."

They also refused to discard any ideas. Instead of focusing their energy on one topic, they used all their original footage, combined the two topics that they had brainstormed, and edited the result to fit the desired maximum length of 5 minutes:

Ahmed: "There are actually two parts. One part is entertainment wise, and the other one gives knowledge wise. It gives you information. We took the two aspects of TV: entertainment and documentary, and we put it together to make our movie."

On the other extreme, another group created a short movie, only 1 minute long, and iteratively revised and refined it. They wrote a detailed script and filmed multiple versions of each shot, including one shot that required eight takes. Following the discussion of moviemaking techniques, they chose to edit the video footage carefully:

David: "In one of the scenes, every time somebody else speaks, it [the camera] is changing back and forth, so there are four different times we change it in five seconds!"

When the lighting was imperfect, they reshot the video sequences. They listened to the instructors' feedback and incorporated a new shot using an overhead camera angle. These improvements required extra time, which they could only afford because the movie was short.

Tools like MAD that facilitate easy and rapid reworking and editing of digital video must be used so that students can create quality projects and show them with pride to media-savvy peers.

> **Gabriel:**   "I was really surprised at how it came out because I wasn't expecting it to come out that good. I was expecting it to look like a low-budget one that someone spent two days doing, but it turned out really good for what I was expecting."

Effect of the Work with Children on Our Technology Design

Clearly, the children pushed and challenged the then-current limits of our technology. By analyzing our data, but to a greater extent just by watching, listening, and thinking about what we have seen and heard, we have learned a lot that has allowed us to improve our design. Here are a few examples:

- The children requested new functionality—for example, the ability to record to a VCR, to add titles, and to sketch overlays, as well as many other ideas still under development or consideration.

- Watching our users work suggested simplifications to the conceptual structure and mental model associated with a MAD movie, namely, the use of a three-level hierarchy of acts, scenes, and shots in place of an arbitrarily deep nested hierarchy.

- Watching our users work suggested the need for improved interfaces to existing functionality (e.g., to the film clip editor).

- Watching where the campers and counselors had trouble and how they spent their time suggested pragmatic needs (e.g., easier and safer management of media resources).

Opportunities

MAD allows video authoring to be used in schools in significant and educationally valuable ways:

- Bringing to life projects in traditional subject areas such as history, geography, English, and science by creating video essays

- Learning and working with filmmaking in classes and in dramatic productions

- Analyzing film and video for courses such as science (e.g., recording and analyzing video data on force, mass, and motion), English (e.g., comparisons of versions of *Hamlet*), and media studies (analysis of television techniques and impacts)

- Teaching planning, project management, communication skills, collaborative work, and problem solving using filmmaking as a significant engaging activity

- Combating technophobia by introducing computers through filmmaking activities that are fun and nonthreatening to both children and technophobic adults

- Creating school video yearbooks and class reunion videos

- Documenting school activities with video-enhanced Web pages

- Developing after-school activities and summer camps

- Enhancing the understanding of learning processes by teachers and learners by videotaping, annotating, analyzing, and discussing classroom situations (Cohen et al. 1996)

- Supporting the development of student portfolios in elementary and high schools and student teacher portfolios in teacher training colleges and universities

Movie Authoring as a Vehicle for Improving Literacy

The level of literacy varies greatly among students, as evidenced by large differences in the responses to our questionnaires. Andrew, a very sociable and energetic seventh-grade student, turned in questionnaires riddled with spelling and grammatical errors far below the seventh-grade level. If Andrew writes a story in class, it will be full of errors and will receive a low grade. His reported daily activities indicated that he does little homework, *never* reads, watches a lot of television and videos, and plays sports. Yet multimedia is compelling to children even if they are not interested in reading and writing, and Andrew's extensive viewing habits make him an experienced media consumer. Thus, given the right tools, he may be able to prepare a higher-quality story using a movie than by writing. Perhaps we can "trick" Andrew into writing if he needs to develop a script in order to create a movie. There is some evidence from our camp that this can happen.

Student Excitement

The biggest complaint at the end of summer camp was that the students didn't like to climb three flights of stairs to get to the lab. The campers' dedication, excitement, and emotional involvement with the camp was intense.

When we were unable to make video copies of two of their movies because of technical difficulties, we received repeated distressed and almost threatening phone calls from campers and their parents. Wouldn't it be nice to have students as excited about school as they were about the camp?

> **David**:   "It's a lot of fun to work with MAD making movies. It's one of the best experiences I've had. Peter is an amazing counselor and I had a lot of fun working with him. I think it's really good that you guys are doing something like this . . . A lot of fun. Interesting. I learned a lot. I will come back next year."

> **Mark**:   "IT WAS GREAT!!! . . . Like I said before, it was what I always wanted to do. Act, go to the computer, do editing and directing on the computer and stuff like that . . . It had everything, all my hobbies, except for sports . . . Because I always have said to my mom that I wanted to be an actor or someone to do with computer animation, and this week I got to do everything that I always wanted to do all in one: using the computer, using the camcorder, directing, acting."

> **Deborah**:   "My comment for this camp is please continue this next year so other kids could have the once-in-a-lifetime experience that I had to learn everything about computers."

Future Directions

We are greatly encouraged by our work thus far. We are beginning to experiment with 1- and 2-day multimedia workshops to see if students can learn and develop educationally valuable projects within a single day or two. We are beginning to run workshops for teachers and to work with them to create curriculum-based projects and to develop supporting materials for students and teachers. By turning our prototype software into a product, we hope that it will be used widely in real classroom settings and that we can gather further evidence about the value of digital video authoring for providing meaningful and engaging projects to children, for documenting the products of their research and learning, and for acting as a Trojan horse to seduce them into writing despite their belief that they hate writing.

We are also planning experimental uses of MAD among distributed learning and filmmaking communities and look forward to the day when children throughout the world will be able to create and interact in digital video as they now do with text. Imagine students in northern Ontario, Vancouver Island, Chile, and Russia jointly collaborating on a project dealing with issues of logging, clear-cutting, and reforestation in their various environments. Imagine women in a variety of countries and cultures, all interested in a career in a particular profession, documenting and sharing what it is like to enter that profession, incorporating and sharing interviews and video footage that bring to life experiences in those countries and cultures. Imagining these examples is easy. But our goal in the next year or two is to realize and prove the viability of the vision.

Acknowledgments

We are grateful to the MAD developers, Alan Rosenthal, Eric Smith, Vanessa Williams, Isabel Jevans, Alexandra (Ali) Mazalek, and David Golden for creating and supporting excellent prototypes; Eric for extraordinary technical and software design leadership; Isabel for assistance with design and running of the first camp; Ali for energetic technical and creative assistance during both camps; Mary Alton for superb interface design work; Agnes Oullette for creative filmmaking; Mike Ananny for thorough software testing; Philip Stern and Marylyn Rosenblum for advice and encouragement on the commercial potential of MAD; Ann-Barbara Graff for administrative support; Steve Poplar for organizing the camps and allowing us to use them as a basis for our studies; University of Toronto Schools for providing equipment, facilities, and the support of their students—Prashant, Rosanna, Denis, Eric, Adrienne, Mike, Eli, Jonathan, and Sebastian; Andrew Cohen for helping design the first study, and Bruce Homer for analyzing the data; the campers from the Scarborough Board of Education; and to the CulTech Collaboative Research Centre, the Natural Sciences and Engineering Research Council of Canada, the Information Technology Research Centre (now Communications and Information Technology Ontario), and the Networks of Centres of Excellence on Telelearning of Canada for financial support.

References

Baecker, R., Rosenthal, A., Friedlander, N., Smith, E., and Cohen, A. 1996. A multimedia system for authoring motion pictures. In *Proceedings of ACM Multimedia '96*. Reading, MA: Addison-Wesley, 31–42.

Buckingham, D. 1990. *Watching media learning*. Bristol, PA: Falmer Press.

Cohen, A., Friedlander, N., Baecker, R., and Rosenthal, A. 1996. MAD: A Movie Authoring and Design system—Making classroom process visible. In *Proceedings ICLS 96: International Conference on the Learning Sciences*.

Friedlander, N., Baecker, R., Rosenthal, A., and Smith, E. 1996. MAD: A Movie Authoring and Design system. In *Companion Proceedings to CHI '96.*

McGrath, J. 1995. Methodology matters: Doing research in the behavioral and social sciences. In R. Baecker, J. Grudin, W. Buxton, and S. Greenberg, eds. *Readings in human-computer interaction: Toward the year 2000.* San Francisco: Morgan Kaufmann, 152–169.

Paley, N. 1995. *Finding art's place: Experiments in contemporary education and culture.* London: Routledge.

Papert, S. 1991. Situating constructionism. In I. Harel and S. Papert, eds. *Constructionism.* Norwood, NJ: Ablex, 1.

Posner, I., Baecker, R., and Homer, B. 1997. Children learning filmmaking using multimedia tools. *Proceedings of ED-Media/Telemedia 1997,* book and CD-ROM. Charlottesville, VA: Association for the Advancement of Computing in Education.

Reilly, B. 1994. Composing with images: A study of high school video producers. *Proceedings of Ed-Media 94.* Charlottesville, VA: Association for the Advancement of Computing in Education.

Reilly, B. 1996. New technologies, new literacies, new problems. In C. Fisher, ed. *Education and technology: Reflections on a decade of experience in the classroom.* San Francisco: Jossey-Bass.

Rosenthal, A. 1995. Computer support for authoring motion pictures. M.Sc. Thesis, University of Toronto.

Rosenthal, A., and Baecker, R. 1994. Multimedia for authoring motion pictures. In *Proceedings Graphics Interface '94,* 133–140.

Scardamalia, M., and Bereiter, C. 1993. Technologies for knowledge-building discourse. *Communications of the ACM* 36(5): 37–41.

Chapter Nine

Making Programming Easier for Children

David Canfield Smith

Stagecast Software, Inc.

Allen Cypher

Stagecast Software, Inc.

9.1 Introduction

There is a new approach that now makes it possible to teach children to program computers. We briefly argue in this chapter that it is worthwhile to do so. Some people teach programming because the learner acquires logical thinking skills that apply to other domains of problem solving. That's an acceptable reason in itself, but we think that there is an even more worthwhile goal: programming enables users to get more power out of their computers. Specifically, we are interested in children—and parents and teachers for that matter—creating learning simulations. The benefits of this approach are much greater.

The general problem of programming by novices is a tough one and has resisted solution for three decades. So we decided to attack it in a limited domain—the domain of symbolic simulations. A symbolic (as opposed to numeric) simulation is a computer-controlled microworld made up of individual objects that move around a display screen interacting with each other. Most video games are symbolic simulations. We chose as our target audience children in the age range of 5 to 18 years old (K–12).

Why simulation? Simulation is a powerful tool for education. It makes the abstract concrete. It encourages unstructured exploratory learning, which fosters creativity. It allows children to construct things, supporting the constructivist approach to education. As Alan Kay says, "We build things not just to have them, but to learn about them." The philosopher Cesare Pavese contends: "To know the world, one must construct it." Scardamalia argues that children learn best when constructing things (Scardamalia and Bereiter 1991). Simulation encourages experimenting, helping children to learn the scientific method. Children make hypotheses about what will happen in a simulation, then run it and observe the results. The wonderful thing about simulations—something that never happens with animations—is that their hypotheses can be refuted. When that happens, children become engaged. They lean forward, point to the screen, turn to their partners, and exclaim, "What? Why did that happen?!" They never remain passive. They become actively engaged in problem solving. They must (1) analyze the data to understand what happened, (2) figure out how to change the simulation to get the desired result, (3) form a new hypothesis to predict the outcome, and then (4) conduct a new experiment by running the simulation again. This is the scientific method. It teaches children to think logically and clearly. It fosters peer-to-peer communication as children work together to solve problems. We believe it is the best kind of learning.

One of our favorite descriptions of why we want kids to program computers comes from Ken Kahn (also an author in this book; see Chapter 10):

The neatest thing about computers is that they can be programmed to be so many different things. Software can be made to make computers into fancy typewriters, calculators, drawing and painting media, video-editing equipment, music systems, spell checkers, games, chess players, weather simulations, and so on. The biggest limitation to what software can turn computers into is our imagination. The kind of software for children that really excites me is software that gives this power to children. I would rather see children make computers into neat things than simply use a computer that someone else has turned into a neat thing.

The problem up to now has been that creating computer software is a difficult task, out of the reach of all but professional programmers. It is simply too difficult to program computers. During the past 30 years, there have been many attempts to make it easier. Researchers have invented languages such as Logo, Smalltalk, Basic, Pascal, and HyperTalk. They have developed techniques such as structured programming. They have approached it from a pedagogical perspective with technology such as the goal-plan editor (Soloway 1986) and from an engineering perspective with computer-aided software engineering (CASE) tools. Each of these has made a significant contribution to the process of programming. Yet today only a small percentage of people program computers—certainly less than 10 percent and probably less than 1 percent. The remaining 90+ percent can't or don't want to. A single-digit percentile is not success.

What's the problem? Is programming inherently too difficult for the average person, as some people have suggested? Or have we computer scientists not done a good enough job of making it easy? Or perhaps it *is* easy enough, but educators have not found an effective way to teach it. One possibility that we reject out of hand is that programming is useless to most people. The computer is the most powerful information processing tool ever invented. Yet much of its potential power will remain unattainable as long as people can only use programs written by others. In the 21st century, using computer power effectively will be a survival issue for many. So we think that nearly everyone would program computers if it were easy enough.

We take the position that programming computers is well within the reach of the majority of computer users, and we offer Cocoa as a proof.* Figures 9.1 and 9.2 (Color Plates only) show two Cocoa games that were created by children.

Up until now, there have been two problems with the traditional approach to programming: First, programming forces the user to learn a new language, the programming language. Learning another language is difficult for most people. Consider the years of effort that it takes to master a

*Cocoa is a trademark of Apple Computer, Inc. It is available at *www.stagecast.com*.

foreign language. Second, programming languages are *artificial* rather than *natural* languages. They have a different epistemology. Imagine if, in learning French, say, you also had to learn what a house is, or a car, or food. But that is exactly the case with programming languages. They deal with the unfamiliar world of computer data structures and algorithms. You must not only learn the language, you must also learn how a computer works. This makes programming even less accessible to people.

The solution is to *make programming more like thinking*. In this chapter, we will show how a new approach to programming attempts to do this for children. The key ideas are (1) to use representations in the computer that are analogous to the objects being represented and (2) to allow those representations to be directly manipulated in the process of programming.

9.2 The "Grand Canyon" Conceptual Gap

We define an "end user" as anyone who uses a computer but is not a professional programmer. End users want to use a computer as a tool to accomplish some task. Most end users have never taken a programming class. They use computer programs written by others, called "applications." The great majority of computer users are end users.

The core problem in programming is that there is a conceptual gap between the representations that people use in their minds when thinking about a problem and the representations that computers will accept during programming. For most people, this gap is as wide as the Grand Canyon. Norman (1986) calls it the "gulfs of execution and evaluation." He notes that "there are only two ways to . . . bridge the gap between goals and system: move the system closer to the user; move the user closer to the system." For programming, this translates into either teaching people the computer's epistemology (i.e., teaching them to think like computers) or teaching computers to accept representations that people find convenient.

Most people have great difficulty in "moving closer to the system." They may have tried a variety of ways to do it (Spohrer 1992). The most direct is to take formal programming classes. The purpose of programming classes is to teach people to build a mental model of computers. Most people, especially children, don't enjoy those classes. Even if they learn the techniques, they don't like where they end up. They don't want to think like computers; they want to control computers. Regardless of the approach, historically, trying to move most people closer to the system has not worked.

9.3 Analogical Programming

It is time to try the other approach: "move the system closer to the user." That is, we need to change the nature of programming to make it more like thinking. To characterize the type of thinking that we want to support, we have come to rely on a remarkable paper by Aaron Sloman (1971, 273), in which he draws a distinction between "analogical" representations and "Fregean" (after Gottlob Frege, the inventor of predicate calculus) representations:

> In an analogical system, . . . the structure of the representation gives information about the structure of what is represented. As two-dimensional pictures of three-dimensional scenes illustrate, the correspondence need not be simple . . . By contrast, in a Fregean system there is basically only *one* type of 'expressive' relation between parts of a configuration, namely the relation between 'function-signs' and 'argument-signs'. . . . The structure of such a configuration need not correspond to the structure of what it represents or denotes.

An example of an analogical representation of San Francisco is a map of San Francisco. From the map, you can tell the relationships between streets, how far it is between two points, where the bay is, and the locations of landmarks. If you're walking the streets, the map can tell you which way to turn when you come to an intersection. By contrast, an example of a Fregean representation of San Francisco is the term "San Francisco." Although it can represent the city in a suitable context, it bears no relationship to the city's structure. There is little you can learn about the city by examining this term. Sloman (1971, 274) continues:

> The generality of Fregean systems may account for the extraordinary richness of human thought (e.g., it seems that there is no analogical system capable of being used to represent the facts of quantum physics). It may also account for our ability to think and reason about complex states of affairs involving many different kinds of objects and relations at once. The price of this generality is the need to invent complex heuristic procedures for dealing efficiently with specific problem-domains. It seems, therefore, that for a frequently encountered problem-domain, it may be advantageous to use a more specialised mode of representation richer in problem-solving power.

In a nutshell this is what we propose to do to bridge the conceptual gap between computers and end users: *"for a frequently encountered problem-domain, . . . use a more specialised mode of representation richer in problem-solving power."*

Of course, we are not advocating eliminating Fregean representations. Rather, we suggest supplementing them with analogical ones when dealing with computers in certain domains. Well then, what representation should we use? Bruner (1966) believes that

> any domain of knowledge (or any problem within that domain of knowledge) can be represented in three ways:
>
> • by a set of actions appropriate for achieving a certain result (enactive representation). We know many things for which we have no imagery and no words, and they are very hard to teach to anybody by the use of either words or diagrams and pictures. If you have tried to . . . teach a child to ride a bike, you will have been struck by the wordlessness and the diagrammatic impotence of the teaching process.
>
> • by a set of summary images or graphics that stand for a concept without defining it fully (iconic representation). [Children learn what a horse is by seeing pictures of horses or actual horses. That is why we have zoos.]
>
> • by a set of symbolic or logical propositions drawn from a symbolic system that is governed by rules or laws for forming and transforming propositions (symbolic representation).

The first two are what Sloman terms analogical representations; the third is a Fregean representation. Piaget believed that children grow out of their early enactive and iconic mentalities; most adult thinking takes place at the symbolic level. By contrast, Bruner recommends that children be taught to utilize all three of their mentalities when solving problems: enactive, iconic, and symbolic. All three are valuable in creative thinking. Indeed, in a survey of mathematicians Hadamard found that many mathematicians and physicists think visually and reduce their thoughts to words only to communicate their ideas to other people (Hadamard 1945).

9.4 An Example of Fregean Programming

To illustrate the difference between analogical and Fregean programming, we will examine the same program—an electric train simulation—programmed in both ways. First the Fregean approach. Figure 9.3 shows a stack that is included with every copy of HyperCard. It is a model of an electric train set. If we place the engine on the track and click on the "Run" button, the engine moves around the track making whistle sounds and blowing smoke. If we change the track layout, the engine follows the new layout. All well and good. Everyone can do this. The problem comes if we try to change

Figure 9.3

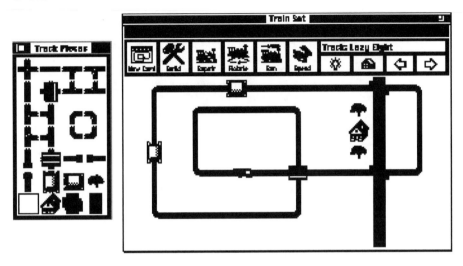

A train set in HyperCard with its palette of elements

the behavior of the model. Suppose we want to put two engines on the track and make them collide, which is the first thing that occurs to many kids. But there is no engine in the palette of train pieces. The simulation has not been programmed with that in mind.

Here is where simulations such as SimCity or SimAnt break down. You can alter the *arrangement* of the elements in the simulation but not their *behavior.* For example, in SimCity you can control the zoning of tracts of land and the layout of roads and railroads, but you can't affect the built-in assumptions. If you find that you have a pollution problem from roads, all you have to do is put in a railroad, and the problem goes away. Not too realistic. That is why many teachers, even those teaching city building, do not use SimCity in their classrooms. In order to change this assumption, the user must descend to a lower level, into the programming itself. This is not allowed in SimCity, but it is in HyperCard.

In the case of the train set, Figure 9.4 shows a slice of the code relevant to adding a second engine. This is just one of 78 routines in the simulation, although it's the longest one. Altogether there are over 1,100 lines of code. Understanding and modifying representations like this is difficult for children (of all ages). We tried to modify it to add a second engine, and we must confess that we didn't succeed. There isn't a single line in the code in Figure 9.4 that has to do with trains and tracks. Instead, it is all about maintaining data structures and interroutine communication—purely computer concepts. It's a classic example of a Fregean representation.

Figure **9.4**

```
on runTrain
  global AutoSwitch,BtnIconName,PrevBtnIconName
  global Dir,PrevDir,LastLoc,PrevLocs,LookAhead,TheNextMove
  global LastMoveTime,SoundOff,MoveWait,Staging,TheStage,TheEngine
  global TheMoves,Choices,Counter,EngineIcon,XLoc
  -- This routine is long.
  -- Most of the code is inline for acceptable speed
  lock screen
  setupTrain
  unlock screen
  repeat
    if the mouseClick then checkOnThings the clickLoc —check user action often
    -- get iconName of current position
    put iconName(icon of cd btn LookAhead) into BtnIconName
    if the number of items in BtnIconName > 1 then
      put "True" into Staging
      if TheStage = 0 then put BtnIconName into PrevBtnIconName
      if BtnIconName contains "roadXing" then put LookAhead into XLoc
      if BtnIconName contains "Rotatetrain" then put 1 into TheStage
    end if
    if the mouseClick then checkOnThings the clickLoc
    put LastLoc & return before PrevLocs
    put LookAhead into LastLoc
    put Dir & return before PrevDir
    if the mouseClick then checkOnThings the clickLoc
    add 1 to Counter
    checkSound
    if the mouseClick then checkOnThings the clickLoc
    -- set up the next position of the engine, all code inline for speed
    if counter <> 1 then
      put char offset(Dir,"RLUD") of BtnIconName into Dir
    end if
    put item offset(Dir,Choices) of TheMoves into TheNextMove
    if TheNextMove is empty then
      if item 2 of BtnIconName is "switch" AND not AutoSwitch
      then
        put char 1 of PrevDir into Dir
        switchTrack
        put item offset(Dir,Choices) of TheMoves into TheNextMove
        if TheNextMove is not empty then do (TheNextMove && "of LookAhead")
        else crash
      else
        put (item 1 of PrevLocs) + (item 1 of LastLoc) into horz
        put (item 2 of line 1 of PrevLocs) + (item 2 of LastLoc) into vert
        if EngineIcon contains "Tunnel" then set icon of cd btn TheEngine to 0
        set loc of cd btn TheEngine to trunc((horz)/2),trunc((vert)/2)
        if BtnIconName contains "rotateTrain" then
          put LastLoc & return before PrevLocs
```

HyperTalk code to make the engine move

Figure 9.4 continued

```
             put LookAhead into LastLoc
             put Dir & return before PrevDir
             put (item 1 of PrevLocs) + (item 1 of LastLoc) into horz
             put (item 2 of line 1 of PrevLocs) + (item 2 of LastLoc) into vert
             set loc of cd btn TheEngine to trunc((horz)/2),trunc((vert)/2)
             rotateTrain
             send mouseUp to bg btn id 224
           else
             crash
           end if
         end if
       end if
     else
       do (TheNextMove && "of LookAhead")
     end if
     if the mouseClick then checkOnThings the clickLoc
     if not SoundOff and the sound is done then play "Chug-Chug"
     -- set engine icon for that Dir
     if not Staging then
       add 1 to word 3 of EngineIcon -- cycle thru engine icons
       if word 3 of EngineIcon > 3 then
         put 1 into word 3 of EngineIcon
         set icon of cd btn TheEngine to EngineIcon
       end if
     end if
     if the mouseClick then checkOnThings the clickLoc
     wait until the ticks - LastMoveTime > (MoveWait div 2)
     if Dir = "-" then crash
     send item 2 of PrevBtnIconName to this bkgnd
     put (item 1 of PrevLocs) + (item 1 of LastLoc) into horz
     put (item 2 of line 1 of PrevLocs) + (item 2 of LastLoc) into vert
     set loc of cd btn TheEngine to trunc((horz)/2),trunc((vert)/2)
     set icon of cd btn TheEngine to EngineIcon
     unlock screen -- locked from the send above
     if the mouseClick then checkOnThings the clickLoc
     wait until the ticks - LastMoveTime > MoveWait
     if not SoundOff and the sound is done then play "Chug-Chug"
     if the mouseClick then checkOnThings the clickLoc
     -- move engine to new position
     if Dir = "-" then crash
     if not Staging then put Dir into char 1 of EngineIcon
     send item 2 of PrevBtnIconName to this bkgnd
     set loc of cd btn TheEngine to LastLoc
     set icon of cd btn TheEngine to EngineIcon
     if there is not a cd btn (LookAhead) then crash
     unlock screen -- locked from the send above
     put the ticks into LastMoveTime
   end repeat
 end runTrain
```

HyperTalk code to make the engine move

We're not picking on HyperTalk per se. In fact, routines like the one in Figure 9.4 are probably more readable in HyperTalk than in other programming languages such as Logo or Basic. The trouble is with *all* current programming languages: they force people to use Fregean representations, even when other representations would be easier for people. We will now show how to program the same simulation analogically in Cocoa.

9.5 An Example of Analogical Programming

Cocoa (originally called KidSim) is an environment designed to allow end users to construct and modify symbolic simulations by programming them (Smith, Cypher, and Spohrer 1994; Smith and Cypher 1995; Cypher and Smith 1995). A symbolic simulation is a computer-controlled microworld in which objects move around on a display screen interacting with each other. Most video games are examples of symbolic simulations. Cocoa takes a new approach to programming by getting rid of the programming language syntax. Instead, it combines three powerful ideas: programming by demonstration, visual before-after rules, and analogical representations.

- Programming by demonstration (Cypher 1993) is a technique in which users program a computer by operating it just as if they weren't programming. In the background, the computer records their actions in scripts. The scripts can be re-executed later on new data.

- Visual before-after rules provide a "memory jogger" for the scripts. They remind people what the scripts do. They are a visual version of the if-then rules used in production systems (Davis and King 1975). A few other researchers are also using them for programming (Repenning 1995; Bell and Lewis 1993; Furnas 1991).

- Analogical representations will be discussed in detail below.

Cocoa was designed to allow children to apply all their mentalities—enactive, iconic, and symbolic—to programming. To our knowledge, it is the first system to do so. In the remainder of this chapter, we will show that combining the three ideas supports these ways of thinking.

Figure 9.5 shows the same model of an electric train set, programmed in Cocoa instead of HyperCard. This is the Cocoa programming environment. It consists of

- a *stage* divided into discrete spaces, like a checkerboard (the upper left area above)

Figure **9.5**

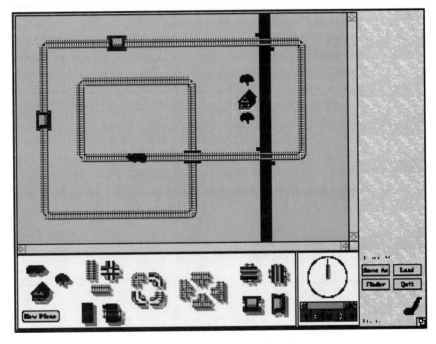

A train set in Cocoa modeled after the HyperCard version

- a *clock* whose time is divided into discrete ticks

- one or more *characters* or simulation objects

- a *copy box*, which is the source of new characters

- a *rule editor*, where rules are defined and modified

- various other elements

Here we will only describe the nature of rules.

The characters above—the track pieces and so on—were all defined and drawn by a Cocoa programmer. Each character starts out as an inanimate object, with no behavior. The programmer draws one or more appearances for the object and then defines some behavior for it in terms of visual before-after rules. Figure 9.6 shows an example of a rule for the engine. A visual before-after rule replaces one region in a simulation (the picture on the left) with another (the picture on the right). Cocoa executes such rules the way other languages execute statements. This rule may be read as follows: "If the engine is on a horizontal piece of track, and there is a horizontal

Figure **9.6**

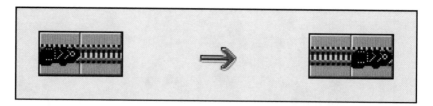

A visual before-after rule to make the engine move to the right

Figure **9.7**

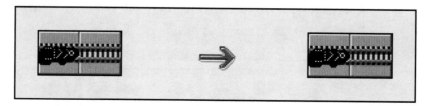

An identity rule

piece of track to its right, and the engine is facing to the right, then move the engine onto the track to the right."

Children define such rules as follows:

1. First they specify the region of the simulation to be dealt with. In this case they're interested in the piece of track to the right of the engine. This results in an "identity" rule, in which the picture on the left is the same as the one on the right, as shown in Figure 9.7.

2. This provides a framework for specifying behavior. Children define the semantics of the rule by editing the picture on the right. They perform actions on the actual objects in the picture. For example, they move the engine by dragging it with the mouse. This is *analogical programming:* the actions performed are analogous to the desired effects. If they want the train to move to the right, they drag it to the right. If they want it to move to the left, they drag it to the left. If they want it to move twice as fast, they drag it twice as far. If they want it to face in the opposite direction, they drag a different appearance onto it. If they want to change its internal state, say, its fuel level, they display its variables and edit the appropriate one *in place* until it contains the desired value. They continue performing actions until the picture on the right looks the way they want it. Cocoa remembers the actions performed and records them in a script. This is *programming by demonstration.*

In this case, only one action is performed: dragging the engine to the right. The result is the creation of a new rule that adds behavior to the engine.

Notice that dragging objects involves kids' enactive mentality, changing appearances and looking at rules involves their iconic mentality, and editing objects' variables involves their symbolic mentality. Indeed, we have found that younger children have an easier time with the first two types of actions, and only older kids can deal with variables—children who have developed "operational thinking," to use Piaget's term.

If children want to see the recorded actions, they can cause them to be displayed. They appear as shown in Figure 9.8. Contrast this representation with the HyperTalk code above. Notice that both the actions the child performs and the representations of the actions are in *model* terms. For example, the action above deals with train engines. Nevertheless, children rarely want to see even this representation for the actions; just seeing the visual before-after rule is enough for them to remember what the rule does. We have seen children go down long lists of rules identifying each one. Thus visual before-after rules appear to provide an effective representation for programs. Kids have an easy time understanding them because they are in model, or analogical, terms.

Programming the train simulation with rules like the one above requires many similar rules: in fact, it requires a rule for every possible combination of two pieces of track. However, in Cocoa, there are ways to reduce this complexity. For example, Cocoa can associate variables with objects such as pieces of track. This allows symbolic representations to be mixed in with visual representations. If we attach a "Directions" variable to pieces of track—so that a four-way intersection has "North South East West" for its "Directions" and a horizontal piece of track has "East West" for its "Directions"—then a train needs just four rules to move along any layout of track.

The problem in designing a child's authoring program is not to invent new computer science technology. There is already plenty of technology. The problem is to select features that ordinary mortals can understand and to recast them with a good human-computer interface. Indeed, in the interest of simplicity, Cocoa deliberately omits some features commonly available in

Figure 9.8

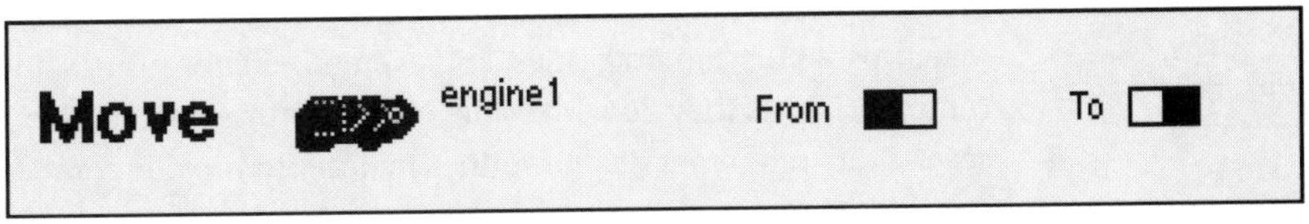

The actions recorded for the move-right rule

other programming languages. Nevertheless, Cocoa is a full programming system (we're trying to avoid calling it a language). It is Turing complete. Of more interest to our audience is that it is what we might call "PacMan complete." That is, it has enough features and power that users can implement the game of PacMan in it. This is a more challenging goal: we want to empower kids not only to *play* video games but also to *write* the games. We believe that any video game can be turned into an educational experience by allowing kids to modify it.

The elements of programming technology that we've included in Cocoa are the following:

- *Object-oriented programming:* Cocoa is object-oriented programming for kids. Characters in Cocoa have object identity (the system can tell one piece of track from another), state (the value of all of the character's variables), and behavior (the character's rules). We are strong believers in the value of object-oriented programming for programmers of all skill levels, but particularly for novices.

- *Conditionals:* Conditionals are pervasive in Cocoa. All visual before-after rules are conditionals. They may be read as "If the left side matches the simulation, then execute the actions on the right side." A rule is the Cocoa equivalent of a "statement" in other programming languages; it is the basic unit of computation. But Cocoa has just "if-then" conditionals, no "if-then-else" or nested conditionals; those constructs have been shown to cause novice programmers difficulty.

- *Iteration:* Iteration is also pervasive in Cocoa. The basic execution cycle is the following. On every tick of the simulation clock, the system goes through all the characters on the stage, giving each one a turn to run. Being given a turn means that the system starts at the top of the character's list of rules and works its way down, trying each rule in order. As soon as a rule matches, it executes, and the character's turn is over. When all characters have had a turn, the clock advances one tick, and the cycle starts over. Thus the system is constantly iterating through every character's rules. This is the reason that the move-right rule in Figure 9.8 will move the train over any amount of horizontal track. Iteration, like conditionals, has historically been a difficult concept for novice programmers; by making them part of the basic structure of Cocoa, they almost recede into invisibility. They become second nature. We find that kids have no trouble with either concept in Cocoa.

- *Subroutines:* A subroutine in Cocoa is a box of rules. It is much like a folder in the Macintosh. Kids can drag rules, and even other subroutines, into and out of subroutines, just as they do with folders and documents in a Mac. Cocoa introduces several different types of subroutines in order to provide some fairly sophisticated capabilities:

1. *Normal:* Cocoa tests each rule inside it in top-to-bottom order, in the normal way. The main purpose of this subroutine is to group related rules together.

2. *Random:* Cocoa scrambles the order of the rules inside each time it enters the subroutine. This allows kids to introduce random behavior into simulations, essential to making them interesting. This is a good example of the Cocoa approach to programming technology: instead of using random numbers and making kids discriminate on numeric values, Cocoa allows kids to deal with randomness at the rule level.

3. *Do all:* Cocoa executes *all* of the rules inside, even if more than one matches. This is the way kids can make a character do more than one thing in its turn. For example, if a character has an "age" variable, they can increment its age on every clock tick, in addition to its normal rules.

4. *Sequence:* Cocoa executes the rules one at a time in strict top-to-bottom order, one rule on each clock tick. The rules must be executed in sequence. If a given rule can't be executed in a turn, that rule will be tried again on the next clock tick, and every tick after that, until it finally executes. Only then will Cocoa move down to the next rule. This lets kids create "stories," such as leave the house, then go to the store, then buy bread, then return home, then give the bread to your mother.

- *Variables:* A variable is a container for a value, such as "name" or "age" or "appearance." Variables allow more sophisticated modeling to be done. For example, a character might have an "energy level" variable. When the character moves around, its energy level goes down because it takes energy to do things. When it runs out of energy (i.e., the value becomes zero), it dies. So now we could introduce the concept of food. When the character eats food, its energy level goes up. But soon it will eat up all the food and die anyway. So there needs to be a way to get more food. In this way, a single energy variable can lead to the classic predator–prey scenario.

- *Variable assignment:* Kids assign values to variables by editing them. For example, they select a variable's value and type a new one. If a rule is being defined, this action is recorded as a "put <value> into <variable>" action. This is programming by demonstration, the same technique that Cocoa uses to record all other actions. There is no assignment statement as in other programming languages.

- *Go to's:* Don't exist in Cocoa.

- *Syntax:* Doesn't exist in Cocoa (more or less). We like to say that Cocoa is "programming without a programming language." There is no language syntax in the traditional sense. There are no "begin-end", "if-then-else", semicolons, parentheses, and so on. Of course, a visual before-after rule does have syntactic structure, so there really is a syntax. But there is very little of it, and kids don't type it. It is created automatically in the background as kids perform actions.

Now let's see how we can accomplish in Cocoa what we tried to do with the HyperCard train set: put a second engine on the track and make them crash. Creating a second engine is easy. We simply drag it out of the "copy box" in the lower-left corner of the window in Figure 9.5. Every time we do this, Cocoa makes a new copy of the item and puts the original back. We drop the new engine somewhere on the track facing in the opposite direction from the first one. Now when we run the simulation, the engines race around the track. When they meet, they simply stop with their noses touching because they don't have a rule for what to do in that situation. That's no fun.

Here's where Cocoa simulations differ from Fregean ones: a child can change the behavior by reprogramming the simulation. For example, a child might add a "crash rule." Figure 9.9 shows what it might look like at the beginning.

The engines just sit there facing each other. To make them do something different, the child drags onto each engine a "crashed" appearance that she has previously drawn, thereby changing its appearance. She then drags a "pow" sound into one of the engine's "Sound" variables, thereby playing the sound. Each of these actions gets recorded as shown in Figure 9.10.

Figure 9.11 shows the final appearance of the crash rule. Now when the two engines meet, something dramatic happens.

Although Cocoa makes programming easier for novices, it is not a panacea for programming. While Cocoa is Turing complete, it is tailored to the specific purpose of implementing symbolic simulations, a domain that is of interest to our audience of K–12 children and their teachers and parents. But we would not try to implement a text editor or operating system in it. Furthermore, the logic of programming is just as hard in Cocoa as it has always been. Children still have to think through all the cases that can arise, handle each one, and debug them when they don't work. This is inherent in the activity of programming. What Cocoa does is to simplify programming by moving the activity of programming into the target domain of simulations.

Figure 9.9

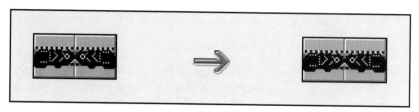

The crash rule as it starts out (an identity rule)

Figure 9.10

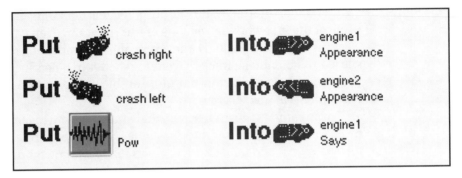

The actions recorded for the crash rule

Figure 9.11

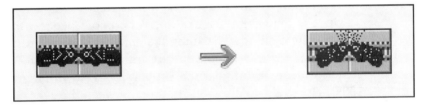

The final crash rule

9.6 User Testing

We began user tests of Cocoa even before we had written a single line of code. The first thing we wanted to know was whether children would be able to understand visual before-after rules. So we posed a variety of problems to a class of fifth-grade students, such as creating a character that could walk to the right and jump over obstacles. We asked them to draw before-after pictures on Post-It notes, and we then had them act out the roles of characters in the simulation, following the rules they had written. We were encouraged that the students were able to write rules in this format and that they quickly understood how to test the rules against the current state of the "world." Furthermore, children were able to understand rules that had been written by other children.

In another informal study, four students created a video prototype of the Cocoa stage, in the style of Vertelney (1989), using magnets under a piece of

Plexiglas to move their characters. This gave us confidence that our use of a clock, with characters taking turns to act, was appropriate.

Even more informally, three fifth-grade teachers were early (and patient) users of the first working versions of our program. Even when the program was crashing quite regularly, they were able to construct a scenario where it started to rain and characters went for shelter in a nearby house. Once the prototypes became somewhat more stable, we tested Cocoa regularly on the students in their classes.

These early tests with teachers and students were invaluable for finding problems in specific user interface objects and interaction techniques. For instance, we found that a trash can was inappropriate for disposing of characters, so we switched to a vacuum cleaner icon.

An encouraging result of these early studies was that girls seem to enjoy using Cocoa just as much as boys. We want to design a system that does not have a gender bias, and we are interested in conducting further studies to better understand which features of an interactive environment are particularly appealing to girls and which are particularly unappealing.

Once we had created a working version of Cocoa, with all of the basic features functioning as we intended, an informal user study of Cocoa was conducted by David Gilmore at the Centre for Research in Development, Instruction, and Training at the University of Nottingham (Gilmore et al. 1995). The study involved 56 children between the ages of 8 and 14. Minimal instruction in Cocoa was provided, consisting of approximately 10 minutes with an introductory worksheet. The sessions were quite open-ended. Initially, the students were given some ideas of rules to write, such as "move a creature rightwards along the ground." Almost all of the children found the rule-writing interface easy to use and were able to generate multiple rules for their characters. Furthermore, the system provoked their imaginations, and the children invented goals for themselves and created their own characters and situations. They created a soccer game, PacMan, a maze traversal game, ninja turtles, and an aquarium. This study showed that children can create rules and that they can read an individual rule. However, it was not clear from the study whether they can understand sets of rules and how multiple rules and characters interact.

9.7 Changing the Design

Our main design goal was to produce a tool that children would be able to use to create their own simulations. Every step in the design involved trade-offs between making Cocoa powerful enough that children would find it expressive and engaging and making it simple enough that they would not find it frustrating or confusing. Our periodic user testing helped us to see where our initial design choices erred in one direction or the other.

In the original version of Cocoa, it was possible to create arbitrarily deep hierarchies of character types. For instance, you could create clown fish, which are a type of fish, which are a type of animal, which is a type of character. We wanted users to create new rules and variables by adding them to a particular character on the stage, but we were not satisfied with any of our schemes for determining how to propagate new rules and variables up the inheritance hierarchy. Furthermore, the deep hierarchy led to potentially confusing situations since users could instantiate abstract superclasses. That is, it was possible to have an object on the stage that was an instance of animal, while other objects were instances of clown fish and sharks.

As a result of these difficulties, we changed to a simple inheritance scheme that admits only a single level of character types. This mechanism is certainly less powerful. For example, to add a "swimming" rule to all clown fish, sharks, and whales, users must put a copy of that rule in each of these three character types.

Our initial implementation assumed that every character fits into a single square on the stage. This simplifying assumption makes it much easier to specify rules in terms of the squares neighboring a character. Although we were quite content with this simple approach, our users were not. They frequently want to create worlds where some characters are much larger than others. This means that our initial design decision resulted in a tool that was not sufficiently expressive. For instance, one user wanted to create a large horse that could carry several riders and found it very unsatisfying to have to draw the horse in a single square. Therefore, our user studies convinced us to modify Cocoa to allow characters larger than a square, even though this complicates the rule system.

To date we have tested Cocoa on over 300 children between the ages of 5 and 15. All of them have learned to program in Cocoa, usually with only 5–30 minutes of instruction. All have been able to create characters, draw appearances for them, and give them rules to make them move and interact with each other. Furthermore, children seem to like it. It is not uncommon for them to stay inside during recess to work on their simulations. Several independent researchers have verified this (Gilmore et al. 1995; Underwood et al. 1996; Sharples 1996; Brand and Rader 1996). Although these are only small-scale tests, they indicate that children can learn and do enjoy this style of programming.

9.8 Summary

We feel that Cocoa has made programming simulations easier for children. Cocoa works because it relies on analogical representations for programs, allowing kids to think in model terms and eliminating the need to learn a programming language syntax. Programming by demonstration lets kids directly manipulate the representations, and visual before-after rules provide an understandable representation for the recorded programs.

In the next 10 years, end user programming may become an important human-computer interface theme. It allows the greatest degree of tailorability for "agents," MUDs and MOOs, games, and educational software. We predict that end user programming will require many domain-specific programming environments, all supporting analogical representations, possibly programming by demonstration, and perhaps visual before-after rules. Repenning (1993) gives a glimpse into this future: each environment will be special purpose. That seems to us to be the only approach that will succeed in practice. If we rely only on Fregean approaches, then we will lose nearly everyone who wants to learn programming. Although it is a long way from controlling trains to calculating spreadsheets or programming agents, we believe that the basic approach is widely applicable. We encourage researchers interested in this topic to contact us for the purpose of collaboration.

References

Bell, B., and Lewis, C. 1993. ChemTrains: A language for creating behaving pictures. In *Proceedings of IEEE Workshop on Visual Languages,* 188–195.

Brand, C., and Rader, C. 1996. How does a visual simulation program support students creating science models? In *Proceedings of IEEE Symposium on Visual Languages.*

Bruner, J. 1966. *Toward a theory of instruction.* Cambridge, MA: Harvard University Press.

Cypher, A., ed. 1993. Watch what I do: Programming by demonstration. Cambridge, MA: MIT Press.

Cypher, A., and Smith, D. C. 1995. KidSim: End user programming of simulations. In *Proceedings of CHI '95.* New York: ACM Press, 27–34.

Davis, R., and King, J. 1975. An overview of production systems. Rep. STAN-CS-75-524, Computer Science Dept., Stanford University, Stanford, CA.

Furnas, G. 1991. New graphical reasoning models for understanding graphical interfaces. In *Proceedings of CHI '91* New York: ACM Press, 71–78.

Gilmore, D., Pheasey, K., Underwood, J., and Underwood, G. 1995. Learning graphical programming: An evaluation of KidSim. In *Proceedings of Interact '95*. London: Chapman and Hall, 145–150.

Hadamard, J. 1945. *The psychology of invention in the mathematical field.* New York: Dover.

Norman, D. 1986. Cognitive engineering. In *User centered system design: New perspectives on human-computer interaction.* Hillsdale, NJ: Lawrence Erlbaum.

Repenning, A. 1993. *AgentSheets: A tool for building domain-oriented dynamic, visual environments.* Ph.D. dissertation, Dept. of Computer Science, University of Colorado, Boulder.

Repenning, A. 1995. Bending the rules: Steps toward semantically enriched graphical rewrite rules. In *Proceedings of Visual Languages,* 226–233.

Scardamalia, M., and Bereiter, C. 1991. Higher levels of agency for children in knowledge building: A challenge for the design of new knowledge media. *Journal of the Learning Sciences* 1(1): 37–68.

Sharples, M. 1996. *How far does KidSim meet its designer's objectives of allowing children of all ages to construct and modify symbolic simulations?* Internal report of the School of Cognitive and Computing Sciences, University of Sussex, Falmer, Brighton, England.

Sloman, A. 1971. Interactions between philosophy and artificial intelligence: The role of intuition and non-logical reasoning in intelligence. In *Proceedings of the Second International Joint Conference on Artificial Intelligence,* 270–278.

Smith, D. C., and Cypher, A. 1995. KidSim: Child constructible simulations. In *Proceedings of Imagina '95,* 87–99.

Smith, D. C., Cypher, A., and Spohrer, J. 1994. KidSim: Programming agents without a programming language. *Communications of the ACM* 37(7): 54–67.

Soloway, E. 1986. Learning to program = learning to construct mechanisms and explanations. *Communications of the ACM* 29(9): 850–858.

Spohrer, J. 1992. *Marcel: Simulating the novice programmer.* Hillsdale, NJ: Lawrence Erlbaum.

Underwood, G., Underwood, J., Pheasey, K., and Gilmore, D. 1996. Collaboration and discourse while programming the KidSim Microworld simulation. *Computers and Education.*

Vertelney, L. 1989. Using video to prototype user interfaces. *SIGCHI Bulletin* 21(2): 57–61.

Chapter Ten

Helping Children Learn Hard Things:

Computer Programming with Familiar Objects and Actions

Ken Kahn
Animated Programs

10.1 Introduction

Some children, when introduced to something new and complex, will jump in and explore because they enjoy exploration and are good at it. Others are much more timid and will explore only if coached or guided. Others ask for instructions and follow them meticulously. Some children will carefully watch a demonstration, while others are impatient to try things themselves.

It may be possible that there is a style of learning that dominates others in effectiveness and appeal. However, we take the position that children differ and that all these learning styles have their place. Even an individual child may switch styles as circumstances and experiences change.

Given the wide variety of ways that children learn, how should we design software for children? This chapter attempts to answer this question by looking closely at our experiences with the design and testing of ToonTalk.

ToonTalk (Kahn 1996, 1998) is an animated world where children build and run programs by performing actions upon concrete objects. The child builds real computer programs by doing things like giving messages to birds, training robots to work on boxes, loading up trucks, and using animated tools to copy, remove, and stretch items.

ToonTalk has been tested with fourth-grade classes in the United States for the last 3 years.* Initially, it supported only an exploratory learning style. Some children quickly began exploring and tried to figure out what each item does and how to combine them. Most, however, asked for guidance, which led to enhancements of ToonTalk that cater to children with different learning styles. ToonTalk now includes a puzzle game that plays the role of a tutorial, which appeals most strongly to children who tend to like to solve problems but are less comfortable exploring on their own. An animated character named Marty was added to ToonTalk that acts like a software coach or guide. Some children like to hear suggestions from him and follow his advice. Others quickly send Marty away because they find him annoying. A set of narrated demos of ToonTalk was created for those who like to sit and passively be shown how to make things. Illustrated instructions on how to build some programs were produced. These too appeal to a subset of the children.

Children of different ages, experiences, and learning styles approach the same software in very different ways. The main lesson we can take away from this experience is that children differ in the degree to which they are motivated and effective at exploring (on their own or with an animated

---

*ToonTalk is currently available for beta testing. It has been published in the United Kingdom and Sweden and soon will be available in other countries. Visit *www.toontalk.com* for more details.

guide), or following instructions, or solving a puzzle sequence. Even the same child will prefer different styles of interaction depending upon her prior experience with the software. Ideally, a software program should be designed so that a wide variety of children might enjoy and benefit from it.

10.2 A Brief Introduction to ToonTalk

Efforts to give children the opportunity to do real computer programming began over 30 years ago. The Basic programming language began as an ordinary programming language with as much as possible removed (Kemeny and Kurtz 1985); over the years, procedures, recursion, data structures, and so on have been put back into it. Logo and Smalltalk, in contrast, were designed to give children the best possible state-of-the-art programming tools (Papert 1980; Kay et al. 1981).

After 30 years of mixed results, many educators today question the value of teaching programming to children. It is hard, and there are now so many other things children can do with computers. Proponents of programming argue that programming can provide a very fertile ground for discovering and mastering powerful ideas and thinking skills (Papert 1980). Furthermore, programming can be a very empowering and creative experience. Children who can program can turn computers into electronic games, simulators, art or music generators, databases, animations, robot controllers, and the literally millions of other things that professional programmers have turned computers into.

Why do we rarely see these wonderful results from teaching children to program computers? The answer seems to be that programming is hard—hard to learn and hard to do (see Chapter 9 for further discussion). ToonTalk started with the idea that maybe animation and computer game technology might make programming easier to learn and do (and more fun). Instead of typing textual programs into a computer, or even using a mouse to construct pictorial programs, the idea is that real, advanced programming can be done from inside a virtual animated interactive world.

The ToonTalk world resembles a 20th-century city. There are helicopters, trucks, houses, streets, bike pumps, tool boxes, handheld vacuums, boxes, and robots. Wildlife is limited to birds and their nests. This is just one of many consistent themes that could underlie a programming system like ToonTalk. A space theme with shuttlecraft, teleporters, and so on would work as well. So would a medieval magical theme or an Alice in Wonderland theme.

The user of ToonTalk is a character in an animated world. She starts off flying a helicopter over the city. After landing she controls an on-screen persona. The persona is followed by a doglike tool box full of useful things.

An entire ToonTalk computation is a city. Most of the action in ToonTalk takes place in houses. Homing-pigeon-like birds provide communication between houses. Birds are given things, fly to their nest, leave them there, and fly back. Typically, houses contain robots that have been trained to accomplish some small task. A robot is trained by entering into its "thought bubble" and showing it what to do. The robot remembers the actions in a manner that can easily be abstracted to apply in other contexts.

A robot behaves exactly as the programmer trained it. This training corresponds in computer science terms to defining the body of a method in an object-oriented programming language like Java or Smalltalk. A robot can be trained to

- send a message by giving a box or pad to a bird

- spawn a new process by dropping a box and a team of robots into a truck (which drives off to build a new house)

- perform simple primitive operations such as addition or multiplication by building a stack of numbers (which are combined by a small mouse with a big hammer)

- copy an item by using a magician's wand

- terminate a process by setting off a bomb

- change a data structure by taking items out of a box and dropping in new ones

The fundamental idea behind ToonTalk is to replace computational abstractions by concrete familiar objects. Even young children quickly learn the behavior of objects in ToonTalk. A truck, for example, can be loaded with a box and some robots (see Figure 10.1 [see also Color Plate]). The truck will then drive off, and the crew inside will build a house. The robots will be put in the new house and given the box to work on. This is how children understand trucks. Computer scientists understand trucks as a way of expressing the creation of computational processes or tasks.

10.3 How Children Learn to Master ToonTalk

ToonTalk provides four fundamentally different ways for children to learn:

1. *Free play:* An open-ended, unconstrained, rich environment to explore and create things

Figure **10.1**

A truck being loaded

2. *A puzzle game:* A sequence of puzzles that gradually introduces the elements of ToonTalk and techniques for building programs

3. *Pictorial instructions:* Sequences of pictures that show how to build programs

4. *Demos:* Narrated demos showing various elements of ToonTalk and construction techniques

Safe Self-Revealing Environments

Proponents of constructivism (Papert 1993) argue well for the position that the best, deepest, longest-lasting learning happens when the learner discovers and constructs the knowledge herself. ToonTalk has a "free play" mode designed to accommodate this kind of learning.

Exploratory learning is best supported by an environment that is *safe* and *self-revealing.* An environment is safe to explore if novice actions will not cause any permanent damage. For example, in ToonTalk there is a character named Dusty that acts like a handheld vacuum. A beginner exploring ToonTalk might pick up Dusty and vacuum up something important. However, Dusty doesn't destroy things, and he can be used in reverse to spit out all the things he has ever vacuumed up.

A self-revealing environment is designed so that an inquisitive explorer can discover what objects exist and how they behave. ToonTalk, for example, contains boxes. Even very small children discover on their own how to move boxes, how to put things into them, and how to take things out of boxes.

Good animation and sound effects help greatly in making an environment self-revealing. If a user holds something over an empty compartment of a ToonTalk box, she sees that part of the box wiggles in anticipation. If she then clicks the mouse button, she sees an animation of the item leaving her persona's hand and falling into the compartment and hears an appropriate sound effect. If a force-feedback joystick is connected to the computer, she even *feels* the weight and other properties of objects.

It is very difficult to make a completely self-revealing environment. For example, in ToonTalk, boxes can be joined together and broken apart by actions that are often not discovered by children on their own. To completely explore ToonTalk, children need help.

ToonTalk includes an animated talking guide or coach named Marty to help a child explore the software (See Figure 10.2 and Color Plate). Marty keeps track of what actions a user has performed. He also is aware of what item a user is holding or pointing to and tries to suggest an appropriate action in the current context. For example, a child holding a box who has put things in and taken them out of boxes but hasn't joined two boxes together will hear a suggestion from Marty about how to join boxes.

Some children send Marty away, preferring to explore without any help. Others can be seen trying Marty's suggestions one after another. Children react to Marty differently depending upon whether he communicates by talk balloons, as in comics, or uses a text-to-speech engine to actually speak. For some children, reading is a slow and burdensome task.

Ideally, a self-revealing environment should also be *incremental*. An incremental environment may feel open-ended and rich but is designed so that certain objects or actions can be discovered only after others have been mastered. This helps reduce confusion and frustration that often results from the initial explorations of a rich and complex environment. Popular video games such as Nintendo's *Mario Brothers* or Sega's *Sonic the Hedgehog* games are excellent examples of incremental self-revealing environments. When a player starts these games, she finds herself controlling an on-screen character. Initially, all she needs to do is move. Soon she sees some coins and by walking into them they are acquired. Soon after there are coins that are not reachable without jumping, and the player experiments with a small set of buttons on the controller to discover how to jump to get those coins. After hours of play, the player has discovered a wide variety of actions her persona can perform and the properties of many different objects in the environment. Some video games have on-screen characters that reveal some of the harder-to-discover game elements. Such characters were the inspiration for Marty, ToonTalk's guide.

Puzzle Sequences as Tutorials

A carefully designed sequence of puzzles can be very effective pedagogically. Many computer and video games use puzzles as an effective and fun tutorial. *Lemmings* and *The Incredible Machine* are two good examples. The idea is to present a sequence of puzzles that introduces new elements or actions one at a time in a simplified or constrained environment.

A series of puzzles is more appealing to most children when it is embedded within a narrative adventure. The ToonTalk puzzle game starts with a brief "back story." An island is sinking, and a friendly Martian named Marty happens to be flying by and rescues everyone. He is nearly finished rescuing them when he crashes and is hurt. The player volunteers to rescue Marty. Because he is hurt (you can see his arm in a sling and his bruises), Marty can't get out and build the things needed to fix his ship. So he asks the player to make things for him. The player goes nearby where the components she needs can be found. She has to figure out how to use and combine them. When stuck or confused, the player can come back to Marty, who provides hints or advice about how to proceed. If a player is really stuck on a particular problem, then Marty gives her detailed instructions so she can proceed to the next puzzle. Note that getting advice or hints from Marty fits the narrative structure since Marty knows what to do but is too badly injured to do it himself.

In order to fix Marty's ship, the first job is to fix the ship's computer. The computer needs numbers and letters to work. The goal of the first level is to generate the numbers needed. The culmination of the level is the construction of a program that computes powers of two (1, 2, 4, 8, and so on, to 2^{30}). The next level involves the construction of a program that computes the alphabet. The task after that is to fix the ship's clock. Solving these puzzles involves measuring time, mathematics, and some new programming techniques. At one point in this level, the player has constructed a number that shows how old she is in seconds. And the number changes every second!

It is instructive to look at some puzzles in detail. The first real program a player builds is in the ninth puzzle. Marty needs a number greater than 1 billion for the computer. The player needs to train a robot to repeatedly double a number. Several of the earlier puzzles prepare the player for this task:

1. The first three puzzles introduce numbers, addition, and boxes (data structures).

2. In the fourth puzzle, Marty needs a number greater than 1,000 (see Figure 10.2, [see also Color Plate]). When the player goes next door, on the floor is just the number 1 and a magic wand that copies things (see Figure 10.3). The trick to this puzzle is to repeatedly copy the number and add it to itself, thereby doubling it each time (see Figure 10.4). In addition, the magic wand has a counter that is

Figure 10.2

The injured alien introducing the fourth puzzle

initially set to 10. After 10 copies, it has run out of magic and won't work any-more. This helps constrain the search for a solution. The solution requires the player to repeat the same action 10 times.

3. In the eighth puzzle, the player is introduced to robots and builds her first pro-gram. This puzzle is very simple. Marty needs a box with two zeros in it. When the player goes next door, she sees a robot with a magic wand and a box with one zero in it (see Figure 10.5). The wand is stuck to the robot and can't be used to copy the box. Most players discover that you can give the box to the robot (and those that don't, do so soon after getting hints from Marty). The player trains the robot to copy the box and drop the copy. Giving the robot the box activates him. He repeats what he was trained to do and copies the box.

These early puzzles are designed to simplify some programming tasks. For example, the player doesn't need to know how to terminate the training of a robot. When the limit on the number of steps that the robot remembers is exceeded, his training is automatically terminated. Similarly, the counter on the magic wand ensures that the robot will stop after the correct number

Figure 10.3

The initial state of the fourth puzzle

of iterations. In later puzzles, arranging for robots to stop when a task is completed becomes the player's responsibility.

By the time the player starts the ninth puzzle, she has performed the prerequisite actions and must combine them properly to train a robot to repeatedly double a number. The player is presented with a robot holding a wand good for 30 copies and a box with a 1 in it. Because the player has only the robot and the box to work with, and because of the limitations imposed on the robot, this otherwise overly ambitious early programming example can be solved by most players with few or no hints. And yet the constraints do not make the puzzle trivial: experimentation, thinking, and problem solving are necessary to solve the puzzle.

A good series of puzzles leads a player step by step where the puzzle designer wants to go. The players don't feel as if they are being led anywhere but have the illusion that they are in control. The puzzles constrain the set of objects that can be used and how they can be used so that the player has only a few choices. If designed well, the puzzle sequence can be challenging without being frustrating.

Figure 10.4

Using the magic wand to copy a number during the fourth puzzle

Even among those children for whom the puzzle game is well suited, there is variation—from those who want to figure out everything themselves to those who very quickly want hints. In ToonTalk, if you come to Marty empty-handed or with the wrong thing, he will give you a hint. Each time you return during the same puzzle, you get a more revealing hint, until eventually you get detailed instructions from Marty on how the puzzle should be solved. This behavior accommodates a wide range of learning styles, from independent problem solving to following directions.

A good puzzle sequence has a "self-testing" character. ToonTalk puzzle number 15, for example, is a difficult programming task for novices—generating a data structure containing 1, 2, 4, 8, and so on up to 1,073,741,824. The prerequisite knowledge for constructing such a program was acquired in solving puzzle 9 (constructing a program to compute 2 to the 30th power) and puzzle 13 (constructing a data structure filled with zeros). These puzzles in turn rely upon having learned in earlier puzzles how to double a number and how to train robots (i.e., construct programs). The fact that the children

Figure **10.5**

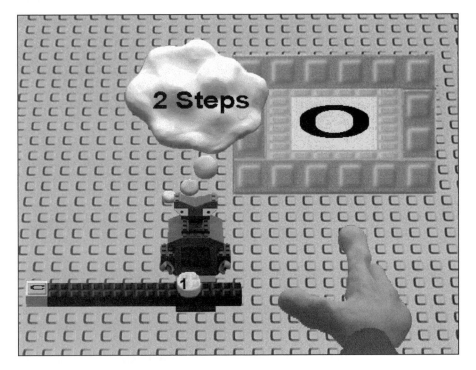

The initial state of the eighth puzzle

succeeded in solving the puzzles indicates that the puzzles have succeeded and that the children are learning ToonTalk and computer programming.

This kind of tutorial puzzle sequence is strictly linear. A less linear game based upon the idea of a treasure hunt or an adventure game should also be considered. The player would explore and find puzzles to solve. The game designer could still maintain some control by making certain areas open only to those who have succeeded in solving some prerequisite puzzles.

Pictorial Instructions

Children can often be seen building a toy or a kit by following instructions that consist of a series of pictures. Many children, for example, enjoy building LEGO constructions by following pictorial instructions. They learn design and construction techniques in the process, as evidenced by their own subsequent creations. Might not this technique work for children's software as well?

To explore this question, a sequence of approximately 60 screen snap-shots was generated for building an exploding object in ToonTalk, involving the use of collision detectors, sound effects, and a change in an object's ap-pearance. While children were able to follow the instructions, we learned that generating good instructions requires good graphic design, lots of test-ing and revision, and a good understanding of the required prerequisite knowledge and experience. In particular, we found the following:

- Pictures should show what is necessary and nothing more. Screen snapshots were a poor substitute for a good drawing because there are too many irrelevant details in each snapshot that made it hard to find the important parts of a picture.

- The step size should be just right. Too big or too small a transition between suc-cessive pictures confuses the children.

- Instructions should be appropriate for the level of experience of the child. The exploding-object instructions were too hard for children with just an hour or so of experience with ToonTalk.

We plan to generate and test new sets of instructions, taking into account the above lessons.

You might question the focus on *pictorial* instructions. What about tex-tual instructions? Textual instructions for building things in ToonTalk tend to be awkward and hard to understand. The world of ToonTalk is so visual that text without accompanying illustrations or animations is not very ef-fective. Consider how hard it is to explain to someone how to tie a knot over the phone. Nonetheless, a few children have been observed to repeatedly get hints from Marty to solve a puzzle until they receive full textual instruc-tions, and only then do they try to solve the puzzle.

Passive Watching of Demos

Instructional films and educational TV are generally accepted as effective for some kinds of learning. Why not apply them to the task of learning to program inside of ToonTalk?

ToonTalk includes eight different automated demonstrations. They are simply a replay of someone using ToonTalk, accompanied by narration and subtitles. Most of the demos are not different from watching someone give a demo to an audience. They tend to highlight different features or tech-niques. As with TV, there is no opportunity for the student to ask questions.

Two of the demos are unusual. One is scripted like an introductory tour. The viewer imagines she is on a guided tour of the ToonTalk world. The tour guide welcomes the visitor and greets characters in the ToonTalk world and proceeds to show how the basic objects and tools in ToonTalk work. The other demo has a soundtrack of two children trying to build a Ping-Pong game in ToonTalk. One of the children, Nicky, is a novice; the other, Sally, has a fair amount of experience but still finds building a Ping-Pong game challenging. Nicky frequently asks questions, and consequently explanations of what is happening are given in a natural context. Most importantly, the children frequently make mistakes. This demo shows the *process* of building something in ToonTalk—including how to deal with bugs and mistakes. This demo illustrates the process of building small pieces, testing them, tracking down and fixing bugs, and then integrating the pieces.

It is important to pay attention to production values when making software demos. Children will, quite naturally, compare them to TV shows. If the narration, script, or voice acting is amateurish, for example, the demos will not be as appealing.

Another important thing that these demos attempt to communicate is good programming style in ToonTalk. By watching a demo of an expert building something, an observant student will notice not just the necessary actions but all the other actions that constitute the style of the expert.

Other Ways to Learn

Absent from this discussion of ways of learning are the traditional ones like listening to lectures by teachers, asking questions, or doing homework assignments. These techniques can work quite well, especially when the teacher is knowledgeable. In such cases, the techniques described above can augment the activities of the teacher. Unfortunately, not all teachers are good at teaching complex subjects like computer programming (Yoder 1994). And computer programming is something interested children may wish to learn on their own. The hope is that a child can learn on her own with software that supports exploratory learning, problem solving, detailed instructions, and demonstrations.

Also absent from this discussion is learning in a social context. Children frequently play or study in pairs or teams, and they help and teach each other in the process. How can we design software to facilitate this kind of group activity? The software should do the following:

1. *Work with a long viewing distance:* Most software is designed to work for a user who is 12–18 inches from the display. When two or three children work together, the distance usually increases. ToonTalk, like most video games, was designed to

work in a typical living room, where the display may be 4–10 feet from the player: text and objects are large.

2. *Support multiple players:* Nearly all children's software is designed to work with a single child using the mouse, keyboard, and possibly a joystick. In contrast, most video games today support two to four simultaneous players, each with their own joystick or game pad. ToonTalk could be enhanced to support multiple users, each with their own controller and screen persona.

3. *Support networked collaboration:* For software to support children playing or learning together over a network, it must deal with many technical issues such as voice communication, latency, and reliability, as well as social issues such as privacy, inappropriate behavior, and trust.

4. *Support an online community:* Web sites, email, chat rooms, and discussion groups all can contribute to a support network to help children master complex subjects like computer programming.

10.4 Dimensions of Learning Techniques

We can analyze the techniques described here along various dimensions:

1. *Active-passive:* The techniques differ along a spectrum from passively watching or listening to actively exploring (see Figure 10.6). Note that there is an analogous spectrum along the cognitive dimension. A child watching a demo may be thinking very hard about what she is watching. Or a child engaging in free exploration may be randomly clicking on things without much thinking. It is beyond the scope of this chapter to attempt to place activities on this cognitive active-passive spectrum.

2. *Creativity:* The techniques also differ in the extent to which the child is instructed versus creatively exploring or constructing (see Figure 10.7). Notice that pictorial instructions require lots of activity but very little creativity.

3. *Planning-tinkering:* Turkle and Papert (1990) discuss these two learning styles in the computer culture. Some children prefer to understand and plan before attempting to build things, while others like to intertwine planning, learning, building, testing, and revising.

There are other spectrums along which these techniques differ. Appeal and effectiveness are two dimensions that are specific to the individual child. Some children like watching demos, and some don't. Some seem to learn best by free exploration; others don't.

Figure 10.6

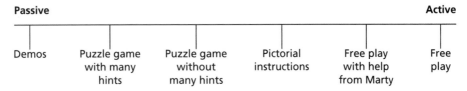

The active-passive dimension

Figure 10.7

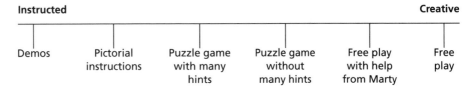

The creative dimension

 **Testing**

ToonTalk has been tested with fourth-grade classes in Menlo Park, California, from January 1995 to the present (June 1998). Pairs of children were observed using ToonTalk for about three 40-minute sessions apiece. For the first year and a half of testing, only free play was available, and most of the children continually sought guidance from an adult. After the puzzle game was implemented, a new class of children tested it exclusively. No formal testing was performed, but nearly all the pairs of children solved the first 25 puzzles without assistance. The children had no prior exposure to ToonTalk, and only two had any prior exposure to computer programming.

Beginning in September 1997, the fourth-graders were given the freedom to choose and switch between free play, the puzzle game, and demos. (The pictorial instructions were not yet ready for additional testing.) The informal observations of these 24 children confirmed the thesis of this chapter. The children tended to try the different modes and switch between them. Preferences varied as to which activities they would do.

ToonTalk has also been tested in hundreds of homes. The resulting anecdotal evidence is that most testers tried all three modes and learned different things from each. Preferences also varied.

10.6 Kids as Critics and Designers

The design of ToonTalk and its learning aids was heavily influenced by over 3 years of use and feedback by children. Simply watching children use the software led to two major redesigns and hundreds of smaller improvements. For example, the initial design provided three kinds of magic wands—for copying, for changing sizes, and for removing things. Observing frequent confusion and frustration led to replacing the wand for changing sizes with a bicycle pump and to replacing the wand for removing things with a hand-held vacuum.

Children, unlike adults, have rarely provided criticism. They are, however, often eager to provide all sorts of creative suggestions. For example, in ToonTalk, you can only land your helicopter on the street. Many children have suggested that you should be able to land on the roofs of houses. When asked what would happen then, responses varied, from "the house blows up" to "you climb down the chimney." Others suggested that you should be able to walk into the water that surrounds the island. Some wanted to add boats, drowning, and sharks.

Very few suggestions from children for changes to ToonTalk have actually been followed because every item or action in ToonTalk supports the fundamental purpose of the system—enabling its users to create programs. Much effort went into making them fun and appealing as well. ToonTalk has a magic wand because there is a need for copying things when programming. Many children find it fun to play with the wand, but it also serves an essential function. Blowing up houses (by landing on them) or drowning not only do not serve useful functions, but they interfere with the task of programming.

Some suggestions are very good ones—for example, that there should be more than three styles of houses or there should be more than one room per house. These would be both functional and add appeal. They haven't been implemented, however, because of resource limitations and the large number of higher-priority changes.

My son, David, who was 7 years old when ToonTalk was started over 5 years ago, has been an invaluable source of ideas. He has also played a very important role as a sounding board. As I considered design changes and alternatives, I would frequently explain them to him first. Unlike focus groups, David had years of experience with ToonTalk but still had a child's perspective.

10.7 Related Work

Rocky's Boots and *Robot Odyssey,* two games from the Learning Company in the early 1980s, excited many computer scientists. In these games, you can build arbitrary logic circuits and use them to program robots in the context of an adventure game. The user persona in the game can explore a city with robot helpers. Frequently, in order to proceed, the user must build a logic circuit for the robots to solve the current problem. The design of ToonTalk and its puzzle game were inspired by *Robot Odyssey.* The most important difference is that ToonTalk is capable of supporting arbitrary user computations—not just the Boolean computations (AND, OR, and NOT) of *Robot Odyssey.*

Many computer and video games use puzzles as an effective and fun tutorial. *Lemmings* and *The Incredible Machine* are two good examples. Scott Kim has written about puzzle design and the pedagogic role of puzzles (Kim 1995).

Pictorial instructions are very commonly used in building a model airplane, a LEGO set, or furniture. We are not aware of any attempts to use them for other tasks such as learning to program a computer. In the context of textual programming, it is unclear what the instructions could do other than tell the student what needs to be typed.

Safe, self-revealing, incremental exploratory environments are very common in computer and video games. They are not common in textual programming environments like Logo or Basic. Someone exploring Logo, for example, needs to be told that "FORWARD N" will move a turtle forward *n* units; she is unlikely to discover it by exploration.

In the last 15 years, there have been several attempts to build intelligent tutors that can teach programming or math (e.g., Selker 1994; Corbett and Anderson 1992). They give explanations, propose problems, and, most importantly, can give intelligent feedback when students fail to solve problems. These tutors are much more sophisticated than Marty, the ToonTalk guide. A tutor based upon this research could be built to help children in free play, solving puzzles, or even following pictorial instructions. Such a tutor could analyze a student's behavior and give much more appropriate and intelligent advice than Marty is capable of.

10.8 Conclusion

We have presented self-revealing exploratory environments, puzzle sequences, pictorial instructions, and demos as aids for students to learn hard things. Currently, the evidence for their effectiveness and appeal is informal and anecdotal. We hope to find and collaborate with another group interested in studying the effectiveness of these techniques and their combinations in a more formal manner.

It seems likely that these techniques could be combined effectively to learn to use complex software like Windows 98 or Adobe PhotoShop. Perhaps software can be made that uses combinations of these techniques to teach science, engineering, or math.

The lesson that I hope you take away from this chapter is that video games and toys are an important source of ideas and techniques for introducing rich and complex things to children in a fun and effective manner.

Acknowledgments

I wish to thank Mary Dalrymple for her comments on early versions of this chapter. Special thanks go to Ruth Colton, who permitted me to test ToonTalk with her fourth-grade students. And I am very grateful to David Kahn and all of the other ToonTalk beta testers.

References

Corbett, A. T., and Anderson, J. R. 1992. The LISP intelligent tutoring system: Research in skill acquisition. In J. Larkin, R. Chabay, and C. Scheftic, eds. *Computer assisted instruction and intelligent tutoring systems: Establishing communication and collaboration.* Hillsdale, NJ: Lawrence Erlbaum.

Kahn, K. 1996. ToonTalk™—An animated programming environment for children. *Journal of Visual Languages and Computing.* (An abbreviated version appeared in *Proceedings of the National Educational Computing Conference.* Baltimore, MD, 7(June): 197–217, 1995.)

Kahn, K. 1998. ToonTalk home page. *www.toontalk.com.*

Kay, A., et al. 1981. *Byte* 6(8).

Kemeny, J., and Kurtz, T. 1985. *Back to BASIC.* Reading, MA: Addison-Wesley.

Kim, S. 1995. Puzzle games and how to design them. *Proceedings of the Ninth Annual Computer Game Developers' Conference.* Computer Game Developer Association.

Papert, S. 1980. *Mindstorms: Children, computers, and powerful ideas.* New York: Basic Books.

Papert, S. 1993. *The children's machine: Rethinking school in the age of the computer.* New York: Basic Books.

Selker, T. 1994. COACH: A teaching agent that learns. *Communications of the ACM* 37(7): 92–99.

Turkle, S., and Papert, S. 1990. Epistemological pluralism: Styles and voices within the computer culture. *Signs* 16(1): 128–157.

Yoder, S. 1994. Discouraged? . . . Don't dispair [sic]. *Logo Exchange* 12(2).

Chapter Eleven

Middle Tech:

Blurring the Division between High and Low Tech in Education

Mike Eisenberg

Department of Computer Science, Institute of Cognitive Science, and Center for Lifelong Learning and Design, University of Colorado, Boulder

Ann Nishioka Eisenberg

Department of Computer Science, Institute of Cognitive Science and Center for Lifelong Learning and Design, University of Colorado, Boulder

11.1 Introduction: Blending Bits of Information and Bits of Stuff

In 1997, the most prestigious high school science fair in the United States—the Westinghouse Science Competition (Berger 1994)—was won by Adam Cohen, then a senior at Hunter High School in New York City. Cohen's project, "Near-Field Photolithography," involved the construction of a home-built scanning tunneling microscope (STM), a high-resolution microscope that uses the extent of quantum tunneling between a metal reading head and a conducting surface to map the contours of the surface. To build his microscope, Cohen not only programmed a home computer, but also employed a wide variety of quirky materials. As he wrote (Cohen 1997):

> The mechanical structure of the STM used in this study is made of LEGO (a plastic building toy). The LEGO provides a rigid structure and shields the sample from air currents . . . To isolate against high frequency vibrations, the entire microscope is encased in about 7 kilograms of plasticine (a kind of modeling clay). Bungee cords suspend the microscope from the concrete ceiling to isolate the STM from low frequency vibrations.

Bungee cords, plasticine, LEGO, and digital electronics—looking at Cohen's project, it is hard to draw any firm lines between high and low tech in this young scientist's work. After all, LEGO bricks, plasticine, and the rubber thread of which bungee cords are made are all relatively new materials: none of them existed a century ago. For Cohen's brand of science, then, there is only a spectrum of material: neither high tech nor low, but simply a wide range of available stuff—some of it on the old side, some new, some modular (like LEGO), some moldable (like clay), some programmable.

The history of scientific investigation is deeply and profoundly woven with the history of crafts—of building and perfecting homemade or informal instruments, of creating new materials for new purposes, of putting old materials to new uses. Sometimes the scientist makes brilliant use of an everyday object: Ben Franklin and his kite come to mind, as does Helmholtz's description of Michael Faraday that "a few wires and some old bits of wood and iron seem to serve him for the greatest discoveries" (quoted in MacDonald 1964, 16). Or perhaps the scientist constructs an instrument (e.g., van Leeuwenhoek's microscope, Galileo's telescope) out of relatively newer or suddenly cheaper materials. Or, in another variation, perhaps the scientist invents a new material (like polyethylene) and only later comes to visualize novel uses for it. For such individuals, the world is filled with scientific objects of all kinds, and this culture of craftspersonship confounds the educational theorists. After all, in the realm of educational technology, we tend to see computers (half-century-old devices) as the epitome of high tech and the rest of the material world as low tech. In the practice of real science, both among professionals and among students like Adam Cohen, the truth is considerably more complex, and more fun.

This chapter is an exploration of the notion of *middle tech* in mathematics and science education. Middle tech, for us, connotes two related ideas. On the one hand, the term suggests a panoply of new materials—temperature-sensitive films, cheap diffraction gratings, glow-in-the-dark dyes, fiber optics, reflective mylar—that sit somewhere between the obvious high-tech world of electronics and the obvious low-tech world of wood, clay, and stone. But middle tech also describes another notion—namely, the creative reinterpretation and integration of high- and low-tech educational materials. Rather than viewing computers as a world unto themselves, ethereal and abstracted from the realm of handicrafts, we prefer to think of middle tech as the unexplored terrain in which programs and materials, complexity and concreteness, blend into new media.

Our interest in this notion of blending bits of information and bits of stuff arose from our work in developing and using a software application named *HyperGami*. HyperGami is a program for the design and creation of polyhedral mathematical models and sculptures in paper, and as such it represents one approach to the integration of craft materials and computational media. We will use HyperGami in this chapter as a major source of ideas and issues for exploring middle tech, but HyperGami represents only one point in the vast space of design alternatives. There are many other craft materials to play with (and to invent), and there are many other ways of blending computation into those materials. In this chapter, we will attempt to look well beyond our initial work with HyperGami and to outline some possibly productive research and development themes for middle-tech education.

Section 11.2 provides a brief outline and history of the HyperGami system, with the primary goal of providing a foundation for the issues raised in the remainder of the chapter. In Section 11.3, we focus on the computational (as opposed to material) side of middle-tech education, discussing how computers may aid in the design of new sorts of craft objects. Section 11.4 looks at the other, tangible, side of middle tech, describing how both new and ancient materials may be enriched by technology. In Section 11.5, we take a step back and look at middle-tech education as a whole; we discuss how this style of design can revitalize science and math education, and we use our experiences with HyperGami in particular to highlight some otherwise easily overlooked issues that emerge from the notion of middle tech. In Section 11.6, we look toward the future, describing what we believe are fruitful directions for research in middle-tech design. Finally, in Section 11.7, we conclude with some reflections on the insufficiency of "purely virtual" environments as the foundation of a rich educational experience in math and the sciences.

11.2 HyperGami—A Tool for Integrating Computers and Papercrafts

HyperGami is a software application designed by us and implemented in the MacScheme language environment (Lightship Software); it runs on all Macintosh computers with at least 16 MB of memory. We have described HyperGami at length elsewhere (Eisenberg and Nishioka 1997a, 1997b) and so will only present a short description of the program here.

An Overview of HyperGami

The essential activity in HyperGami is the design of customized three-dimensional polyhedral shapes, represented on the computer screen. These shapes may then be unfolded by the program into two-dimensional *folding nets:* flat patterns that can be printed out and refolded into the specified three-dimensional form. The HyperGami user may choose to decorate folding nets with an extensive variety of tools prior to printing; by this means, and by combining polyhedra together into composite forms, she can create an endless collection of decorated mathematical models and sculptures.

Figure 11.1 shows the HyperGami screen in the course of a typical scenario. Here the user has selected a particular polyhedron—the truncated octahedron, one of the thirteen Archimedean (semiregular) solids—from the Archimedeans palette shown in the figure. The solid is shown in a three-dimensional rendering in the ThreeD window and in its unfolded form in the TwoD window. The user has begun decorating the net using a selection of paint tools: some faces have been filled with textures, solid colors, or patterns; some have been decorated with hand-drawn lines; some have been decorated with geometric patterns; some with text; some with Logo-style turtle graphics designs. There are still other decorative options available to the HyperGami user: filling patterns may be defined via the extended Scheme language provided with the program (we'll return to this general topic in a moment); a recently completed "surface turtle" package may be used to create designs in which a turtle executes a walk over the entire surface of the polyhedron (see Chapter 6 in [Abelson and diSessa 1980] for an

Figure **11.1**

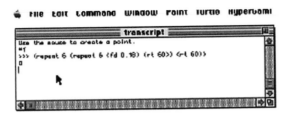

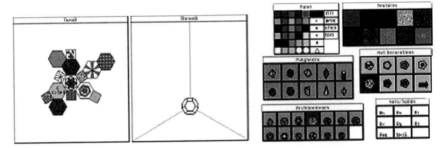

A view of the HyperGami screen in the course of a typical scenario. The TwoD and ThreeD windows toward the bottom left show the folding net and three-dimensional rendering of a truncated octahedron, respectively. The folding net has been decorated with textures, patterns, solid colors, a hand-drawn figure, a turtle-drawn design, text, and geometric designs. The transcript window at top allows the user to type expressions into the MacScheme interpreter. The windows toward the bottom right include tools for choosing, decorating, and viewing polyhedra (several other optional windows are not shown).

extended example of this idea); or the folding net may be saved and re-loaded into other graphics applications.

Two major points deserve emphasis even within this telegraphic discussion of HyperGami. First, although the system provides the user with a large collection of starting polyhedra (including the five regular solids, the thirteen Archimedean solids and their duals, prisms, and pyramids), the true power of the program derives from the user's ability to create new customized polyhedra. HyperGami includes an extensive collection of mathematical operations that may be used to alter shapes in systematic ways—adding a new vertex here, stretching or shrinking there, and so forth. Figure 11.2 provides a simple example of the idea. Here, we have sliced the truncated octahedron into two halves and retained the upper half. This "half-shape" has been stretched vertically, and a "vertex cap" has been added to the top of the shape. Finally, the system has unfolded the newly created shape into a folding net, which may then be decorated and printed out just

Figure 11.2

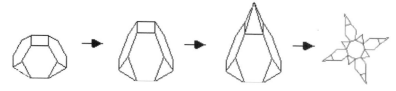

The top half of a truncated octahedron (left) *is stretched, then capped. The resulting shape is unfolded by HyperGami to produce a folding net* (right).

like any other HyperGami net. Besides the operations shown in Figure 11.2, many other solid-customization operations are available to the HyperGami user. (See [Eisenberg 1996] and [Eisenberg and Nishioka 1997a] for more discussion of these techniques and for discussion of limitations of the unfolding algorithm.)

A second and perhaps even more important point is that HyperGami is designed as a *programmable* application: it is built on top of the MacScheme system and includes not only the core Scheme language environment but also a huge and growing library of specific procedures and data types useful for the creation of polyhedral models. This permits the advanced HyperGami user to express ideas (e.g., new customization procedures) well beyond those directly built into the original system (we will return to this issue shortly).

The Design of HyperGami: A Short History

Before moving on to a more general discussion of middle-tech design, it is worth pausing at this juncture to provide a historical sketch of the Hyper-Gami application in particular. We would like to be able to claim that we began with a clear vision of the system that we wanted to build, with a cogent set of requirements and specifications (as the software engineering texts recommend), and with a strong theoretical grounding in the integration of computation and crafts. But the actual history of HyperGami is considerably messier and less organized (and perhaps more interesting) than that.

HyperGami in fact began approximately 5 years ago as an addition to a graphics application named SchemePaint (created by the first author). The goal of SchemePaint was to demonstrate the power of programmable applications generally by integrating elements of direct manipulation interfaces with elements of interactive programming (see [Eisenberg 1995] for a discussion—maybe an overly emotional discussion—of this idea). In particular, SchemePaint employed features typical of most paint applications (e.g., using the mouse to paint lines on the screen or to select regions for filling with colors), but it combined these features with Scheme graphics primitives (e.g., for producing turtle graphics designs). The resulting application lacked many advanced features of commercial paint programs, but it did permit users to create pictures with an appealing mixture of hand-drawn and "linguistic" (often mathematical) elements.

HyperGami, then, originated as a library of procedures within Scheme-Paint—a library geared toward the decoration of simple polyhedral nets and classical origami figures and primarily aimed at students of geometry ([Eisenberg and Nishioka 1994] provides a relatively early description of the system). Since that time, the paint application origins of the program have faded in importance, and the polyhedral-modeling aspects of the program have grown. What was originally a paint application has become, steadily and by degrees, a papercraft application.

There are several reasons behind this evolution of SchemePaint into HyperGami. First, we observed that both we and our students seemed to take far greater enjoyment in the creation of tangible papercraft objects than in the creation of computer-generated pictures. (We'll revisit this observation in Section 11.5.) Second, as we explored the domain of polyhedral modeling in paper, we became progressively more fascinated in our students' understanding of three-dimensional forms; over time, this interest has blossomed into a much broader interest in spatial cognition, its development in children, and its role in mathematical and scientific thinking. Finally, we found that the domain of papercrafts provides fertile ground for experimentation in software. Thus, many of HyperGami's features have been designed with an eye toward the special needs and problems of craftspeople working in paper. A recent addition to the program allows the creation of "tabs" that aid in the folding together of solids. The program includes tools that help advanced users rearrange the folding nets that they create, making them easier to decorate or fold; and many of the decoration tools (such as the aforementioned "surface turtle" or the built-in geometric designs) are geared specifically toward ornamentation of geometric solids. ([Eisenberg and Nishioka 1997b] and [Eisenberg and Eisenberg 1998] include more discussion of these topics.)

Since HyperGami's beginnings, we have worked intensively with over 50 children (ranging from third- to twelfth-graders) on a wide variety of mathematical papercrafting projects, and we have made energetic use of the program ourselves, creating a gallery of polyhedral models and sculptures. Figure 11.3 (see also Color Plate) illustrates four representative HyperGami objects resulting from this effort. Two are constructions of our own: a polyhedral sculpture (an "orihedron") of a pineapple and a lattice structure composed of antiprisms and cuboctahedra. Two others are constructions by

Figure **11.3**

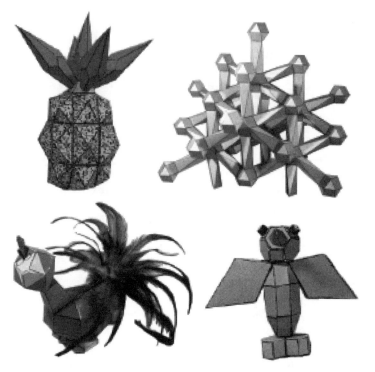

HyperGami constructions. Upper left: *a HyperGami "pineapplehedron";* upper right: *a lattice figure composed of cuboctahedra (as nodes) and antiprisms (as struts);* lower left: *a polyhedral sculpture of a rooster by a middle school student;* lower right: *a duck with "radioactive green feet" by a fifth-grader.*

students: a sculpture of a rooster created by a 13-year-old girl and a "Super-Duck" figure created by a fifth-grade boy. ([Eisenberg and Nishioka 1997a] includes much more description of work with students using HyperGami, and our Web site [*www.cs.colorado.edu/~eisenbea/hypergami/*] presents many more examples of HyperGami constructions, though these are still a small subset of those created by our students and us.)

Are there any lessons in this history for the prospective designer of children's software? Perhaps. On the one hand, we have been pleased to see the rich intellectual rewards that followed from pursuing an offshoot of a (much more conservative) graphics application. And we regard it as especially important that we ourselves play with the software, just as our students do: rather than ghettoizing "educational software" as something designed by adults and used by children, we prefer to create tools that afford a wide range of projects suitable for elementary school students, high school students, undergraduates, and professional mathematicians. On the other hand, while there are some edifying morals to be extracted from the history of HyperGami, we would not want to portray the application as an unmitigated success story nor as a shining exemplar of a sound design process in operation. The application is still, after 5 years, "homegrown software," and many aspects of its interface could benefit from an overhaul (we are currently at work on a reimplementation of at least a portion of HyperGami in Java; this should afford the opportunity to perform a thorough redesign of the interface). For our own part, we have focused a greater portion of our energies on developing compelling examples, new curricular activities, and papercraft-related software features than on rethinking the fundamental design of the system.

 ## 11.3 Middle-Tech Design: The Computational Environment

This section and the next explore a variety of recurring issues in middle-tech design. For organizational purposes, we separate the issues into those that arise primarily from the computational side of the subject and those that arise from the material side (though the division is of course not always clear-cut).

Computers in the Design of Mathematical and Scientific Craft Objects

The HyperGami system represents one style of application design integrating computation and materials. Broadly speaking, this style of design emphasizes the use of the computer as a tool to expand the creative range of mathematical and scientific crafts. In the particular case of HyperGami, this expansion of creative potential occurs for three reasons. First, HyperGami allows the user to create a far wider variety of polyhedral models than would be possible in the absence of computational media. Noncomputational polyhedral kits composed of predesigned pieces (e.g., flat snap-together polygons or plastic struts and joints) are capable of producing only those shapes whose faces or edges are given by the specific (and limited) dimensions of the pieces themselves. To take a simple example: a snap-together kit whose quadrilateral faces are all squares may be used to make a cube but not an arbitrary rectangular prism. Of course, you could argue that this is an advantage of HyperGami's chosen material—paper—over plastic pieces, but a math student working in paper, and without a computer, is faced with the daunting task of creating a folding net for any shape that she wishes to create. HyperGami allows the mathematical crafter to describe and create complex, never-before-seen shapes precisely because of the combination of its eminently accommodating physical medium (paper) and the computational support that it provides.

A second important reason that HyperGami expands the creativity of the mathematical crafter is because it takes advantage of a range of computational facilities related to the central task of making polyhedral models. Specifically, HyperGami's decorative tools allow the user not only to create multicolored models, but to do so in novel ways suggested by (or solely enabled by) computational tools. The HyperGami user may decorate models with solid colors, patterns, or textures; she may use the system's built-in tools to add complex geometric designs of various sorts to solids (as mentioned in the previous section); or she may read a HyperGami net into some other graphics system (e.g., Adobe Photoshop or Canvas) and decorate her net using the vast assortment of features offered by those other systems. Because the computer is itself an instrument of such sprawling capabilities, it permits the user to take advantage of tools not only for the specific aims of creating a particular shape but of enhancing that shape in hitherto unrealizable or unimaginable ways.

Finally—and perhaps most importantly—HyperGami's associated language offers a new and powerful medium in which to describe, express, and think about the shapes that people create. As we and others have argued (Abelson 1991; Eisenberg 1995), a programming language is not simply a convenience for the user of a computer application, nor is it merely a tool with which to add new customized features to an application. Most crucially, a programming language is a means by which to express procedural ideas—perhaps otherwise hidden or subtle ideas—about some particular domain. In the case of HyperGami's expanded Scheme dialect, the language permits thinking about solid geometry in procedural terms. New polyhedra may be created via an "algebra of solids," starting from simple solids and performing sequences of operations upon them. Shapes are sliced apart into pieces, joined together at faces, stretched, shrunken, and capped, and any shape created by previous manipulation is a candidate for further manipulation. This is a style of creation peculiarly linguistic in nature—the language of creation becomes in itself a language for the description of polyhedra. (A new shape, for example, might be a "slice of an icosahedron, two of whose triangular faces have been exchanged and one of whose faces has been capped with a pyramid"—a description reflecting the sequence of procedural operations used to design the solid.)

This last point is perhaps worth dwelling upon just a bit longer. Computers enhance craftwork not only because they allow new physical artifacts to be created, nor only because they allow for more precision or more decorative options to be employed in those artifacts. Computers enhance craftwork most surprisingly because they allow for new languages, new formalisms to be developed around the creation of artifacts—and these new languages allow the student to think in novel, productive terms. Languages and notations are the media through which our thoughts are structured, and computers are tools by which new languages and notations may come to be considered as designed artifacts in their own right.

It is likewise important to note that these arguments, while derived from our HyperGami experience, do not at all depend on that particular example. Indeed, it is a fruitful exercise to think about other mathematical/scientific crafts and to imagine how computational tools for design could extend those crafts in wondrous directions. What would a computational tool for the creation of new kaleidoscopes look like? Or a tool for the creation of tops? Or a tool for the creation of topological puzzles? Or a tool for the creation of balancing toys? In every case, we might begin by thinking along the three major lines suggested by our HyperGami example: the increase of potential complexity, the use of related computational tools, and the power of a programming language. A balancing-toy design system, for instance, might begin by allowing us to create (on the computer screen) novel asymmetric forms that, when realized in wood, will balance at the edge of a shelf or athwart a string (increase in complexity). It may allow us to experiment with new forms created by mixing together materials of multiple densities (increase in complexity). It may allow us to experiment with decorations of our creations (related computational tools). And it may allow us to imagine sequences or algebras of operations that alter or extend balancing toys in various ways while preserving their fundamental property of balance (the addition of a programming language).

Computers as Advisors in the Creation of Craft Objects

We ourselves have barely begun to explore the myriad ways in which computational design tools may lend themselves to new forms of mathematical and scientific crafts. But this is only one way in which computers may enhance the design of educational objects. Here our ideas are shaped not by something that HyperGami does but by something that (in its current version) it fails to do—namely, to offer anything in the way of help, advice, or guidance to the student in the creation of some new form. The HyperGami user, when faced with, say, an octahedron on the computer screen, may have no clue as to which interesting operations might be performed on this shape. He is simply left with an array of options, and while sometimes that array may be construed as an invitation to explore, it may likewise represent a conceptual reef on which the novice craftsperson may founder.

We are currently at work on a collection of embedded *advisors* to incorporate within HyperGami—software tools to suggest potentially interesting geometric operations to perform upon solids. One such advisor, for example, examines a starting polyhedron to see whether it contains a planar set of vertices through which the shape may be sliced (see Figure 11.4). Here we begin with an icosahedron; the HyperGami advisor finds a set of five vertices through which the shape may be sliced to produce two component slices. An advisor such as this is similar in spirit to the computational coaching facility pioneered years ago by Brown and Burton in their creation of the WEST system (Burton and Brown 1982), and it has a family resemblance as well to the "critics" incorporated in design applications by Fischer and his colleagues (Fischer et al. 1991).

Space does not permit more than a cursory discussion of this topic, but the notion of creating useful craft advisors for middle-tech applications raises a host of interesting research questions. First—looking back to the original WEST work, which focused on the identification of important "issues" that students should be aware of in playing a mathematical game—a craft advisor should crucially have some notion of what constitutes worthwhile advice. Why, after all, should, say, HyperGami's polyhedron-construction advisor suggest several operations but not others? Such questions inevitably lead to the larger task of attempting to formalize (but not rigidify) principles of good taste in design. And there are educational issues to be raised as well. Is the purpose of an educational craft advisor to suggest new directions for design? Or is it perhaps more importantly to develop cognitive skills in the student? To take the specific case of HyperGami's polyhedron-construction ad-

Figure 11.4

*One of HyperGami's experimental "spatial advisors" in operation.
Starting from an icosahedron* (left), *a set of five planar vertices
is found by the software advisor and identified for the user*
(center), *who may then slice the shape through the suggested
plane to produce two pieces* (right).

visors: are these tools supposed to help the student create especially novel forms, or are they primarily aimed to promote specific skills in spatial cognition? Different answers to this question might well lead us, as researchers, to explore vastly different sorts of craft advisors in our work.

Computers as Elements of Crafted Objects

While HyperGami does blend the use of computational media into the process of creation of crafted objects, it still maintains a sort of division between the "virtual" and "real" worlds. The HyperGami user employs the computer during the first (design) stage of her work and then moves over into the physical world for the subsequent (construction) stage. Although this division is perfectly appropriate for the sort of materials employed by HyperGami, it obscures still other directions for exploration in which computational media are themselves embedded within mathematical and scientific craft objects.

Groundbreaking work in this direction was done by Druin (1987) in her creation of NOOBIE, an appealing stuffed creature that served as the interface to a computer, though in this case only the system designer (not the users) took the role of "physical craftsperson." More recently, related ideas have been creatively pursued by Resnick and his colleagues at the MIT Media Laboratory in the incorporation of computational elements (the Programmable Brick and its descendants) into scientific constructions of all sorts (see Chapter 7) (Resnick et al., 1996; Umaschi 1997).

Over the past year we and several colleagues at the University of Colorado have employed the Media Lab's most recent generation of Programmable Brick (dubbed the "Cricket" by its inventors) to create prototypes of scientific toys, kits, and exhibits in which computational and craft elements are blended. Figures 11.5, 11.6, and 11.7 show specific examples along these lines.

Figure 11.5 depicts a "programmable kaleidoscope" (created by A. Warmack). Here three large mirrors are arranged in an equilateral triangle over a wooden base. When the user peeks over the edge of one of the mirrors, she sees an endless array of triangular prisms filling the space of her vision. A programmable motor is placed through the base so that it may churn up objects such as metal balls that are placed between the mirrors of the kaleidoscope; this produces a visually dynamic effect, suggested by the picture at right in Figure 11.5.

Figure 11.6 depicts another example (this one created by T. Wrensch). Here a Cricket has been programmed to move a pair of metal coils in oscillatory fashion, measuring any increase in current through the coils and

Figure **11.5**

Left: *A view of a Cricket-enhanced kaleidoscope from the outside.* Right: *The view of the interior, reflected endlessly by the kaleidoscope's mirrors. At the center is a Cricket-operated motor that churns the objects placed inside the kaleidoscope.*

Figure **11.6**

A Cricket-operated magnetic field sensor. The Cricket (bottom left) *turns copper coils on the stand* (right), *and senses current through the coils to detect a magnetic field.*

thereby acting as a magnetic field detector (in much the same fashion as in Faraday's original 19th-century experiments).

Finally, Figure 11.7 (see also Color Plate) depicts a programmable color display (created by M. Burin, K. Johnston, and D. Olvera) in which programmable pumps alternately fill and empty three rectangular tanks with dyed

Figure 11.7

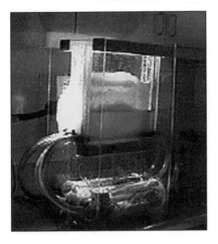

A Cricket-operated color display. Light shines through three water tanks filled (via pumps) with blue-, red-, and yellow-tinted water. The pumps are operated by Crickets, causing the water tanks to fill and empty in programmable patterns.

water in red, yellow, and blue shades. By shining a light through the three tanks as they fill and empty in ever-changing patterns, you may see different colors shining through the tanks. All these examples (and numerous others that we and our students have made) illustrate the basic idea of taking some traditional scientific toy or exhibit—a kaleidoscope, an experiment in magnetic field detection, a color wheel—and seeing what happens when a bit of computation is incorporated.

11.4 Middle-Tech Design: The Materials

The previous section focused on the computational side of middle-tech design, exploring the notion of computers as design tools, as advisory devices, and as elements of craft materials themselves. In this section we turn to the more explicitly material, tangible aspect of middle-tech design.

Figure **11.8**

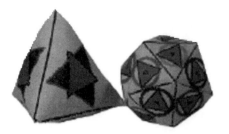

"Pillowhedra" created from sewn fabric

The Evolution of Traditional Materials, or Everything Old Is New Again

In our earlier accounts of the HyperGami system, we often found ourselves referring to the application as a blend of high tech (computers) and low tech (paper). Over time, we have come to revise our view—not about the "high techness" of computers but about the "low techness" of paper. A visit to any large office supply store reveals that the range of expressiveness of paper—even restricted to those grades of paper available for color printers—is immense. There are relatively inexpensive grades, glossy papers, thick cardstock, papers in pastel shades, and papers with background designs. And beyond these paper grades, there are still other types that we have incorporated into HyperGami creations by gluing them onto already-constructed models: glow-in-the-dark adhesive sheets, holographic design paper, and reflective mylar sheets. One grade of paper may be run through a color printer and transferred via ironing to fabric; this is usually employed for creating decorated T-shirts, but we have transferred folding nets to fabric and sewn them into the "pillowhedra" shown in Figure 11.8. There are still other types of experimental paper that we have yet to try in HyperGami constructions: temperature-sensitive films that change color over a given temperature range, sheets with embedded diffraction gratings, paper that changes color when exposed to sunlight, polarizing filters, and so forth. In short, paper considered purely on its own is a medium that defies categorization as high or low tech.

Indeed, many traditional materials are evolving in similar, wonderfully bewildering ways. While most elementary classrooms have a supply of yarn, there are now easily available glow-in-the-dark and magnetic strings—not to mention extremely strong Kevlar fibers or the fiber optic cables and "muscle wire" described later in this section. Most children have worked with traditional paints; now craft stores market a variety of novel paints

Figure **11.9**

*A small stellated dodecahedron
decorated with copper finish*

(including rubbery "3D" paints, glow-in-the-dark varieties, and "antiquing finishes" of the type used to make the copperlike polyhedron shown in Figure 11.9). Commercial kits for molding rubber into high-bouncing balls are available. Over and over, the uncharted possibilities for cross-fertilization with computational media are promising, to say the least: software tools might, say, model the dynamic behavior of a magnetic string design, or suggest ways in which glow-in-the-dark dyes might be combined with polarizing filters in new types of classroom sculpture, or help in creating rubber balls of nonuniform composition to provide customized patterns of bouncing.

Materials Specifically for Science Education

The previous paragraphs focused on the ways in which even traditional low-tech classroom materials—string, paint, paper—have come to take on remarkably new forms. We may likewise turn our attention to materials (some new, some old) specifically geared toward science education, just to see how those scientific materials might lend themselves to integration with computational media. Consider, for instance, the venerable crystal-growing kits, in which crystal structures accrete (typically over a period of hours or days) from saturated solutions. As far as we know, no one has attempted to employ computational control in the classroom to render these crystal kits more customizable: conceivably, by using a computer to systematically vary, say, the temperature, solute concentration, chemical composition, or mixing rate, you could create new or offbeat varieties of "crystal artwork." (At least such an idea is worth a try!) Fiber optic cables, not long ago the epitome of futuristic materials science, are now available at low cost and suggest some potentially fruitful directions for integration with computational devices like the Media Lab's Crickets: although the Crickets are designed to communicate "through the air," by sending infrared signals to one another, we might imagine instead an arbitrary network of Crickets communicating via light signals in point-to-point fashion merely by rearranging patterns of fiber optic cables. Or consider the myriad uses to which inexpensive piezo films (which convert pressure to electrical current) may be put in creating touch-sensitive surfaces as interfaces to small computers. Just as the materials of the art studio offer new avenues for computational integration, then, so do the affordable materials of the classroom laboratory.

New Materials Well-Suited to Computational Control

There are several specific instances of new and affordable materials that seem especially ripe for integration in computational projects; we can't resist mentioning those materials here. One example is "muscle wire" (Nitinol), a nickel-titanium alloy that can be used to convert an electrical current into a powerful pull along a length of wire (Gilbertson 1993). This type of material seems perfectly suited to devising programmable marionettes or dynamic sculptures, for example. Yet another family of examples are the various temperature-sensitive films and paints that change color within selected temperature ranges: by coating an arbitrary surface with a temperature-sensitive dye and using a computer somewhere inside that surface to gently heat or cool specific locations on the surface, you can make unique multi-colored output devices. A less exotic but still potentially interesting example involves the use of iron filings suspended in transparent viscous fluid; such substances are marketed as ways of demonstrating magnetic field patterns in a manner that is easily seen in a sheet of paper or viewable on an overhead projector screen. By using computers to control the timing and placement of small magnets near these viewable fields, you could easily create dynamic displays.

The Question of Cost

It should be noted that all of the sample materials mentioned in the previous paragraphs are available at relatively low cost—at least well within the budget of a modest home or classroom laboratory. In much the same manner as high-tech digital electronics, the cost of middle-tech materials is (by and large) dropping precipitously, so that even topics such as holography and superconductivity may be demonstrated through kits marketed at far lower cost than might have been imagined a generation ago.

Some middle-tech materials are still at the research stage but are likely to become affordable in the foreseeable future. Recent work in computationally enriched fabrics of various sorts—"wearable computing"—has garnered a tremendous amount of popular attention and interest (Mann 1997). Less glamorous but nonetheless fascinating work in basic material science has produced astonishing advances in such areas as the creation of synthetic diamond at prices that may ultimately be within the range of the home hobbyist (Amato 1997, 154). Overall, this burgeoning activity in affordable new materials—when combined with computational media—could, we believe, result in a marvelously democratic revival of the culture of serious scientific amateurism (the culture exemplified by pioneers such as Boyle, Lavoisier, and Franklin, all of whom explored scientific questions at their own personal expense). We will return to this issue in the following section.

11.5 Middle Tech in Science and Mathematics Education

To this point, we have described our own system and discussed what we believe are central issues in middle-tech design; but we have not paused to explain our own interest in the subject. In this section, then, we present several arguments for the importance of middle tech in science and mathematics education.

The Cognitive Role of Middle-Tech Materials

Consider the following typical scenario from an undergraduate astrophysics course: the professor describes the notion of an ever-expanding universe, mentioning that galaxies further from our own are rushing away from earth faster than galaxies close to ours. He goes on to state that this phenomenon of expansion is seen throughout the universe; that is, an observer within some distant galaxy would witness the same sort of expansion that we on earth do. Here several students object: if we see further galaxies rushing away faster from us than do the closer galaxies, doesn't this imply that our own galaxy is at some sort of distinguished "center" of the universe? How could a distant observer experience the same phenomenon? The professor replies that there is no paradox and by way of illustration takes a rubber balloon and some white paint; he paints an assembly of white dots on the balloon's surface and then proceeds to blow up the balloon with air. As the balloon expands, the professor points out that, from the vantage point of any dot D on the balloon's surface, all the other dots are rushing away from

D at a rate that increases with distance from D. No dot is unique in this respect.

The balloon demonstration is a staple of physics classes—a marvelously simple, low-tech illustration of an otherwise hard-to-visualize concept. But is the demonstration really quite as low tech as all that? After all, rubber balloons—inexpensive toys for children—are made of a substance that has only come into widespread industrial use during the past century and a half (Amato 1997, 49–51). Rubber balloons did not exist, either for children or scientists, in the mid-19th century. Quite arguably, the very idea of a uniformly expanding universe would have been far harder to understand in the absence of material illustrations through which to seed the idea; at any rate, the notion would have undoubtedly been harder to teach.

Materials are the concrete, day-to-day, tactile illustrations of difficult scientific concepts. Rubber balloons illustrate the notion of an expanding universe. Curves drawn on rubber sheets are used to illustrate basic ideas of topology. Pond water illustrates the transverse wave phenomena through which light waves are understood. Metal springs illustrate longitudinal waves as well as harmonic motion. When Kepler developed his laws of motion for the planets, he employed magnets as an exemplar of the idea of action at a distance (Kearney 1971, 130–137). Descartes used the image of fluid moving through a conduit as a basis for his model of reflex actions in muscles (Flanagan 1984, 1–3). The first understanding of polarization emerged from the examination of the mineral calcite (Halliday and Resnick 1962, 1148). Paper is a good material approximation to a two-dimensional space, thread to a one-dimensional space; soap films illustrate minimal surfaces. The theory of evolution has traditionally been understood through the image of a thickly branching tree, as eloquently described by Gould (1996). Freud's theories of the mind borrowed imagery from fluids under pressure (Baars 1997, 84). In this century, clouds and coastlines have been used as illustrations of fractal sets (Mandelbrot 1988); water dripping from a tap becomes an illustration of chaotic dynamics (Shaw 1984); and froth or soapsuds are said to resemble the large-scale arrangement of galaxies in the universe (Taubes 1997).

Many, many more examples along these lines could be offered. Indeed, even the apparent counterexamples—those instances of scientific ideas not strongly linked with material illustrations—are striking for that very reason; arguably, it is the absence of obvious material analogies that make the theoretical ideas of quantum mechanics (especially those of wave/particle duality) so difficult to visualize (Miller 1984, 154–174). And even the short list given in the previous paragraph demonstrates some interesting variety. Some of the materials and objects mentioned (water, froth, clouds) are natural, occurring in the environment of every human culture; others (thread, soap, paper), while possessed of long histories, are nonetheless artificial, engineered materials. Importantly, these latter materials were not invented for educational purposes—there is no evidence that the earliest manufacturers of soap had any interest in the study of minimal surfaces—but once these materials became common cultural artifacts, they enabled still other, more abstract ideas to enter the cultural consciousness.

Everyday materials, simple objects, are more than carriers of potentially powerful scientific metaphors. They are also capable of emotional resonance, of being irresistible sources of wonder to the student of science or mathematics. Morgan's book on the geometry of minimal surfaces (Morgan 1988) opens with a marvelous photograph of the author as a tiny child watching with serious and rapt attention as his mother blows soap bubbles into the air. In a famous autobiographical anecdote, Einstein mentioned that his interest in science was piqued by an early gift of a compass (Bernstein 1993, 161). For some children, tops or gyroscopes become joyful illustrations of angular momentum; mirrors arranged into kaleidoscopes beautifully present ideas of symmetry; and crystals are gorgeous, collectible snapshots of solid geometry. And even adult scientists derive wonder and inspiration from toys, objects, and gadgets. The birth of the Gestalt movement occurred when the psychologist Max Wertheimer found himself thumbing through a children's "flip book" and reflecting on the perception of movement that it produced (Goldstein 1989, 193–194). Or, to take another example: the physicist Richard Feynman reported in his autobiography (Feynman 1985, 157–158) that his Nobel-prize-winning work was first inspired by the visual image of dishes wobbling as they rotated.

For educational technologists, the immediate implications of these notions are twofold. First, the burgeoning world of new and affordable materials, new stuff, should be taken as an opportunity for an expanded repertoire of visual images and analogies; that is, we should be on the alert for difficult scientific and mathematical concepts that may suddenly become illustratable through the means of new things. Velcro, fiberglass, silly putty, styrofoam, and so forth may be new concepts in the making or old advanced concepts rendered comprehensible. Second, we should perhaps begin to regard materials, objects, and everyday stuff as artifacts that can potentially be designed, or redesigned, with an eye toward educational purposes. To some extent, the well-established tradition of scientific toys, kits, and exhibits already represents a step in this direction. But is it so much more quixotic to wonder whether the day-to-day materials of our culture could be looked at afresh in the hope of making them more provocative, compelling, self-explanatory, or fun? Might not electrical wires, for example, be designed to somehow display the fact that a current is running through them? What if adhesives were designed to make a sound as they formed chemical bonds with the surfaces that they contacted? Might not string instruments be designed to somehow enhance the user's awareness of the vibrations in their strings? Or might not drums somehow display the vibration patterns of their surfaces? We will return to these issues, and the role that computation might come to play in conjunction with them, a bit later in this chapter.

The Social Role of Objects—Examples from HyperGami

The previous paragraphs highlighted the cognitive (and to some degree the affective) role of objects and materials in science and mathematics education. For many educational technologists, this taste for the tangible, for the physical, might well be viewed as oddly nostalgic. Aren't animations, simulations, and virtual laboratories more powerful and expressive than any physical toy or object? Aren't cyberspace and virtual reality the educational and professional environments of the future? Isn't tangibility . . . well . . . a rather musty, obsolescent notion?

We have three major thematic responses to this sort of objection. First, the world is a rich and complicated place, capable of more than one cultural development at any given time. Simulations, virtual reality, and cyberspace have an undeniable appeal, and (from the educational standpoint) they embody some remarkable strengths in presenting scientific ideas. Often, the real world is not especially good at illustrating phenomena at very large or small scales. Simulations can help us understand the behavior of the unfamiliar, or of large and complex systems, or of systems evolving over long periods of time. None of this is controversial, and none of it contradicts the equally great potential, and appeal, for objects and materials in a full scientific and mathematical education. The world of educational technology, in short, can accommodate more than one intellectual development at a time.

Second—as we have argued—there are especially strong opportunities for integrating the strengths of computation, simulations, and cyberspace, with the educational strengths of materials, toys, objects, kits, and exhibits. We will return to this theme once more in the final sections of this chapter.

Third, our experiences with HyperGami have convinced us that in fact there is a unique and special educational role for physical (as opposed to virtual) objects in the lives of young mathematicians and scientists. As computer scientists, we weren't initially very acute; these ideas actually crept up on us. It was only after working with our first bunch of students that we began to notice how real objects function over the course of an educational lifetime. We saw that our students would put their objects on display or give them as gifts to adults. One younger student bestowed a nickname upon a polyhedron that she had built; another (somewhat older) student reported to us that he had proudly showed his HyperGami construction to his classroom teacher. Even our adult visitors, after viewing the program, would often ask to take a construction back as a gift for their children at home.

We began to notice, over time, how HyperGami objects—unlike most artifacts of a mathematical education—took on what we have referred to as "social currency" (Eisenberg and Nishioka 1997b). Even mathematical objects such as HyperGami polyhedra have the potential of being souvenirs, expressions of affection, personal statements, and imaginary friends. We ourselves have used HyperGami constructions as wedding gifts, holiday ornaments, and thank-you notes. Virtual objects, in contrast, simply don't carry the same kind of weight, emotionally or literally (Csikszenthmihalyi 1993).

The fact that a physical object such as a HyperGami sculpture can just be *present*—can be in the room, unobtrusive, but noticed at odd moments—has a sort of importance that itself can be almost too simple to notice. When an object merely hangs out on the shelf, we find ourselves talking about it with visitors: we explain and reexplain the object from time to time. Or perhaps we pick it up in absent moments just to reflect on it anew. Most educational artifacts—and especially classroom software applications—are conceived of as having a built-in time clock: you use the arithmetic program until you have mastered the skill (the quicker the better), and then you put the program away for good. In contrast, a physical object has a hope of sticking around on the shelf for a few months, maybe a few years. The object first created by a fourth-grader may be reflected upon all over again years later by an eighth-grader. And while the eighth-grader is now ready to view the object in a new light, she still imbues the object (particularly if it is a creative product, like a HyperGami sculpture) with emotional meaning. Objects have stories attached to them; they have personal narratives. In contrast, it is the rare simulation or virtual experience that could ever have the personal meaning of even the simplest keepsake or souvenir.

Middle Tech and the Culture of Professional Science

Our focus throughout this chapter has been on the role of middle tech in science and mathematics education. But it is worth pausing at this juncture to reflect on the culture of professional science as well. After all, middle tech is not a notion that applies exclusively to children or novices: it is an idea that could increasingly find expression in the lives and practice of professional scientists as well.

Indeed, we would argue that professional science needs a dose of middle tech. The past half century of scientific research has been identified in the public mind with expensive, gargantuan, multiperson efforts: the Manhattan Project, the Apollo missions, the human genome project (Galison 1992). It wasn't always so. When we think of 17th- and 18th-century science (the Scientific Revolution), we tend to think of the individual, amateur scientist working out of his own home and laboratory: Robert Boyle, Antoine Lavoisier, Christian Huygens. Often, these individual scientists were wealthy men—only men were provided the education with which to participate in the scientific community, and few but the wealthy could afford the time and materials for scientific work. The opportunities, then, to practice science were anything but democratic. Nonetheless, there is a certain appeal about the practice of early science when compared to "big science": the resources of the individual could be sufficient to make huge progress, and the idiosyncratic taste and style of the individual shone in his work.

We believe—and hope—that professional scientists in the next century may increasingly come to resemble their predecessors of the Scientific Revolution, at least in their ability to do important science on their own, in home laboratories and workshops. Twenty-first-century scientists will be able to work with a huge range of new, relatively inexpensive materials—in conjunction with a huge range of inexpensive computational devices. (Just to mention Adam Cohen's Westinghouse Competition project once more: he estimated the construction cost of his home scanning tunneling microscope at a mere $50.) This second Scientific Revolution can be expected to be more democratic than the first. The cost of participating will be far less daunting than in the 18th century, and consequently the participants themselves are likely to be more demographically varied (and their styles and interests more widespread). Although doing science may not soon, or ever, be universally affordable, it could well be as common a personal hobby as skiing or playing a musical instrument, and importantly, the quality level of amateur science could compare favorably to that of the 17th-century pioneers.

11.6 Middle Tech: Potential Directions for Future Research and Development

In this section, we look to the future of middle-tech design, again (somewhat arbitrarily) separating the subject into its "material" and "computational" aspects.

Looking to the Future: The Materials Side

The past decade has seen a blossoming level of progress in materials science, including work on "smart" materials—that is, materials endowed with (typically small but highly useful) elements of computational behavior (see [Amato 1997] for a readable overview of this research). Likewise, there has been extensive and creative work in adding computational capabilities to furniture (Zimmerman et al. 1995), clothing (Mann 1997), and numerous other basic materials and artifacts. Perhaps only a bit more futuristically, Berlin and Gabriel (1997) describe the notion of realizing computation in large numbers of elements in distributed media (they refer to the idea as "programming a cloud of dust").

Although we see this work as exciting—even awe-inspiring—it should be noted that as a body of work it only partially overlaps with the notions of middle tech described in this chapter. First, our own preferences in material design run toward those that have some sort of educational use or intention. Materials, as we have argued, can be seen as tangible expressions of important ideas. A magnet evokes the idea of action at a distance. A diffraction grating evokes ideas of wave interference. Soap films evoke ideas of minimal surfaces. Merely making a material "smart" may not be especially useful from the educational standpoint, if the material fails to evoke these sorts of ideas or to promote productive imagery in its users. Indeed, we might view much of the research in "smart" materials as following in the (we believe unfortunate) tradition of embedding more and more incomprehensibility, more opacity, into engineered artifacts.

As a first research step, then, we would advocate studying materials from the educational/cognitive standpoint, a stance not usually taken in thinking about material design. What is it about certain types of "stuff"—craft materials, everyday objects, perhaps toys and kits—that gives them evocative power in science and math education? What is the role of working with materials—rubber, plasticine, paper, string—in developing mathematical or scientific ideas? Once we have a better understanding of materials as educational catalysts, we can begin to design new materials not to be more efficient insulators, fabrics, dyes, or whatever, but rather to make them more provocative, more wonderful, and more inspiring.

By the same token, our interest in "smart materials" is less in embedding computation per se within materials and objects and more toward endowing materials with *expressive* computation—at least some measure of programmability or communication with programmable media. Resnick and his colleagues' work, mentioned earlier, is directly in this spirit, but there are many more directions still to try. For example, craft work is characterized by the use of numerous small and cheap elements—hinges, screws, tacks, wires, paper, felt, adhesive, and many more. We believe that there is tremendous opportunity in adding very tiny amounts of programmability—perhaps a dozen instructions' worth of program—in these widespread crafting elements. To take a few (admittedly speculative) examples:

- Programmable string or thread might be constructed so that it snaps or breaks after a certain discrete number of small tugs; for instance, you could program a "three-tug string" that severs itself after three pulls, a "four-tug string" after four pulls, and so forth. Alternatively, you might imagine a type of string that (upon some given signal, such as a tug) will stretch and contract itself in some sort of repeating pattern; string of this type could be used (among many other possibilities) to make a variety of marionettes with complex behaviors.

- You might imagine programmable thumbtacks that double as simple "button" inputs to craft objects; that is, if the thumbtack had a single ("flag") bit of memory, then pressing on the tack would set the flag to high, while otherwise the flag is set to a low value. In the same vein, materials (e.g., new types of felt or construction papers) into which the tacks are pushed might have simple means whereby they could read the values communicated by the embedded tacks.

- Programmable hinges might allow for simple dynamic motions (e.g., the hinges might periodically open and close or might alter their state in response to, say, a light input). Such hinges might find especially interesting uses in scientific modeling kits like those used by students of anatomy: a "visible man" model containing a few tiny programmable hinges might be able to demonstrate the movements of muscles in an especially informative way.

Yet another direction might be to look at recent work in "augmented reality" (Feiner, MacIntyre, and Seligmann 1993), in which researchers endeavor to permit greater levels of communication between computer applications and physical artifacts, to enhance the expressiveness of middle-tech scientific crafts. Imagine, for instance, strings that can communicate (to a computer application) the level of tensile forces being applied to them, or perhaps adhesives might be designed to communicate the force with which they are holding two surfaces together, or a felt surface might be able to communicate a level of static charge. While some or all of these examples might be a bit fanciful, at least at present, we believe that the philosophy behind them is quite reasonable: they allow small increments of computational behavior to be distributed inexpensively throughout the types of craft projects that typify scientific education and homespun scientific work.

Looking to the Future: The Computational Side

On the computational side, we believe that the proliferation of middle-tech materials and projects offers new directions for research. Certainly, it would be worthwhile to develop a greater range of powerful HyperGami-style applications to assist in the creation of homemade scientific experiments and instruments; in effect, we might ask what sorts of programs might be of assistance to the Adam Cohens of the next century. Computer applications could assist in the choosing of materials (alloy compositions, types of plastic, grades of paper) for certain construction projects. Programs might be able to take large lists of available materials—an inventory of those things that a student happens to have handy—and to suggest scientific projects or research areas that could be accomplished using those materials. Programs could assist with specific formalized aspects of more complicated craft projects (e.g., how to arrange a collection of lenses and mirrors to achieve a specific optical effect or how to create a certain type of mechanical linkage).

At least some sort of development could readily be undertaken in making computer applications more powerful tools in the service of informal, homespun scientific and mathematical crafts. Pushing some of this research a bit more in the direction of artificial intelligence leads to the sort of efforts that we mentioned earlier in conjunction with HyperGami: developing intelligent advisors for scientific and mathematical crafters. Programs might assist students in the creation of topological or geometric puzzles, or they might advise students of graphics on the use and creation of visual illusions, or they might advise a student on how to create and maintain a terrarium. Rather than pursuing the traditional lines of AI research in creating "intelligent tutoring systems," we might imagine trying to create a line of "intelligent science project judges" that would assist students in building, presenting, and assessing entries in science contests. Although research in this area might not produce truly automated science fair judges (our guess is that it wouldn't), the effort could not help but yield new insights into the ways that science fair judges encourage—or maybe fail to encourage—the development of young researchers.

Another major line of research would look toward enhancing the computational infrastructure that contributes to middle-tech education. It might become common practice, for instance, to endow the creations of scientific workshops with Web sites (much as a signature is placed on a painting, or explanatory documentation beside a museum exhibit). In this way, students encountering home-crafted objects would have a standard means of finding documentation on the composition and creation of those objects. Likewise, science museums could take on an increasing role as local middle-tech crafting centers, offering new materials to students for experimentation and offering remote links to useful workshop equipment that could be made available to the public. For example, high school students might be able to design customized plastic pieces on their school computers and then retrieve the manufactured pieces at their local science museum (Eisenberg and Eisenberg 1998).

11.7 Conclusion: Filling the Room with Stuff, or Why Virtuality Isn't Enough

Much of the last decade's writing about educational technology seems to imply a decreasing role for real, physical objects. Students are portrayed as increasingly virtual creatures, spending their time in virtual laboratories, taking virtual measurements, collaborating within virtual scientific communities, and communicating their results in virtual notebooks and journals.

It is strange that educational technologists, of all people, should be so cavalier about the need for physical objects in students' lives. As educational technologists—computer scientists—we have become aware over time of an emotional tension felt by many members of our profession: "yearning" might not be too strong a word. Computer scientists, after all, work with an instrument that remains majestically impervious in its outward appearance to all the labor that we bestow upon it. Day after day, the computer scientist returns to his or her office, and the computer looks exactly the same as it did a week ago, a month ago, a year ago. All the programming work, all the communication, all the email, all the documents, fit into a box that looks pretty much as it did when we installed it. Contrast the situation of the sculptor, the woodworker, the gardener, the mechanical engineer: these people's efforts are reflected, day by day, in their surrounding environments. Each day they return to work and see evidence of their creative and intellectual growth made manifest in the objects that they own and touch and stand among. It is perhaps the need for this experience that accounts for the poignant efforts that computer scientists make to reflect their work in their own environments (e.g., by putting screen dumps or conference poster presentations up on the walls).

Students of science and mathematics—at least many students, ourselves included—need to breathe the atmosphere of science and math in their surroundings. They miss the sense of wonder invoked by a setting: the local science museum, or the planetarium, or the botanical garden. They need the sense of place experienced by the young Arrowsmith in Sinclair Lewis's novel:

It was the central room of the three occupied by Doc Vickerson . . . This central room was at once business office, consultation-room, living-room, poker den, and warehouse . . . Against a brown plaster wall was a cabinet of zoological collections and medical curiosities, and beside it the most dreadful and fascinating object known to the boy-world of Elk Mills—a skeleton with one gaunt gold tooth . . . The wild raggedness of the room was the soul and symbol of Doc Vickerson; it was more exciting than the flat-faced stack of shoeboxes in the New York Bazaar; it was the lure to questioning and adventure for Martin Arrowsmith.

In this chapter we have argued that middle tech is a broad notion that can revive this sense of excitement in the physical materials, objects, and settings of science. It points to the introduction of new materials, new objects, new scientific stuff for students to play with, and explores techniques of integrating these materials (as well as traditional materials) with computation. In doing so, middle tech can remake the surroundings of young scientists and mathematicians, enriching their lives by merging a sense of intellectual mission with a sense of physical place.

Acknowledgments

Three anonymous reviewers had extremely helpful comments on an earlier draft of this chapter; our thanks to them. We are indebted to the ideas and encouragement of Hal Abelson, Robbie Berg, Fred Martin, Michael Mills, Mitchel Resnick, Brian Silverman, Jim Spohrer, and Carol Strohecker, among many others. Adrienne Warmack, Tom Wrensch, Andee Rubin, and Vennila Ramalingam have all collaborated on the work described here. Thanks to Gerhard Fischer, Hal Eden, and the members of the Center for Lifelong Learning and Design at the University of Colorado for providing an intellectual home for our efforts. This work has been supported in part by the National Science Foundation and the Advanced Research Projects Agency under Cooperative Agreement CDA-9408607 and by NSF grants CDA-9616444 and REC-961396. Ann Nishioka Eisenberg is supported by a fellowship from the National Physical Science Consortium; Mike Eisenberg, by a Young Investigator Award IRI-9258684. Finally, we would like to thank Apple Computer, Inc., for donating the machines with which our research was conducted.

References

Abelson, H. 1991. Computation as a framework for engineering education. In A. Meyer and J. Guttag, eds. *Research directions in computer science: An MIT perspective.* Cambridge, MA: MIT Press, 191–213.

Abelson, H., and diSessa, A. 1980. *Turtle geometry.* Cambridge, MA: MIT Press.

Amato, I. 1997. *Stuff.* New York: Basic Books.

Baars, B. 1997. *In the theater of consciousness.* New York: Oxford University Press.

Berger, J. 1994. *The young scientists.* Reading, MA: Addison-Wesley.

Berlin, A., and Gabriel, K. 1997. Distributed MEMS: New challenges for computation. *IEEE Computational Science and Engineering* 4(1): 12–16.

Bernstein, J. 1993. *Cranks, quarks, and the cosmos.* New York: Basic Books.

Burton, R., and Brown, J. 1982. An investigation of computer coaching for informal learning activities. In D. Sleeman and J. S. Brown, eds. *Intelligent tutoring systems.* New York: Academic Press.

Cohen, A. 1997. *Near-field photolithography.* Westinghouse Competition paper (unpublished), 1996–1997 (1st prize).

Csikszentmihalyi, M. 1993. Why we need things. In S. Lubar and W. D. Kingery, eds. *History from things.* Washington, DC: Smithsonian Institution Press.

Druin, A. 1987. Building an alternative to the traditional computer terminal. Master's thesis, MIT Media Lab.

Eisenberg, M. 1995. Programmable applications: Interpreter meets interface. *SIGCHI Bulletin* 27(2): 68–83.

Eisenberg, M. 1996. The thin glass line: Designing interfaces to algorithms. In *Proceedings of CHI '96.* New York: ACM Press, 181–188.

Eisenberg, M., and Eisenberg, A. 1998. Shop class for the next millennium. To appear in the *Journal of Interactive Media in Education.*

Eisenberg, M., and Nishioka, A. 1994. HyperGami: A computational system for creating decorated paper constructions. In *Origami Science and Art (Proceedings of the Second International Meeting of Origami Science and Scientific Origami).* Otsu, Japan: Seian University of Art and Design, 259–268.

Eisenberg, M., and Nishioka, A. 1997a. Creating polyhedral models by computer. *Journal of Computers in Mathematics and Science Teaching* 16(4): 477–511.

Eisenberg, M., and Nishioka, A. 1997b. Orihedra: Mathematical sculptures in paper. *International Journal of Computers for Mathematical Learning* 1(3): 225–261.

Feiner, S., MacIntyre, B., and Seligmann, D. 1993. Knowledge-based augmented reality. *Communications of the ACM* 36(7): 52–62.

Feynman, R. 1985. *"Surely you're joking, Mr. Feynman!"* New York: Bantam Books.

Fischer, G., Lemke, A. C., Mastaglio, T., and Morch, A. 1991. The role of critiquing in cooperative problem solving. *ACM Transactions on Information Systems* 9(2): 123–151.

Flanagan, O., Jr. 1984. *The science of the mind.* Cambridge, MA: MIT Press.

Galison, P. 1992. The many faces of big science. In P. Galison and B. Hevly, eds. *Big science.* Stanford, CA: Stanford University Press, 1–17.

Gilbertson, R. 1993. *Muscle wires project book.* San Rafael, CA: Mondo-Tronics.

Goldstein, E. B. 1989. *Sensation and perception.* Pacific Grove, CA: Brooks/Cole.

Gould, S. 1996. Ladders and cones: Constraining evolution by canonical icons. In R. Silvers, ed. *Hidden histories of science.* New York: New York Review of Books.

Halliday, D., and Resnick, R. 1962. Physics, part II. New York: John Wiley & Sons.

Kearney, H. 1971. *Science and change.* New York: McGraw-Hill.

MacDonald, D. K. C. 1964. *Faraday, Maxwell, and Kelvin.* Garden City, NY: Anchor Books.

Mandelbrot, B. 1988. *Fractal geometry of nature.* New York: W. H. Freeman.

Mann, S. 1997. Wearable computing: A first step toward personal imaging. *IEEE Computer* 30(2): 25–32.

Miller, A. 1984. *Visual imagery in scientific thought.* Cambridge, MA: MIT Press.

Morgan, F. 1988. *Geometric measure theory: A beginner's guide.* New York: Academic Press.

Resnick, M. 1993. Behavior construction kits. *Communications of the ACM* 36(7): 64–71.

Resnick, M., Martin, F., Sargent, R., and Silverman, B. 1996. Programmable Bricks: Toys to think with. *IBM Systems Journal* 35(3): 443–452.

Shaw, R. 1984. *Dripping faucet as a model chaotic system.* Santa Cruz, CA: Aerial Press.

Taubes, G. 1997. Beyond the soapsuds universe. *Discover* 18(8): 52.

Umaschi, M. 1997. Soft toys with computer hearts. In *Proceedings of CHI '97.* New York: ACM Press, 20–21.

Zimmerman, T., Smith, J., Paradiso, J., Allport, D., and Gershenfeld, N. 1995. Applying electric field sensing to human-computer interfaces. In *Proceedings of CHI '95.* New York: ACM Press, 280–287.

Index

About the Authors

Preface **Beginning a Discussion about Kids, Technology, and Design**

Allison Druin

Human-Computer Interaction Lab, Institute for Advanced Computer Studies and Department of Human Development, College of Education, University of Maryland, College Park

Allison Druin is an assistant professor focusing on the development of new multimedia storytelling technologies for children. She has written extensively on this topic for numerous publications and is coauthor of *Designing Multimedia Environments for Children* (Wiley, 1996). For more information on her work see *www.umiacs.umd.edu/~allisond*.

Chapter 1 **The Role of Usability Research in Designing Children's Computer Products**

Libby Hanna

IMG Usability, Microsoft Corporation

Libby Hanna is a developmental psychologist who researches children's use of computer products. She has written and presented on the topic of how to conduct usability testing with children. She performed the work discussed in this chapter while affiliated with Microsoft IMG Usability and now is working as an independent consultant in the Seattle area. She can be reached at *libbyh@earthlink.net*.

Kirsten Risden

IMG Usability, Microsoft Corporation

Mary Czerwinski

Microsoft Research, Microsoft Corporation

Dr. Mary Czerwinski is a cognitive scientist in the User Interface group at Microsoft Research. Her research interests include the study of cognitive issues related to 3D and multimodal environments. She is currently an affiliate faculty member in Psychology at the University of Washington. Dr. Czerwinski is an active member of the CHI and

Human Factors communities and has published extensively in those domains. Further information is available at *research.microsoft.com/users/marycz/home.htm.*

Kristin J. Alexander, Ph.D.

Hardware Ergonomics and Usability, Microsoft Corporation

Dr. Alexander is a developmental psychologist providing consultation and research for media products, including software, interactive toys, Web sites, and television programming. While working with the Microsoft Corporation, she played a major role in the research and design of ActiMates, a new line of interactive learning products based on popular children's characters, including Barney, Arthur, and D.W. She is an independent consultant and can be reached at *kalexa@newmediaconsultants.com.*

Chapter 2   Kids as Informants: Telling Us What We Didn't Know or Confirming What We Knew Already?

Mike Scaife

School of Cognitive and Computing Sciences, Sussex University, Brighton, UK

Mike Scaife is an associate professor doing research on the educational value of multimedia and on how to bring child and adult users into the design process. He has several current research projects in the area. Details of these and of relevant publications are available at *www.cogs.susx.ac.uk/users/mikesc/index.htm.*

Yvonne Rogers

School of Cognitive and Computing Sciences, Sussex University, Brighton, UK

Yvonne Rogers is an associate professor in human-computer interaction and cognitive science at the School of Cognitive and Computing Sciences. Her research is concerned with developing innovative and effective interactive multimedia and other forms of external representations for children and adults. For more information see *www.cogs.susx.ac.uk/users/yvonner.*

Chapter 3   Children as Our Technology Design Partners

Allison Druin

Human-Computer Interaction Lab, Institute for Advanced Computer Studies and Department of Human Development, College of Education, University of Maryland, College Park

Benjamin B. Bederson

Computer Science Department and Human-Computer Interaction Lab, University of Maryland, College Park

Benjamin B. Bederson is an assistant professor working in the area of human-computer interaction. His focus for the past few years has been on the development of

Zooming User Interfaces (ZUIs). He has developed a prototype ZUI called Pad++. For more information, see *www.cs.umd.edu/~bederson.*

Angela Boltman
College of Education, University of Maryland, College Park

Angela Boltman is a Ph.D. student at the University of Maryland's College of Education and a research assistant in the Human-Computer Interaction Lab where her research focus is on technology and children. She also holds a joint research appointment with the Royal Institute of Technology in Stockholm, Sweden, where she will be participating in a three-year European Union project. Previously, she was the technology specialist at Hawthorne Elementary School (a K–5 school located in Albuquerque, NM) as well as a research assistant at the University of New Mexico.

Adrian Miura
Distance Education Center/Multimedia Services, University of New Mexico

Adrian Miura is a multimedia developer for the University of New Mexico with an emphasis on the development of Web-based courses.

Debby Knotts-Callahan
University of New Mexico, Albuquerque

Debby Knotts-Callahan is the program director for the University of New Mexico's New Media Centers Program as well as the manager of UNM Multimedia Services. She has collaborated on research with Allison Druin in exploring how participatory design and contextual inquiry can be used with children.

Mark Platt
Louisiana State University

Dr. Platt is assistant director of academic computing at LSU Medical School in Shreveport. He is interested in the interaction between students of all ages and information that is available electronically. He develops software that explains complex medical processes in an interactive format. He can be reached at *Mplatt@lsumc.edu.*

Chapter 4 ## The Researcher's Role in the Design of Children's Media and Technology

Debra A. Lieberman
KIDZ Health Software, Inc.

Debra Lieberman, Ed.M., Ph.D., specializes in educational technology research, design, and evaluation. She was a faculty member at Indiana University, Bloomington, where her research focused on children's processes of learning with interactive media. Subsequent to that she has been a researcher and instructional designer in the educational software industry. At KIDZ Health Software she has contributed to the design and evaluation of interactive games for health behavior change, including Bronkie the Bronchiasaurus (asthma self-management), Packy & Marlon (diabetes self-management), and Rex Ronan (smoking prevention). For more information about these and other interactive health products for prevention and self-care, see *www.kidzhealth.com.*

Chapter 5   Designing Collaborative Applications for Classroom Use: The LiNC Project

Jürgen Koenemann

GMD—German National Research Center for Information Technology

Jürgen Koenemann is currently a researcher at GMD focusing on the design and evaluation of user-tailored information environments. For more information on his past and current work, email him at *jurgen.koenemann@acm.org.*

John M. Carroll

Center for Human-Computer Interaction and Department of Computer Science, Virginia Polytechnic Institute and State University, Blacksburg, VA

John M. Carroll is a cognitive/computer scientist; he is professor of computer science, psychology, and education, and director of the Center for Human-Computer Interaction at Virginia Tech. His research is in the analysis of learning and problem solving in human-computer interaction contexts and in the design of methods, tools, and environments for instruction and design. His most recent books are *Design Rationale: Concepts, Techniques, and Use* (with T. P. Moran, Erlbaum, 1996) and *Minimalism Beyond the Nurnberg Funnel* (MIT Press, 1998). In 1994, he won the Rigo Career Award from ACM SIGDOC for contributions to the design of instruction and documentation. For current information, see *www.cs.vt.edu/~carroll/.*

Clifford A. Shaffer

Department of Computer Science, Virginia Polytechnic Institute and State University

Cliff Shaffer is an associate professor and author of *A Practical Introduction to Data Structures and Algorithm Analysis* (Prentice Hall, 1997). His current research areas are computer-supported cooperative work and problem-solving environments. For more information on his work, see *www.cs.vt.edu/~shaffer.*

Mary Beth Rosson

Department of Computer Science, Virginia Polytechnic Institute and State University

Mary Beth Rosson has been an associate professor at Virginia Tech since January 1994; prior to that, she was a research staff member and manager at IBM's T. J. Watson Research Center. Her research is in the design and evaluation of interactive systems, with emphasis on systems that support learning and collaboration. She has participated extensively in ACM SIGPLAN and SIGCHI activities and has authored numerous technical papers and books, including *Instructor's Guide to Object-Oriented Analysis and Design* (Benjamin-Cummings, 1994). Further information can be found at *www.cs.vt.edu/~rosson.*

Marc Abrams

Department of Computer Science, Virginia Polytechnic Institute and State University

Marc Abrams (*abrams@vt.edu*) is an associate professor in computer science at Virginia Tech. In addition to being one of the designers of the LiNC user interface (*linc. cs.vt.edu*), he works on tools to construct user interfaces for what are called information or Internet appliances and leads a network research group that characterizes World Wide Web users (*www.cs.vt.edu/nrg/*). He is the author of *The World Wide Web: Beyond the Basics*, published recently by Prentice Hall.

Chapter 6 Children as Designers, Testers, and Evaluators of Educational Software

Yasmin B. Kafai

Kids Interactive Design Studies, Graduate School of Education & Information Studies, University of California, Los Angeles

Yasmin Kafai is an assistant professor examining the development of software design environments for young children learning science and mathematics. She is also studying gender differences and children's design of video games. She is the author of *Minds in Play* (Erlbaum, 1995) and coeditor of *Constructionism in Practice* (Erlbaum, 1996). More information about her work can be found at *www.gseis.ucla.edu/faculty/ kafaiintro.html*.

Chapter 7 Constructional Design: Creating New Construction Kits for Kids

Mitchel Resnick

Media Laboratory, Massachusetts Institute of Technology

Mitchel Resnick is an associate professor studying how new technologies can help children learn new things in new ways. He is codeveloper of LEGO/Logo and StarLogo, cofounder of the Computer Clubhouse, and author of *Turtles, Termites, and Traffic Jams* (MIT Press, 1994). For more information, see *www.media.mit.edu/~mres*.

Amy Bruckman

Georgia Institute of Technology

Amy Bruckman is an assistant professor in the College of Computing at the Georgia Institute of Technology. She and her students in the Electronic Learning Communities (ELC) group research online communities and education. She is the founder of MediaMOO (a text-based virtual reality environment or "MUD" designed to be a professional community for media researchers) and MOOSE Crossing (a MUD designed to be a constructionist learning environment for kids). MOOSE Crossing includes a new programming language, MOOSE, designed to make it easier for kids to learn to program. Amy Bruckman received her Ph.D. from the MIT Media Lab's Epistemology and Learning group in 1997, her master's from the Media Lab's Interactive Cinema group in 1991, and her bachelor's in physics from Harvard University in 1987. More information about her work is available at *www.cc.gatech.edu/~asb/*.

Fred Martin

Media Laboratory, Massachusetts Institute of Technology

Fred Martin is a research scientist with the Epistemology and Learning Group at MIT's Media Laboratory. Dr. Martin's research interests include the role of experiential knowledge in the learning of formal scientific and engineering methods, design-rich environments for learning, and the use of robotics as a medium for the exploration of engineering practice.

Chapter 8   Children as Digital Motion Picture Authors

Ronald Baecker

Collaborative Multimedia Research Group, Dynamic Graphics Project Laboratory, Department of Computer Science and Knowledge Media Design Institute, University of Toronto

Ronald Baecker is professor of computer science, electrical and computer engineering, and management at the University of Toronto; codirector of the Dynamic Graphics Project; founder and director of the Knowledge Media Design Institute; and founder and CEO of Expresto Software Corp., recently formed to commercialize the MAD system. His research focuses on human-computer interaction and user interface design, multimedia, computer-supported cooperative work and learning, and computers in education. For more information on his work, write *rmb@dgp.toronto.edu* or see *www.dgp.utoronto.ca/people/RMB/rmb.html*.

Ilona Posner

Collaborative Multimedia Research Group, Dynamic Graphics Project Laboratory, Department of Computer Science and Knowledge Media Design Institute, University of Toronto

Ilona Posner is a research associate in human-computer interaction and usability. She previously studied children learning collaborative writing using groupware. She is currently involved with development of MAD (Movie Authoring and Design system) and its integration into the curriculum. She may be reached by email at *ilona@dgp.toronto.edu*.

Chapter 9   Making Programming Easier for Children

David Canfield Smith

Stagecast Software, Inc.

Dr. David Canfield Smith is the co-inventor with Allen Cypher of Apple's award-winning Cocoa technology. He is currently user experience architect for Stagecast Software, Inc., the company developing Cocoa into a product called Stagecast

Creator. See *www.stagecast.com* for details. Previously, Dr. Smith was a principal designer of the Xerox "Star" computer (the ancestor of Apple's Macintosh), inventing the concepts of icons, the desktop metaphor, generic commands, and dialog boxes.

Allen Cypher

Stagecast Software, Inc.

Allen Cypher is a researcher in the area of end-user programming. He is co-inventor of Cocoa, now known as Stagecast Creator. He edited the book, *Watch What I Do: Programming by Demonstration* (MIT Press, 1993). For more information on his work, see *www.pobox.com/cypher.*

Chapter 10 Helping Children Learn Hard Things: Computer Programming with Familiar Objects and Activities

Ken Kahn

Animated Programs

After nearly two decades at XeroxPARC, MIT, and other universities doing research on programming languages, AI, animation and software for children, Ken Kahn founded Animated Programs in 1992. Since then he has been pursuing his goal of making programming child's play by building ToonTalk.

Chapter 11 Middle Tech: Blurring the Division between High and Low Tech in Education

Mike Eisenberg

Department of Computer Science, Institute of Cognitive Science, and Center for Lifelong Learning and Design, University of Colorado, Boulder

Mike Eisenberg received his Ph.D. in computer science from MIT in 1991 and is currently associate professor of computer science at the University of Colorado, Boulder. His research interests include the uses of technology in math and science education; end-user language design; the uses of computers to enhance spatial cognition; and the integration of computational media and craft materials. He is the author of a play (*Hackers,* published by Samuel French) and a programming textbook (*Programming in Scheme,* published by MIT Press).

Ann Nishioka Eisenberg

Department of Computer Science, Institute of Cognitive Science, and Center for Lifelong Learning and Design, University of Colorado, Boulder

Ann Eisenberg is a doctoral candidate in computer science at the University of Colorado, Boulder. Her research interests include the development of software to enhance spatial cognition and the role of computers in mathematics education. She is a member of the Educational Board of the Collage Children's Museum in Boulder and does freelance artwork.